Winkler on Marketing Planning

Winkler on Marketing Planning

John Winkler

Cassell/Associated Business Programmes
London

Dedication

To Gillian, who believed my vow
never to write another book,
and did not complain when I broke it.

Published by
Associated Business Programmes Ltd
17 Buckingham Gate, London SW1

Distributed by
Cassell and Co Ltd
35 Red Lion Square, London WC1R 4SG

First published 1972

This book has been printed in Great Britain
by The Anchor Press Ltd and bound by Wm Brendon & Son Ltd,
both of Tiptree, Essex

ISBN 304 29077 7

Contents

Case-History Examples

Acknowledgements

No less than three million words written about marketing have been studied and the personal experiences of twenty years in marketing have contributed to the production of this book. I acknowledge my great debt to these authors and writers, and also my debt to the thousand or so senior executives in this country and overseas who have attended the management seminars upon which this book is based. It was Helen Sasson, of Associated Business Programmes, who had the idea of running a seminar specifically on marketing planning and who encouraged the book; and it was her colleague Aubrey Wilson whose energy and ideas provided the inspiration for the writing.

Sir John Hamilton, the President of the Institute of Marketing, was the first to help actively with material, Mr. Owen Palmer of the City of London College supplied useful material and urged two of his final year students, Andrew True and Stuart Packington, to research and write up two case histories. Phil Morgan did a great deal of the research work and made a significant contribution to the text, writing most of the cases. Any mistakes in the book undoubtedly occur in those places where we both argued and I won. Many of the errors of fact or interpretation were pointed out by Norman Hart who read the manuscript most thoroughly. Between us all, we gave Mrs. Shirley Murray a beast of a manuscript to type which she did expertly and in good humour.

Nearly a hundred authors and their publishers have given permission to quote from their copyrighted works. In particular Michael Rines, editor of Marketing, has let me quote from many cases reported in that magazine. Most companies are reluctant to allow authors or their research assistants to investigate their past or current practices. These companies quibbled not a bit; they gave the time and experience of their senior management even though there was no commercial interest for them: All Precision Engineering Ltd, Audits of Great Britain Ltd, Bird's Eye Foods Ltd, Broads, Builders Merchants, Ltd, Contimart Ltd, Crosfields Farm Foods (S.W.) Ltd, Johnson and Johnson Ltd, J. Walter Thompson Ltd, Yale Security Products Division of Eaton Corporation. My thanks to all these companies and individuals.

My thanks are due also to my colleagues in Winkler Marketing Communications Ltd and Michael Laurie Design Ltd who helped actively with material, and passively by not being cross when I commandeered the vital resources of the organisation to help with problems as they arose.

Introduction

Most books on marketing concentrate upon expansion. This one concentrates upon efficiency. Strange as it may seem, there are not many books about marketing planning specifically: most books on marketing include only a chapter or so about the planning function. Since planning is the name of the marketing game, that hardly seems to do it justice.

The book originated from a discussion with Helen Sasson, Managing Director of Associated Business Programmes Ltd. She felt there was a gap in the management seminar market for an advanced course on marketing planning. The seminar originally researched and presented has been very successful even though the material has been revised radically in the light of constructive contributions from the many hundred executives from some of Britain's top industrial and consumer marketing companies who have attended. These executives are not so interested in advanced operating techniques, except in areas such as model-building. Even then, they do not wish to have the knowledge to develop mathematical models for themselves; they want to know what is available and what it can do to help in the area of marketing.

They are interested in uncovering their planning weaknesses. They are interested in tightening up their operations—in spending less and getting more for it. That is why the seminar session on 'tight budgeting' is more important than any other; it is described in Chapter 6, Resource Allocation and Control.

Another title for the book could have been 'How to be better off from having less to do'. It is not generally recognised that many marketing and management practices may severely harm a business through forcing it to do too much.

As a company's range of products becomes wider it causes corporate indigestion. The effect of product-clutter is similar to that of an unpruned rose bush—it stunts healthy growth. That is why a procedure for the formal elimination and profit-stripping of weak products is proposed in Chapter 8. Although management is reluctant to talk about the subject, there is great profit to be made from the deliberate degradation of products. Someone must say it; it is a fact.

As a company's range of activities and markets becomes wider it suffers from the erosion of power. By power is meant not only the financial support behind each activity, but also the amount of time and attention to which top management is able to give to each activity and market. Management decision-clutter exists in large companies on a wide-scale basis. The effect of it is to jam up the works at the top thereby pushing the operating decisions down the line into the hands of what Professor John K. Galbraith calls the 'technostructure'. And then they, the technocrats, really run things.

The book is aimed at two audiences. The first is the experienced practising manager who is intent on upgrading his planning procedures. The second is the advanced student of marketing who wants to know of the most advanced texts and cases on the subject and who needs to follow up original source material. For him there are over 100 technical references covering the material, most of them recently published.

The problem with a book of this kind lies in the immense variety of market structures and product situations in which companies find themselves. It is becoming steadily more unwise to generalise in marketing—each person's experience is so different. To overcome this problem each chapter has been written from general principles without frills. To most chapters has been added a section in which various types of market and product situations may take a different view or lay an alternative emphasis.

In addition, each chapter concludes with a longer case history which describes how different companies in various markets have approached the subject.

Of necessity, most of the material is heavily influenced by the established experts in these fields. Seminar audiences have contributed some of the original work in Chapter 10 on product planning; particularly in identifying product-range weaknesses. The other original area in the book is a field in which the author has been working personally for some time and which still remains the most under-researched area of marketing—the effect of 'word of mouth' within the marketing communications process, as described in Chapter 15.

The core of the book is about making profits and the emphasis is on making more profit through the better use of resources—about marketing productivity if you like. The examples entitled 'How an increase in your sales may mean a reduction of your profits' (Chapter 10) and 'How you might be better off with less product development' (Chapter 11) and 'How you could be more profitable with a smaller sales force' (Chapter 13) and 'How more sales promotion may harm your product market' (Chapter 17) have been drawn not merely to be provocative—they are real-life decision areas which businessmen should actively consider every day.

Developing the Plan

1. The Approach to Marketing Planning

Marketing plans are developed by many companies in a situation of nearly total ignorance.

Taking the large and small manufacturers of products as a whole, most companies are only hazily aware of such basics as the true size and shape of their markets, and the likely reaction of the market to the various moves they plan.

People's behaviour is amongst the most difficult of all subjects to analyse and predict. And, since marketing is about behaviour, it follows that marketing decisions must be amongst the hardest in business. Production decisions, for example, are concerned more with efficiency and the better use of plant and labour. They lend themselves to work study measurement. They can usually be quantified to the extent that the range of alternative solutions to a given problem is narrow.

Buyers, for example, consider moves to keep down the cost of materials —the prediction of future supplies and prices is based more upon economic analysis than behavioural study. Research and development is concerned with the exploitation of existing technology or with developing new avenues of exploration. Sales try to maximise turnover, accounts try to reduce credit losses. Decisions in each of these areas may be highly complicated. They may involve risk—no one is suggesting otherwise. But for most of the time, such decisions are taken with more knowledge and better data than is available in the marketing function.

The effectiveness of other functional plans, however, depends for success on the accuracy of the marketing plan. In many companies, if the sales deviate from forecast by only a fraction then any production efficiencies become meaningless, when measured against the disruption cost. Equally, if the products have not been costed and priced properly, then the gross profit may not be sufficient to allow for an adequate research and development budget. If the product range is not competitive or is directed through the wrong trading channel, then the sales organisation will have poor results.

All these plans, then, are derived from the assumption that the marketing plan is accurate. And that, as we say, is the one plan which is most difficult to produce with confidence. In the first place there is too little information about situations which are both behavioural and dynamic. The market is interactive—a move in one area affects reaction in another. The data is non-linear, and lagged. Furthermore, the marketing plan must take account of other variables; some are within the company's influence but many are not. For example, there are market variables; these are outside the company control and concern economic circumstances, technological, social and cultural forces, and competition.

Then there are product variables. The company's prosperity depends upon the mixture of decisions taken in relation to its products, their relation to competitive products, their pricing levels, their channels of distribution. There are also the operational variables such as selling, advertising, sales promotion, public relations, physical distribution, after-sales service. Each operates within a complex process and each operational plan must be a compromise between what is desirable, what is technically possible, and what is affordable.

Business decisions involve a mass of conflicting interests. Nowhere is this more apparent than in the clash between the marketing interests and those of other departments of the company. 'Production' likes long runs of limited models. It likes standard components. 'Marketing' likes many models, enough to meet each sector of the market. 'Finance' likes fast moving items, with economical levels of stock as against marketing's preference's for high levels of stock cover. 'Accounting' likes standard transactions, 'Marketing' wants special terms. 'Research and development' likes a long lead time, functional features and an emphasis on pushing new technical barriers. 'Marketing' likes short lead time, sales features, and an emphasis on product modification and development.

Without a central focus, not necessarily a marketing plan, each department in the company will pursue its own aims. Without a plan which will hold in check some of their ambitions, each department will set up its own objectives within the budgeting system and subsequent actions will inevitably tug at other departments.

In small companies a common problem is that the resources are so scarce that they require very careful handling. One mistake in a strategy can cost a firm years of development. Small firms have simpler means of making decisions involving fewer people, and the departmental conflicts are more obvious. The planning process in such a company is used to isolate and identify these conflicts and to mesh them together against a background of limited financial and technical means.

Large companies fight against what has been called the 'technostructure'.[1] Decisions are taken by groups, the process can be slow, and the effect of these decisions is to move the company in the way that suits the aims of the

[1] J. K. Galbraith, *The New Industrial State*; Hamish Hamilton, 1967, pp. 69–80.

members of the groups. For example, a high rate of growth and the development of new markets will suit the aims of the marketing and sales personnel, while a high rate of technical innovation will suit development executives, and so on.

In all of this, the control of the company's development is taken from the hands of the Board of Management, and profits drift to the level at which they are acceptable to the shareholders and the financiers. The corporate plan, operated at all levels of the business, is the only way of countering such a tendency.

The planning process does two supremely important things. First, it identifies corporate problems and searches for alternative solutions. Then it provides the corporate body with a focus and a direction. It offers a number of other benefits to the company, also. The process of planning makes management step aside from the day to day problems and causes it to think ahead on a systematic basis. It also encourages the company to examine the dynamics of its situation and to estimate what will be the future of the technical, economic and social forces which act upon its operation.

Planning leads to better co-ordination between departments and facilitates the establishment of performance standards within the organisation. It shows the participating executives how their responsibilities interact upon others.

It is realised that generalities as such are quite useless for the purpose of better marketing planning and that account must be taken of the different kinds of circumstances in which companies are situated. Owing to the nature of its business, or its market situation, each company will approach different aspects of the marketing function with a different emphasis.

To be of practical assistance to managers, this book takes account of the fact that at any one time, it is appealing only to a minority of the audience For example, the reader who is responsible for negotiating shipbuilding contracts will mentally 'switch off' when he reads about a food manufacturer. Equally, a small-company chief executive is likely to skip those parts of the book which deal with the more esoteric decision-making techniques which are available only to those with specialist skills, time and money.

So, in dealing with each aspect of the planning process, only the general principles to be followed have been outlined. At the end of each chapter these general principles are looked at with the eyes of men operating in different kinds of market situations.

Only the most significant divisions of situations, those which affect basic and fundamental attitudes to the subject, have been analysed. There are thousands of ways of classifying market circumstances and these are limited here to those which cause the most obviously different attitudes to fundamental questions of marketing.

Companies in differing types of markets approach the subject of marketing orientation in totally distinct ways. What is commonly mistaken for marketing by the general public is that range of activities engaged in by the producers of fast-selling packaged goods for the consumer. The idea of marketing has become identified with packaged cornflakes, soaps, branded foods and toiletries. Certainly it is true that the most massive programmes of market control, operated by the most specialised marketing talent, are used for such products as these, which can be produced simply and uniformly. Certainly, these manufacturers use the most advanced techniques of market forcing to build large sales volume and to keep price platforms high. It is the success of such techniques applied to such low priority products from a social point of view which provides the opponents of marketing with their ammunition.

Because they involve large numbers, and the patterns of behaviour are repetitive, and because the concepts involved are simple, such markets are easy to analyse and measure. It is when such techniques are applied with little modification to the vastly different behavioural systems involved in industrial marketing that they often fail. This is why marketing has a lower reputation amongst industrial manufacturers. They often 'try a little marketing', and find it doesn't work.

Marketing, as such, cannot be *tried*. It is merely the collection of skills, techniques and attitudes which provides the interface between the company and its market. Marketing is happening, whether it is recognised as such or not.

Marketing emphasis

Let us take a look at the emphasis which is laid naturally on different parts of the marketing process by companies operating in different types of market. (*Figure 1*.) The diagram describes general attitudes which themselves flow from the nature of the business.

PACKAGED GOODS: CONSUMER. We see that the advertising function is critical for companies selling low priced packaged goods; so is merchandising and sales promotion. This is not to say that other things such as pricing and the reaction to economic circumstances will not be important—it is merely to say that their main marketing emphasis lies elsewhere. In a large company manufacturing a wide range of such products, the man who controls and directs the advertising expenditure is usually seen to hold the key to the future of the organisation.

DURABLES: CONSUMER. High priced durables lay more emphasis on face to face selling. These are 'considered' purchases and many questions must be resolved before a buyer commits himself. He wants to talk with an expert, and the salesman fills this role. Such products are traditionally affected by economic circumstances—the prediction of changes in government policy

CONSUMER PRODUCTS

Packaged goods

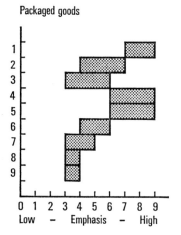

```
0  1  2  3  4  5  6  7  8  9
Low   -   Emphasis   -   High
```

High priced durable goods

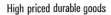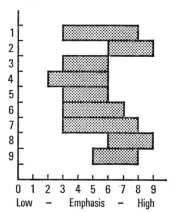

```
0  1  2  3  4  5  6  7  8  9
Low   -   Emphasis   -   High
```

INDUSTRIAL PRODUCTS

Plant and equipment

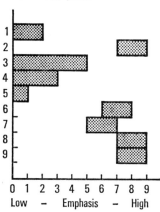

```
0  1  2  3  4  5  6  7  8  9
Low   -   Emphasis   -   High
```

Components

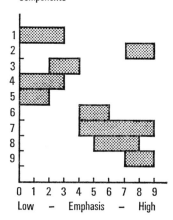

```
0  1  2  3  4  5  6  7  8  9
Low   -   Emphasis   -   High
```

Materials supply

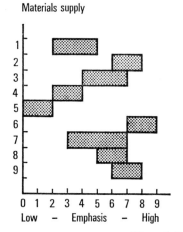

```
0  1  2  3  4  5  6  7  8  9
Low   -   Emphasis   -   High
```

Key

1   Product advertising
2   Personal selling
3   Physical distribution
4   Sales promotion
5   Merchandising
6   Pricing
7   Technical research and development
8   Economic variables
9   Service

Figure 1 The marketing emphasis.

towards credit, for example, may be an important factor in a company's plans.

PLANT AND EQUIPMENT.   When selling plant and capital equipment, the salesman and his team are seen by their companies to fulfil a critical function in the process. Pricing issues predominate in the preparation of tenders, and technical development can provide the mainspring of such a company's future.

The demand for such products is derived from other industries. Movements towards vertical integration, mergers, rapid technological development and general economic circumstances exert heavy pressure on the markets for plant and capital equipment. It is no surprise, therefore, to find that most of what we call marketing decisions in such a company are taken by the heads of the sales operation, in close conjunction with engineering departments. There may be a marketing services department in the organisation whose job it is to provide key data about the market, and the competition, to the decision makers. Companies in this field are nearly always capital-intensive in their structures and their futures depend upon successfully clinching a relatively few orders at profitable prices. Owing to the capital intensity, a supplier may always be liable to cost a particular contract on a marginal basis. Having covered his fixed costs elsewhere, he may want the extra volume to generate net profit. Therefore, tenders can vary widely, and information on pricing activities is the most closely guarded secret in this type of market.

COMPONENTS.   The component and tool type of industrial markets have many similarities. Here there may be wide variations in the types of equipment offered in a given market. The price span will therefore be wide; and to that extent buyers find it more difficult to compare prices. The problem for such companies is to find out where the potential customers are and to identify the decision making units. Here the major emphasis may lie on techniques to build sales enquiries.

In such a company, personal selling will still be the dominant factor. Research and development may be a key factor, and certainly the company will still be affected greatly by the economic circumstances of their customers' industries.

MATERIALS.   In supplying materials to industry, the important factor is the initial sale. This is the biggest area of the industrial market because the sales are repetitive, and ebb and flow in general with the output of the customers' business. Once the initial order has been gained and has been well serviced, it may be worth an enormous volume of business in the years to come. By the nature of such business, the quality levels of the materials may vary for different purposes, but it is often difficult to build a significant product distinction between competitive products.

The market is, therefore, price sensitive. Even though the supplier may have a sound and profitable relationship with a purchasing officer which extends over the years, the fact is that he must not move too far out of line with competitive prices without risking the business. In modern marketing there is no such thing as a perfect free market—all suppliers and all buyers are constrained by artificial forces in some way or another. But with the supply of basic commodities and materials to industry, we come as close as we ever will to a perfect market situation.

Figure 1 is a diagrammatic illustration of the different attitudes towards the importance of parts of the marketing operation by various types of business. There are product fields other than those shown. There are companies operating within these product fields who have a different marketing emphasis from that shown here. And any one company may lay an emphasis on a different aspect of marketing at any one time. But these are the significant splits in attitudes, and examples from these five types of product field are given in each chapter wherever their attitude differs significantly from the general approach.

Market structures

Next in analysing distinctions between companies, we turn to the structure of the market in which the company is engaged. *Figure 2* describes three basic types of competitive structure.

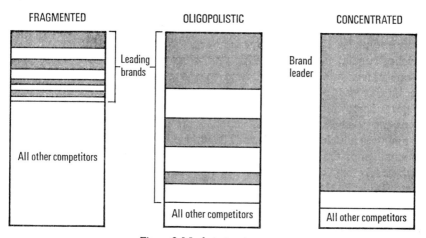

Figure 2 Market structure.

FRAGMENTED MARKETS. The first is a fragmented structure where most of the market is in the hands of a large number of suppliers. The leading suppliers compete from platforms of low market share. Such markets are very difficult to control. They are difficult to analyse, since the basic data is usually hard to find, and it is constantly changing. Sometimes the attempt to measure the market as a whole has no great practical value for a company, even a leading brand, because its ability to do something about it is limited.

Often these markets are labour intensive in their supply. When the going is good and margins are high, companies enter the market with little capital and low risk. When the going is bad, companies are forced out, or they volunteer themselves out, until times are good again. The usual fight is to achieve good trade distribution. Few companies have the power to reach over the heads of their distributors to talk to the users direct; so the main emphasis is on price and promotion techniques to force distribution. In such markets, new products do not remain different for very long. As soon as one company makes a technical breakthrough, unless it is of a radical nature and fundamental in its effect, then the others will copy the innovation and all go back to square one. Nearly all companies have some of their products selling in markets like this, which are of the most common kind. The market for sausages is fragmented; so is the market for builders' services

OLIGOPOLISTIC MARKETS.   The oligopolistic market is the second type of structure and one which is dominated by a few very large suppliers. It is common to find these suppliers with a ready access to raw materials which is technically difficult or financially impossible for others to copy once the market pattern has been established. Such markets are usually capital-intensive in their operation. There is usually a very heavy investment in research and development. Any technical advantage can be expected to score handsomely from the rival products, and the main emphasis is for such companies to establish a direct link, usually through advertising, with their end-users. The competition between such companies is fierce at every level of promotion. There is a high premium placed on market intelligence —one company cannot be allowed to run away with the market simply because he uses a new sales technique successfully. Although competition appears fierce through endless sales promotion offers, giveaways, competitions and other deals, in fact the suppliers to such markets are usually careful to maintain a high price platform. The market itself may not be very sensitive to small price moves, and a high price platform secures the base for their high marketing investment and for the heavy research and development costs. Typically the markets for soaps and detergents are oligopolistic; so is the market for car tyres.

CONCENTRATED MARKETS.   The third type of market is one which is concentrated mainly in the hands of a single supplier, who may have reached this position through some great technical innovation in the past, or who may monopolise all the lines of distribution and communication to his users.

However, more than ever before, such companies are vulnerable. Without the cutting edge of effective competition, their technical staff become concerned with improving productivity within their system, rather than searching for new and better ways to satisfy customers. These companies find it very difficult to satisfy all the market sectors. As economic power moves slowly into the hands of buyers and away from suppliers, such companies find their markets requiring more sophisticated models, different levels of price and service. And when a new, often relatively small, competitor develops a service in their market which appeals to a particular sector, they find it difficult to compete. Their main marketing emphasis is on defence and market support. They can be forced on to the offensive by an up and coming competitor who begins to eat into their business, but this usually takes time. And it is often the case that by the time their counter-attack is launched, the basic market structure has been altered. The market for important types of glass is concentrated; the market for razor blades was, but it became broken up in the manner described. The same thing happened to the market for potato crisps.

It is not suggested that these three types of competitive structure cover all markets comprehensively. But these are the three which will determine basic attitudes to many of the general approaches on marketing plans.

To define a market is a basic and quite difficult task. Some markets are limited first by the immediate and direct competition within the specific product group. Beyond that there is indirect competition from the more general product area. For example, printers with letterpress machines compete directly with both letterpress and offset-litho printers. But they also compete with office printing equipment, copying machines and duplicators. Finally, there is a geographical limit to the description of any market.[2]

Product characteristics

Basic attitudes to marketing and planning will differ also according to the specific characteristics of the product.

UNDIFFERENTIATED PRODUCTS. A cluster of attitudes will surround those products which are virtually undifferentiated from their competitors. There may be small variations in size, shape, colour, but the general levels of quality in such product fields can be matched by all competitors. Such companies lay great emphasis on attempting to build artificial distinctions to their products. One stage further than this they may compete through offering systems or service of a special kind which cannot be matched easily by their competitors. Such companies use advertising and sales approaches which appeal to the imagination. And such companies usually manufacture a wide range of types of the product so that they can offer a universal appeal to all sectors of the market. The market for petrol is typical of an undifferentiated product field.

DIFFERENTIATED PRODUCTS. In contrast to that is the attitude of the company making products which are distinctly different from its direct competitors.

[2] J. F. Winkler, *Marketing for the Developing Company*; Hutchinson, 1969. pp. 9–11.

Such products may be differentiated in a number of ways. First there may be functional differences in that the product works in a way different from its competitors, or its performance is particularly suitable for certain types of use, but not for others. On the other hand, the product may have an appeal for different types of customer satisfaction. For example, two ball-point pens may do precisely the same job of writing. One is made of plastic and is coloured red; the other is of rolled gold. The functional performance is the same, but the customer satisfaction is different. The differences may be perceived by the user, or he may have to take them for granted. The difference which he can see, as in the case of the ball-point pens, is to be preferred to the one he cannot. For example, two hammers may look and feel identical. However, if the haft of one is made of poorer quality wood, the head may snap off earlier. But there is no way of telling at the point of purchase. Two pies may look the same, but they have to be bought, cooked and sliced ready for eating before it is discovered that in one there is more filling than in the other.

Most manufacturers work in markets involving differentiated products. As a result they have two lines of approach. First, they examine individual merket segments in order to identify any gaps which they can fill or any weaknesses they can exploit. Secondly they use promotional appeals which draw the key distinction between their product benefits and those of the competition, and they explain these in user terms. If their product advantage is not obvious, they will stress it through packaging, branding, display and using demonstration in their marketing approach.

CUSTOM-BUILT PRODUCTS. Lastly, custom-built products provide for an entirely different set of attitudes towards marketing. Here the marketing process should be seen as a series of steps, each needing its own careful and rational procedure. For example, the first requirement is for the company to get on to the list of buying firms so as to be asked to tender. Great stress is laid upon desk research and on field sales reports to provide the company with clues as to where future customers might lie. Such companies advertise to build their reputation, usually on the basis of quality and service, rather than low price. Care is taken to service any customer enquiry with great efficiency. The salesman is intent on finding out about the organisation and who within it will influence the decision to buy—maybe up to a dozen or more people, at all levels. He may put his own technical personnel in touch with their opposite numbers so that he can have prepared a detailed technical proposal. This will often be submitted to the highest executive level, as well as the purchasing officer.

Distribution

The last significant split in marketing attitudes which we shall use for this study is related to the numbers and power of the customers. (*Figure 3.*)

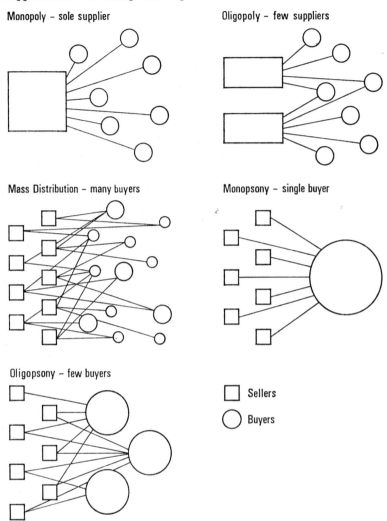

Monopoly – sole supplier

Oligopoly – few suppliers

Mass Distribution – many buyers

Monopsony – single buyer

Oligopsony – few buyers

☐ Sellers

◯ Buyers

Figure 3 The five buying/selling categories.

MASS DISTRIBUTION. If the company sells direct to product end-users or through a widespread retailer network, the power of an individual buyer is small. Companies in markets like these are interested in trend movements and in global changes of buyer behaviour which indicate opportunities, or threats, for the future. The emphasis lies on the prediction of customer group behaviour. From that, the need to influence such behaviour puts a premium on advertising and promotion skills rather than on personal selling.

OLIGOPSONY. In an oligopsonistic situation the buying power rests in the hands of a very few people. There may be many more suppliers than there are buyers. In this case the focus of interest lies on these buyers and their relations with competitors. There is great stress laid on co-operative schemes designed to tie in with the buying organisation and to secure their goodwill. The emphasis will be on personal selling, and promotion techniques may be personalised and discreet. The greatest threat in such circumstances is that buyers will play off suppliers against each other. To counter the threat there is often an understanding reached at trade association level so that, for example, information about rival bids may be exchanged and action taken if one company is seen to diverge from the standard tacitly set by the industry. Equally, the buyers have a habit of forming circles of their own, and the relationship between the two groups is a delicate one. The main power, however, rests with the buying group. Manufacturers selling gas appliances such as cookers find the bulk of their sales moving through the buyers in the 12 Area Gas Boards. This is a typical example of an oligopsonistic market.

Monopsony. If the company sells all its output through one main agent or distributor, and if it is successful in doing so, then a fairly stable but monopsonistic situation can be created. Effectively the distributor is taking on the marketing of the company's products with the supplier responding to the distribution. Each plays very little part in the other's operation. Such relationships can trade well for years, but a disruption in the market, a merger, or a new technical threat can put immediate and severe pressure on one side or the other. From time to time the distributor may feel uneasy about having only one supplier for an important part of his business, and the supplier likewise. They may therefore come to some understanding that each will build up a part of his business separately in order to protect the future. Electronic companies supplying the Post Office or government defence contracts are in a monopsonistic situation.

The effect of planning

There is more emphasis laid on planning of all kinds today than ever before. There is good reason for it, because we live in unusual times. And top management is confronted by new and unfamiliar challenges. One challenge is the phenomenal rate of progress in research and development. The rate of acceleration of technical development is far faster than any advances we are making in understanding or quantifying human behaviour. Over 90 per cent of all the scientists who ever lived are alive today, and the marketing man is taking the fruits of their endeavours and modelling them for the market place. And, in the sense that the cumulative sum of what marketing men do, and the way in which they do it, affects the market place they are, to that extent, moulding the market, too.

Next, the broad social and cultural movements in Western society are leading to an ever more educated public which is articulate and which is beginning to question not only the values and assumptions of its forebears, but also the circumstances and quality of life. Marketing men are affecting that life. After all, marketing men know more about persuasive communication than any other group of people and they are using their powers daily, often without asking to what end.

Business is becoming more capital intensive. Computer systems and management scientists are invading every area of industry. Mechanical skills are developing as never before so that the costs of business are mounting. Large capital requires large markets, preferably of a standard kind. This contrasts with the needs of markets which are becoming ever more sophisticated and diverse. Also, product life cycles are shortening. Companies are faced with the technical obsolescence of their products within a short time span, whereas previously such products would last for years. Competition is sharper technically, and is quick to spot weaknesses in the market. This is throwing more and more strain on applied research and on to product modification programmes.

The last problem relates to what has been called the information explosion. This explosion is in both the volume of information and the substantive content relative to general management decisions. Shortly, system designers will be upon us, who will be responsible for the acquisition, processing, disseminating, displaying and interpreting the information. This will lead to more use of decision analysis systems.[3]

Planning for all this change is inevitable. It might be said that the company with the better planned operation is more likely to be the survivor in an age when great industries will polarise into a few hands. Certainly, the plan will win against management intuition, which, more often than not, is the only alternative.

It is safe to predict, however, that out of all the information that is becoming available, marketing will remain the most baffling and difficult information area for analysis and action.

[3] H. Igor Ansoff, *Top Management; Problems and Process*; Associated Business Programmes seminar, July 1971.

2. Long-range Planning

Industry is moving beyond the production of marketing plans in isolation and into systems of integrated planning for the business as a whole. The days are passing when a marketing plan was the only one produced, used as a sales forecast and assessed for feasibility by production and finance divisions. A procedure of this kind may be a useful means of getting a planning base started in a company, however. From this base an integrated planning system can evolve, leading to corporate long-term planning. But it should be recognised for its limitation, in that it takes a one-sided view of the company's operation. It also presumes that the only part of the organisation which produces profits is marketing, and will miss profit opportunities in other parts of the business. Indeed, by its nature this system may drive other divisions into diseconomies through their attempts to meet marketing goals.

This procedure has one other outstanding flaw. The entire focus of attention of the organisation is upon the marketing plan, from which all else is derived. Because of the difficulties of predicting market reaction, the plan is seldom very accurate. Without contingency plans, therefore, the final outcome will always be adrift from the plan, with a consequent reaction against planning itself, 'it does not work', or against the marketing effort, 'they do not know what they are doing'.

Three degrees of integrated planning have been described.[1]

Blind Management in which few statistical facts are gathered to help in management decisions and in which policy decisions are determined through intuition, judgement and experience.

Management by Approximation in which statistics and facts are gathered with varying degrees of accuracy, but with policy decisions not based on the data.

Integrated Systems Management which is the combination of all applicable scientific techniques, plus empirical judgement.

[1] W. I. Little, 'The Integrated Management Approach to Marketing;' *U.S. Jnl. of Marketing*, Vol. 31, April 1967, pp. 32–36.

If we accept that no one except the smallest businessman can use the blind management system for long, in markets which are competitive and changing, then we should recognise that for most companies a system of Management by Approximation is what is used now and will continue to be used in the foreseeable future. Large multi-product firms, capital-intensive companies, particularly those serving industrial markets, and companies operating in differentiated product markets, will be the first to apply more scientific methods and to use continuously an integrated systems management approach. But for most companies, the monthly 'Executive Meeting' and the 'Monday Morning Managers Meeting' will continue to provide the integrated planning function of the company. This, despite the fact that strength of personality, wit, debating skill, and seniority usually rule such proceedings. Such meetings are governed by short-term considerations, will consider a mass of trivia, and will inhibit the introduction of long-term planning considerations.

Effective integrated management planning involves the establishment of a sequence for problem solutions; that is, analysing problems, gathering data, making computations and applying judgement and creative ability to the findings. In establishing corporate plans, this is precisely the procedure—and it involves all departments of the business.

Simon[2] explains that there are four basic steps in problem solving:

(1) *Perception* of the decision need or opportunity, which he calls the 'intelligence phase'. A method is required to force management away from the operating problems and to recognise the strategic problems facing the company.
(2) *Formulation* of alternative courses of action. At the start of the planning process only a few alternatives are recognised, but others present themselves in a continual stream. A company may choose to be passive and wait for opportunities to come to it. However, it will hardly have much influence over its own destiny, let alone be in control of it.
(3) *Evaluation* of the alternatives for their respective contributions. The rules for search and evaluation of products and markets are not the same for all firms. Objectives will vary from one firm to another, even within the same industry, and there is interaction between the selection of the strategic opportunities and the setting of objectives.
(4) *Choice* of one or more of the alternatives.

There now arises the first practical problem which affects corporate planning as much as it affects short-term marketing planning. It is generally assumed that objectives must be set *before* the strategies are evaluated. In fact, the process is entirely interactive—the means available to reach an objective will help to determine the choice and size of objective.

Given a problem which planners can identify, they search for the means of resolving it. In evaluating the alternative means they quantify the objectives which *can* be reached. Then, having chosen the strategy, set the objective.

[2] H. A. Simon, *The New Science of Management Decision*; Harper & Row, New York 1960.

The corporate planning process

Ansoff describes seven corporate objective-setting areas.[3]

(1) Continuing growth of sales of at least the pace of the industry, to enable the firm to maintain its share of the market.
(2) Increase in relative market share to increase the relative efficiency of the firm.
(3) Growth in earnings to provide resources for re-investment.
(4) Growth in earnings per share to attract capital.
(5) Continuing addition of new products and new lines.
(6) Continuing expansion of the firm's customer population.
(7) Absence of excessive seasonal or cyclical fluctuations in sales or earnings.

An analysis is now required comparing the historical trend in each sector of the business to the immediate future. Forecasts will take into account factors external to the company such as market trends, economic trends, competitive trends, technical trends in both the direct and the indirect markets in which the company is engaged. These are then compared with the likely performance of the company based on internal factors such as product strengths, material costs, labour costs, management skills, distribution costs, technical ability, productivity prospects and financial capacity. The earnings from the existing business can be predicted over the time-scale of the forecasts. These are then compared with the objectives required.

Profit Gap Analysis

What will result is a profit gap (*Figure 4*). Only three methods can be used now to make up the required profit difference from the existing business.

First, is the possibility of increasing turnover either through those products which provide an opportunity for 'economies of scale' production, or through the development of new products and new markets.

Second, is through the reduction of costs in running the organisation, through the better use of materials or labour, or the reduction of distribution or management costs, or through the reduction of other overheads.

Third, through the adjustment of prices and discounts to promote the company to a higher gross profit platform without a matching loss of sales revenue.

There is no other way of proving a company's trading profit, short of selling the business.

If the profit gap cannot be made up through these means, and the long-range objectives for the business are realistic, then a diversification and acquisition policy is required, in addition to optimising the profitability of the existing operation.

Figure 5 shows the breakdown of some data which might be built into the Profit Gap Analysis. The profit gap technique is valid for short-range planning for a year ahead. It provides one of the few techniques available

[3] H. Igor Ansoff, *Corporate Strategy*; McGraw-Hill, 1965.

for tightening up the budgeting procedure so as to force the maximum economies from the current operation. In a time of escalating inflation, the gap analysis technique, applied to the short-term, can be used constantly by companies to guide value analysis projects and to assist them in price change decisions. Through the accurate short-term forecasting of costs, the point at which a price alteration is required becomes clearer to management. Consequently, moves towards industry and company price changes can be prepared well in advance. The case for a price change can be argued more soundly and the usual time lag between, say, material cost increases and

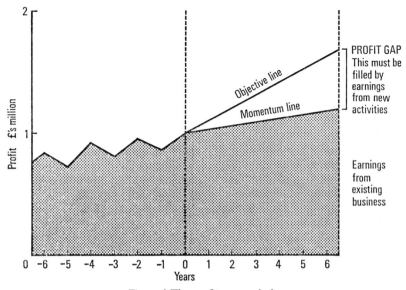

Figure 4 The profit gap analysis.

price increases is thereby reduced. This time lag has been the cause of more losses in industry during periods of spiralling inflation than any other factor; except the downturn of markets themselves.

The Management Audit

From this point, what is now required is an audit of all the key areas of the business. This is a basic attempt to analyse the strengths and weaknesses of the organisation. Even when used for long-term planning, short-term profit opportunities will be uncovered by the audit and should be attacked. This is part of the organic planning process described by Ward[4] in which the best long-term plans are built up as a result of systems developed for resolving short-term problems. An organic situation is one where there is a complex of interacting and perhaps conflicting parts. In this way management be-

[4] E. P. Ward, *The Dynamics of Planning*; Pergamon Press, 1970, pp. 24–35.

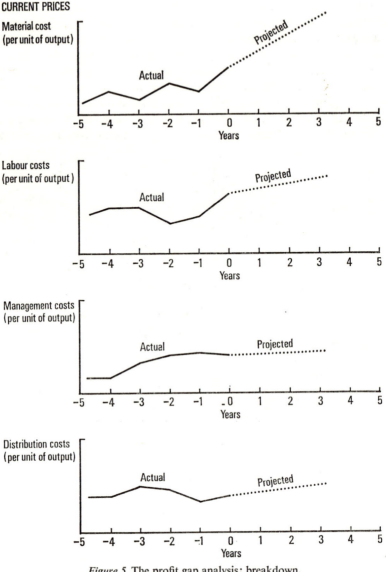

Figure 5 The profit gap analysis: breakdown.

comes experienced in diagnosing problems as well as setting objectives and developing strategies, tactics, and control procedures to meet them. If this is established as part of the day-to-day working routine, then corporate and long-range planning becomes fairly easy as a straightforward extension of the technique.

The basic purposes of the management audit are to improve the deployment of resources, to uncover potential assets still to be exploited, to make good weaknesses, and to determine measures to take to prepare the company for its future controls and planning base. The main areas to be investigated include finance, and the functional divisions such as production and marketing, plus product/market situations, personnel resources, and organisation structure.

In the financial area great stress is laid on a set of financial ratios including return on capital employed, cash/creditors, cash plus debtors/current liabilities, net worth/current liabilities, cash flow measures, turnover/fixed assets, turnover/total assets, stock turn, and working capital turn. Against the analysis of the financial situation must be set two questions. The first is the level of service which is required by the customers. The second concerns the level of risk which is acceptable to management.

In the functional departments, particularly in marketing, the first outstanding question relates to those activities in which the company has established a 'leadership' position or is dominating an area. The second indicates where the company has consistently fallen short of the standards of leading or closest competitors. The really outstanding areas of a business are usually extremely limited, and the source of the advantage may be perishable. For example, it may be located in the ability of two or three managers. The main sources of strength may be vulnerable to outside factors, such as government legislation, or technological change. As Drucker has said, the only distinct resource of any business is knowledge—competitors can attain nearly all other advantages which are not protected in some way.

In the product area, it is usual to analyse the key products of the business. Most companies have too many products for them all to be analysed and the future of most companies will be determined by the performance of a relatively few products in their range. The key product analysis will vary from company to company, but the questions relate usually to the existing size of market share and whether it is prominent, or viable. The questions may refer to a specific market segment or area rather than the whole of the market. Other questions relate to distribution penetration, prices, discount levels and so on. In analysing the human resources, the keynote should be an objective analysis of the performance of managers, rather than a subjective assessment of their capability range. The questions relate to general management's range of skills and abilities, as well as those of specialist managers. An assessment is required of technical management resources operating at staff level, say, in research and development departments, or in line or service positions, perhaps in quality control or work study.

The analysis of the organisation structure should be undertaken after the aims of the company have been clarified and the plans to achieve these aims have been drawn up. Then the organisation structure can be set up to divide the work effectively, to establish a clear line of command, to stretch managerial and technical resources, and to provide for accountability and control.

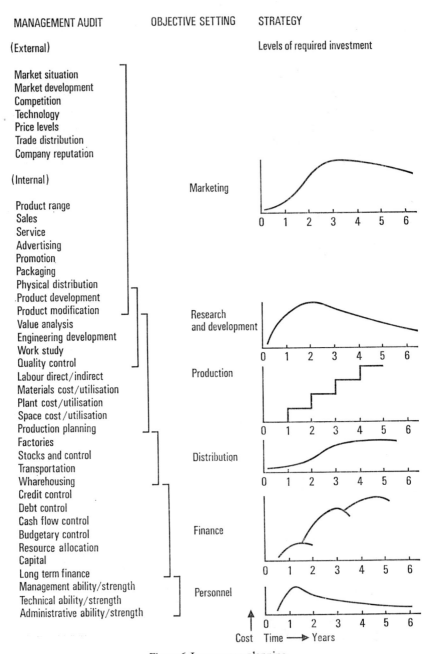

MANAGEMENT AUDIT   OBJECTIVE SETTING   STRATEGY

(External)   Levels of required investment

Market situation
Market development
Competition
Technology
Price levels
Trade distribution
Company reputation

(Internal)

                              Marketing

Product range
Sales
Service
Advertising
Promotion
Packaging
Physical distribution
Product development
Product modification   Research
Value analysis   and development
Engineering development
Work study
Quality control
Labour direct/indirect   Production
Materials cost/utilisation
Plant cost/utilisation
Space cost/utilisation
Production planning
Factories
Stocks and control   Distribution
Transportation
Wharehousing
Credit control
Debt control
Cash flow control
Budgetary control   Finance
Resource allocation
Capital
Long term finance
Management ability/strength Personnel
Technical ability/strength
Administrative ability/strength

                                 Cost   Time ⟶ Years

Figure 6 Long-range planning.

Setting Marketing Objectives. In any company, seven distinct marketing goals have to be identified:[5]

(1) The desired standing of the existing products in their present market, in turnover and percentage share measured against direct and indirect competition.
(2) The desired standing of existing products in new markets, measured as before.
(3) The existing products which should be phased out and ultimately abandoned, and the future product mix.
(4) The new products or modifications needed in existing markets, the number, their properties and the share targets.
(5) The new markets which new products will help develop, in size and share.
(6) The distributive organisation needed to accomplish the marketing goals and the pricing policy appropriate to them.
(7) A service objective, measuring how well the customer should be supplied with what he considers value.

Strategy Formulation. So far the corporate plan has analysed the trend of the business in some detail, it has forecast the profit differences between where it is going and where it wants to be, and it has analysed the strengths and weaknesses of the existing organisation. Thus far, an overall objective has been produced, together with a series of shorter-term departmental objectives. Now comes the question of strategy formulation.

The first procedure is to record the current strategy.[6] This flows from the overall movement of the business as a whole and is made up of a series of sub-strategies operating within the main functions of the business. The next stage is to relate the current strategy against the *core* of the problems which have been analysed. Once the core of the strategic problem has been identified, management can formulate alternative ways of dealing with it. At this stage imagination and creative flair may be required in order to generate the largest number of possible alternatives. The realistic alternatives need now to be evaluated, not only for their power to deal effectively with the immediate functional problem, but also for their ability to contribute to the overall corporate goal. A number of compromises may have to be made within divisions, simply because what is desirable within one division may not be desirable within the overall framework of the organisation.

The alternatives can be compared in terms of:

(1) Relative effectiveness in solving the overall corporate problem.
(2) Degree to which each matches the company's competence and resources.
(3) Relative competitive advantage.
(4) Degree to which they satisfy management's preferences.
(5) Extent to which they avoid creation of new problems.
(6) Risk, in relation to their practical feasibility, long-term commitment, and payoff period.

The last stage is to choose the strategy.

[5] P. Drucker, *The Practice of Management*; Heinemann, London, 1966, p. 64.
[6] F. F. Gilmore, 'Formulating Strategy in Smaller Companies'; *Harvard Business Review*, May–June 1971.

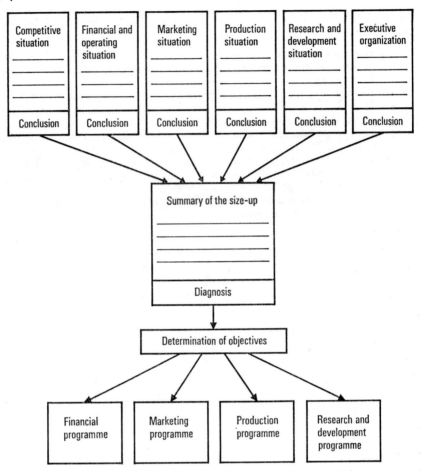

Figure 7 Example of traditional approach to strategy formulation.

(*Adaptation from:* P. F. Gilmore, 'Strategy formation in smaller Companies'; *Harvard Business Review*, May-June 1971)

The accuracy of long-range planning

It will seem doubtful to those in management who are traditionally against planning systems, that long-range corporate planning can be quite accurate. A study published in the u.s. in 1970[7] showed that in most companies, long-range plans are for five years. As to be expected, the shorter-term plans tended to be more accurate; and the longer a company has had a corporate planning system running and continuously updated, the more accurate become its predictions.

Most long-range plans have been conservative in their forecasts in the

[7] R. F. Vancil, 'The Accuracy of Long Range Planning'; *Harvard Business Review*, Sept.–Oct. 1970.

past decade. This is due to two main factors. First, the effect of escalating inflation makes the turnover projections look conservative because prices are continuously being raised. Secondly, during this period, there has been in this country, and in the u.s., a spate of take-overs and mergers. These are seldom planned for, at least in terms of size and timing, although many long-range plans have identified the need for a vigorous acquisition policy.

The factors which have been identified as affecting the accuracy of long-term planning are described as being mainly of two kinds. 'Situational' factors such as a record of low growth in profits tend to make future forecasts conservative; and high growth records tend to make future estimates optimistic. Larger companies do more accurate planning than small ones, and accuracy is lower amongst companies in highly competitive industries.

The other main factor has been called 'system design'. Accuracy is greater in those companies which have used corporate planning to provide a frame of reference for the operating budgets. And it has been proved that the more involved in the planning process is the chief executive, the more accurate will be the plan. On the other hand, plans produced 'from the bottom up' tend to be more accurate than those produced by senior management and 'handed down'. A rigorous discipline in linking the long-term corporate plan to the operational budgets tends also to improve its accuracy.

The question is whether great accuracy is desirable or not. It has been said that the one thing of which we can be certain is that the unforeseen will happen and will upset our plans. But it has also been remarked that the true benefit of corporate planning lies in the routine involved. The routine of analysis of performance, the identification of problems, objective-setting and strategy selection to overcome the problems is the greatest benefit of planning.

Market Situations

Packaged goods: consumer

The low-priced packaged goods produced for consumer markets will be concerned in the long term with social movements and consumer attitudes. A movement towards blander tasting foods, or increasingly towards slimming foods, or towards one main meal a day, will affect branded food companies. The reaction of the consumer movements and their likely effect on legislation will be considered. Already there have been radical changes in legislation (introduced practically overnight) on the contents of soft drinks; sugar-based products may feel it next. A company based on a narrow product range will be looking for acquisition and market development opportunities.

Durables: consumer

High-priced durable manufacturers are more likely to take note of likely government policy with regard to credit and taxation; but they, too, may be affected greatly by the consumer protection movement. Economic circumstances, particularly with regard to consumers' level of disposable income, will affect their markets and their trading channels. Such companies will also be concerned about takeover movements within their industries.

Plant and equipment

The two most vital concerns to these companies are changing industry structures, particularly movements towards closing-off an open market by means of company mergers or reciprocal trading. Industrial markets are becoming more closed-off than ever. Vertical integration has meant that large customers who were previously buying on the open market now buy from suppliers within their group. And the trading links between large industrial companies are drawing tighter together, often for mutual protection against the forces of government and competition. Reciprocal dealing is the practice both of using one's purchasing power to obtain sales, and the practice of preferring one's customers in purchasing supplies. Particularly it is coming under more detailed scrutiny from anti-trust authorities in the States.[8] This may be the next great area for clarifying and tightening company law in this country.

Materials

Owing to the high material cost involved in supplying these products, the profits and prices of suppliers are extremely sensitive to shifts in world material prices. In their corporate planning, such companies look outside the boundaries of Britain and are concerned with two factors. They need accurate predictions of supply/demand factors, so that market prices can be established both for short-range operations and for corporate planning. Also, such companies need long-range forewarning of new technological developments which may act against the continuing scope of their own market.

Changes in technology may affect any part of the chain leading from material procurement to customer use. At the supply end, a development may occur which converts poorer quality materials more easily. There may be radical alterations of processing technology. And there may be a move on the part of the customers out of one type of material and into another.

Such companies are also concerned with their markets being closed off by their competitors, because most of them are large suppliers to industry and also large buyers, so it is in this area where reciprocal trading practices abound.

Fragmented markets

Companies supplying fragmented markets in a minor capacity tend to adopt strategies which can react quickly to external influences. They tend not to

[8] R. Moyer, 'Reciprocity: Retrospect and Prospect'; *U.S. Jnl. of Marketing*, Vol. 34, Oct. 1970, pp. 47–54.

make long-range plans, or they introduce a large element of flexibility into their systems. Leaders in such markets are usually concerned at the strategic level with making certain that the rest of the competition behaves well. They seek to ensure that their competitors do not engage in practices such as price cutting which could lead to destructive price wars and great market disturbance. Such companies are frequently to be found taking the lead in industry co-operative movements in, for example, exchanging product information or discount level information. In the long run, the leaders will be concerned to produce some great leap forward in technology which will alter the basic shape of the market entirely. It has been done, for example, in the ice cream industry, but it is rare.

Oligopolistic markets

Such companies are the real corporate and long-range planners in industry. Their business is very competitive so they must make plans to deal with every kind of contingency. Their investment on fixed and running cost is extremely high and they must protect the profitability of their future installations through long-range planning.

Concentrated markets

The leaders in such markets may be very concerned with long-range planning. Their attitudes are defensive in nature, and may be concerned primarily with the acquisition of likely competitors before they establish too strong a hold on a section of the market.

The fighting brands in such markets tend to push and drive as quickly as their resources will allow, and they consequently tend to be not too bothered about long-range planning, until their own segment of the market begins to 'top out', when sales increase only at diminishing rates. Then they look for new product development, geographical expansion, and new markets to exploit.

Mass distribution

Where a company deals with many thousands of customers and end-users, it is more likely to have a planning function which is closely geared to improving its efficiency and productivity particularly in the area of distribution. Quite simply, the costs of marketing may represent more than half the total costs of the business, and it is such companies which lay great stress on organisation structures, objectives and controls.

Oligopsony and monopsony

The further a company moves towards a situation where all or most of its business is in the hands of only a few buyers, or one major buyer, the less likely it is to produce long-range plans which are independent of the buyers' own plans. Such companies have little alternative but to react to the day-today situation of their buyers. But their long-term thinking tends to be done in conjunction with their small group of buyers who will be traditionally reluctant to assist materially in the preparation of forecasts. Their long-range plans may be made in conjunction with their colleagues in the trade, but this leads to a conflict in that these are competitors also.

In the long run, the cumulative effect of all this long-range planning which is being undertaken at present is bound to be felt in the economy at large. There are already signs of it.[9] For example, the spending on capital goods will become more stable and will be less responsive to the year-to-year profitability of the organisation. Businessmen, because they can predict more accurately their need for finance, will begin to borrow money at a time of favourable interest rates, and not simply when they come to require the cash. Because there will be more planned phasing out of products, more radical innovation, quickly copied by competition, product life cycles will continue to get shorter. And the ultimate effect may be that inflation may become even more difficult to control by fiscal measures—simply because companies can predict the moves more easily and can take avoiding action.

Example: Setting Marketing Objectives

When a company looks at itself in its marketing audit—it should also look at the markets in which it operates, or is trying to reach. At least four questions should be asked:

      (1) What markets are we in?
      (2) What are we trying to sell?
      (3) To whom are we trying to sell?
      (4) Who are our competitors?

Consider the case of a company manufacturing and selling electric food mixers. The narrow answers to the above questions would be:

      (1) The electric food mixer market.
      (2) Electric food mixers.
      (3) People who need/want an electric food mixer.
      (4) Other electric food mixer manufacturers.

1. What markets are we in?

However, as can be seen from the illustration, the company is not in just one, but many markets simultaneously. Obviously they are aiming at the person who likes labour-saving devices in the kitchen. They should also be aiming at the gift market remembering that 46 per cent of mixers found in the kitchen arrive by way of a gift. Other markets also exist, including, for example, what has been termed the Veblenian market. In this market people buy the products not for what they are, but because they add a touch of the prestige associated with their social reference group.

    These markets can be further segmented. Take for example the gift market. Here 17 per cent of the 46 per cent mentioned earlier is taken up by

[9] Dean S. Ammer, 'The Side Effects of Planning'; *Harvard Business Review*, May–June 1970.

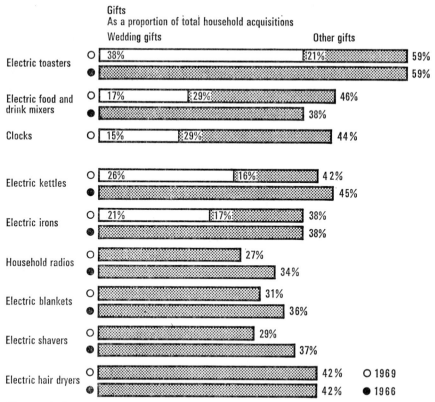

Gifts
As a proportion of total household acquisitions

(*Source:* Audits of Great Britain Ltd., 'The Big Give-away'; *Audit Magazine*, July 1971, p. 9)

Figure A

wedding gifts. However, there are also the birthday, anniversary and holiday (Christmas) segments to this gift market.

2. What are we trying to sell?

The previous sections lead directly to the second question. Using the electric food mixer/gift market example it can be seen that the company is selling a gift rather than a mixer. Consequently their promotion and advertising campaign should be directed accordingly.

3. To whom are we trying to sell?

17 per cent of the electric food mixers arrive in a household as wedding presents. The company must, therefore, sell to two groups. The potential receivers have to be impressed by the advantages of owning an electric food mixer. The potential buyers, the givers of the gift, must be persuaded to purchase the company's particular brand.

4. Who are our competitors?

The company which believes itself to be in the electric food mixer market will consider as its competitors only those companies selling a similar product. Consequently the marketing effort may be directed at establishing, in a potential customer's mind, only the points differentiating his product from those of his competitors. Examples could include colour, size, price and quality.

However, reference to *Figure A* will demonstrate the fallacy of this idea. In the kitchen convenience ware market his product must vie for a sale with electric toasters, electric frying pans, and so on. In the gift market, the competition could arise from similarly priced popular cameras and in the Veblenian market, for example, from electric toothbrushes. These latter two products have nothing to do with kitchen ware in general, let alone food mixers in particular. All these factors will, or should, influence the direction and intensity of the marketing effort.

By segmenting the market one can see that the company is selling in the three markets—and there are probably more.

> (a) a labour saving device
> (b) a gift
> (c) a prestige article

Consequently the company's advertising and promotional campaign, as well as the complete marketing strategy, may need to be expanded or redirected to fulfil its aims and objectives.

P.M.

3. The Process of Marketing Planning

The precise make-up of the marketing plan will vary from organisation to organisation. This is inevitable because it flows from the nature of the business and how it is organised to meet the market. The annual marketing plan will be formulated in much the same way as the long-range marketing plan, but will take note of more recent and surface trends, and will be concerned with short-range projections, primarily to build up a budgeting base.

There is a flaw in thinking that the two kinds of plan are the same, only with different time-scales. This is because some of the investment in marketing, notably in market research and in advertising, should be properly regarded as capital expenditure rather than as revenue. The effect of advertising, for example, is spread over a longer time-scale than the annual plan allows for. And a high investment may be needed in research at a time when the company has only limited knowledge of its environment. Yet this investment may be properly dropped in subsequent years to a level sufficient to allow only for market monitoring, and testing. Basic data is cheaper to up-date than it is to obtain in the first place. Therefore the benefits from market research expenditure incurred in one year may not be felt until subsequent periods, and the information decay rate may be fairly slow. A case for treating advertising as capital expenditure has been made out in the same way,[1] except that the decay rate may be much quicker.

The overall marketing plan usually is built from separate plans prepared and submitted by the heads of the departments within the marketing division. It is a compromise between these short-range plans and the longer-term corporate plan (*Figure 8*). Most companies have a function-based organisational structure. So the subplans will consist of:

A product mix plan, showing the product deletions, the product modifications, the product additions, their timing, and the volume, turnover and profit objectives, broken down by product groups and, probably further, into product items.

[1] Joel Dean, 'Does Advertising Belong in the Capital Budget?'; *U.S. Jnl. of Marketing,* Vol. 30, Oct. 1966, pp. 15–21.

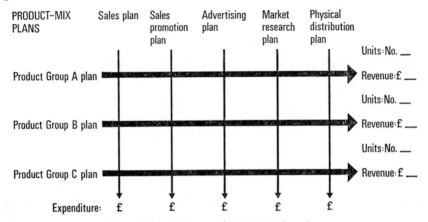

Figure 8 The main operational marketing plans.

(*Source:* J. Winkler, 'Developing the Annual Marketing Plan'; Associated Business Programmes Seminar, October 1971)

Each product group may have its own objectives in terms of market share and distribution penetration. Each plan will show the supporting operational facilities, such as sales assistance, required.

The sales plan will show the strength and direction of the selling effort over time. It will have objectives related to levels of service for existing customers and for new account penetration, split region by region. It may specify conversion rates of orders to calls, recall rates, the rate of introduction of additional products to existing accounts. It should also contain a subplan which relates specifically to the key accounts held by the company, showing where a defensive policy is required and where key accounts can be exploited for further business. The plan will show the deployment of the sales organisation related to journey cycles, sales promotion schemes and featured products.

The advertising plan in companies laying great stress on this activity, may be quite complex in its make-up. In other companies it may be merely a statement showing the timing, nature, weight and media to be used. The advertising plan could, however, be related to communications objectives in those companies to whom the data is available and for whom advertising is critical. For example, the objectives may relate to the description of the audience to be reached; the weight of the message upon different sectors of the audience; the increase in levels of awareness of the brand; the penetration of new users for each main brand.

The sales promotion plan will be set according to the nature of the company operation and its markets. Many companies run promotions continuously to tie in with sales journey cycles. In such companies there may be one major promotion, perhaps related to the product user, plus two minor promotions, one perhaps related to distribution trade incentives, and the other to motivate the sales force itself. In mass marketing, the practice is to phase heavy promotion schemes with consumer advertising.[2] The advertising is run in a pattern of bursts, while the promotion is used to force the trade and to counter competition in non-advertising periods.

These are the four most common plans, but there may be others of equal importance, depending on the type of company.

Physical distribution plan. In a company with a high physical distribution cost, there will be a plan which outlines programmes for the more efficient handling of stock, involving measures of its level of stock holding, its speed of turnround, its level of waste and breakage, or the handling cost. Programmes may be evolved for improving, or cutting the cost of customer service levels involving delivery lag time; for the re-location of distribution points and for the use of different methods of transportation. In transport, objectives may be laid out for better utilisation of vehicles, reduction of drivers' cost, more efficiency in servicing, and re-planning of delivery routes for more efficient working. Increasing emphasis is being given to this function by modern management.

Market research plan. In a technically intensive company, producing numerous new product ideas, there may be a market research plan of some consequence. This will divide into three main areas:

Gathering of establishment data relating to markets or other environmental factors.
Consistent monitoring of operations, particularly in existing key markets and competitor's activity.
A programme of testing products, markets, operations or concepts.

This plan is particularly important for companies in fast-changing markets or for companies in markets which are sensitive to changes in economic or other environmental conditions.

Research and development plan. Most companies with more than a shadow of a research and development unit will produce a plan for it. At some point this must be meshed with the marketing operation. This will show the programmes of work and estimates of the timings and contribution levels to be obtained from value analysis projects; from product modifications, from new product development, and from profit-stripping products which are to be phased out. Of necessity, this plan is essentially a series of projects laid out in order of feasibility and timing. In R. & D. several projects are run concurrently—but this plan needs constant updating during the year, with a consequent effect upon product mix and sales plans. Some projects will take longer than estimated, some will fail altogether, some will be completed

[2] Audits of Great Britain Ltd., 'Do You Plan to Burst Your Advertising Schedules?'; *Audit Magazine*, July 1971.

earlier. So it is usual to keep a degree of flexibility about the latter end of the product mix and sales plans, only firming up as development projects are completed.

Pricing plan. Some companies, notably those with a high material cost, those which exist on large contracts, and multi-product companies, may also have a pricing plan. This is usually prompted and guided by management accounts, although the objectives are set and decisions are taken in marketing or at general management level. The pricing plan outlines the principles and objectives to guide pricing and discounting decisions. Future price changes are built in, often to coincide with product modifications or to relate to a predictable moment when material or labour costs makes an industry-wide price change inevitable.

Regional plan. In a decentralised organisation, running its marketing operations from different geographical centres while using central services, there will be a meshing of some of these plans at regional level. Particularly will this be true of the sales plan, the sales promotion plan, and of physical distribution.

Market plan. In a market-structured organisation, there is less emphasis on product planning and more on the identification of separate market movements and opportunities. This is usual in a single product company. For example, a computer manufacturer can apply his product to a wide variety of uses in different markets. Each marketing manager will then produce a marketing plan for his sphere of responsibility, embracing all the operations he commands, and using the facilities of central services. The overall marketing plan is built up from this base.

Some plans will be developed at much greater length than others. It is desirable to have at least a simple analysis, a statement of key objectives quantified and dated, a method of operation, costs and timing for every plan mentioned here. Some of them will be less important than others, but these are all cost areas, while most of them are revenue producing in their own right. If even a minor operation is working to a plan, then the budgeting process has a focus and a direction so that variances can be traced to their cause more easily. This is putting the benefits of the plan at their lowest level. There is one other great advantage. It makes someone responsible for that part of the operation.

The planning procedure

There are ten steps involved, broken into two halves—situation analysis and programming.

The situation analysis involves two areas, diagnosis and prognosis.

Diagnosis of the present situation in each planning area in terms of costs, revenues, contributions and environmental factors relating to the function. This answers the question: What is our situation now?

Prognosis extrapolates the trends in each area and answers the question: If we take no action, where will we end up?

At this point the next two stages are inter-related. We need to set objectives and to decide strategy. The problem is that we cannot do them in that logical order, because not every strategy is available to us. Some strategies will run counter to other departmental plans, some will be beyond our technical and financial resources, some will not pay off until well beyond the planning period.

Generating alternatives. It is convenient, therefore, to interpose a stage here, which could be called generating alternative and feasible strategies, and quantifying them.

Objective setting. Having narrowed the short-term strategies we can see which short-term objectives are possible to achieve. These should be as few as are reasonable to achieve the main long-term objectives of the company

The overall objective flows from the gap which lies between where we will go if we take no action, and where we desire to go. This requires profit gap analysis, described in Chapter 2.

In preparing detailed functional plans it is not usually possible to use the gap analysis technique, because of the effect of operations overlap between departments. For example, a decrease in physical distribution cost may result in a lower level of customer service, causing in turn a loss of sales revenue. The gap analysis technique can only be used for operations which are internally consistent, self-contained, and to a large degree independent of other operations. Sales planning, for example, may have a use for the technique, and so may research and development in certain circumstances. But a service activity dependent upon other functions for its objectives, such as sales promotion, cannot use it.

The following table illustrates specific marketing objectives for a one-year plan in a consumer product company.[3]

Statement of Goals

A company's marketing goals for the coming year might be as follows:

COMPANY MARKETING GOALS (CONSUMER GOODS)

Sales

5 per cent increase in unit sales
10 per cent increase in sterling sales
No change in unit sales of products *A* and *B*
10 per cent increase in unit sales of product *C*
15 per cent increase in unit sales of product *D*
To complete market tests and obtain £200,000 sales for new product *E*

[3] V. P. Bluell, *Marketing Management in Action*; McGraw–Hill, 1966, pp. 153–54.

Share of Market

To increase overall company share of market by 2 per cent

Distribution

To add 10 per cent class *A* retailers
To add 20 per cent class *B* retailers
No change in number of class *C* and *D* retailers

Retail Promotions

Class of stores	Counter displays %	Co-op ads, %
A	90	100
B	60	75
C	40	30
D	25	0

Sales Coverage and stock

Class of stores	Annual sales calls	Line in stock %
A	24	100
B	12	80
C	6	50
D	4	40

Advertising

5 per cent increase in consumer awareness of company's name and product lines
2 per cent increase in consumer preference
5 per cent increase in co-op advertising space

Marketing Expenses

3 per cent increase in sales expense
5 per cent increase in advertising expense
No change in sales promotion expense
5 per cent decrease in head office expense
1 per cent decrease in stock and distribution expense

These are total company marketing goals. Except for advertising and certain expense items, goals are broken down by region, district, and salesman's territory; or, to be more accurate, the company goals are the sum total of the territory goals. Each territory is analysed by the salesman, his supervisor, and the head office for potential and competitive factors. Individual territory goals are set by agreement among the salesman, his district manager, regional manager, general sales manager, and the marketing manager after a review of economic and industry assumptions and a review of advertising, promotion and new product plans.

Sales goals are then broken down into weeks, taking into consideration seasonal variations. These are set up as budgeted figures against which performance is measured. Sales promotion goals are set up to be measured quarterly. Advertising goals, except for co-op advertising, to be checked only once—at the end of the year—because of the expense of this type of measurement.

The general strategy is to place emphasis on those products that would provide more volume and profit, to emphasise salesman's activities with the larger retailers and to build customer acceptance and retailer traffic through increased national and local co-op advertising.

Adapted from: V. Bluell, *Marketing Management in Action*, p. 153. Pub: McGraw-Hill, 1966.

The next stages of the procedure involve programming. These include strategy selection and tactics.

Choice of strategy. This answers the basic question: How are we going to reach the specific objective? It describes the overall method to be employed. It is different in character from the next stage, which is,

Tactics. Tactical questions concern the specific action which must be undertaken, by whom, when, and within what cost constraints. The tactical question really specifies how the plan is to be implemented.

Controls. Into the plan must be built control procedures. Control means identifying those measures in the organisation which must be watched in order to indicate how well the plan is succeeding. Indicator controls are better than historical data. These are the data which show how well a particular part of the plan is working. For example, if a new product is found to be difficult to sell-in to the trade by the sales force, this may be a strong indication that it will not perform well with the customer.

Tests. All marketing programmes have some element of testing involved. Tests are used to reduce the uncertainties involved in a plan, particularly those which involve putting capital at risk. Most obvious are test marketing schemes for new products; less obvious are the re-routing of delivery journeys using work study analysis in one limited area, to measure the effect on customer service. Testing schemes can confuse a main plan: many of the operations being tested cannot be altered within the time scale of the current plan. So a testing programme can be included as an appendix to the main plan. It may be possible to feed some changes into the current plan should the new operations survive the tests. This is another reason for keeping functional plans a little flexible, particularly towards the year end.

Contingency planning. Some marketing moves must be made in circumstances of great ignorance. Some other moves may be at high risk. On the success of a few plans may hinge the entire company operation. For this reason, it is advisable to identify these critical or core elements and have available a procedure for dealing with the two contingencies which may arise.

The first contingency poses the questions: What will happen if we fail to meet this central objective? Who will it affect? By how much? What are the indicating measures of failure, and who shall be responsible for implementing the contingency procedure?

The second contingency poses the reverse, and much pleasanter, question:

What action should we take if we succeed overwhelmingly in this objective? It would be a pity if we failed to bring up sufficient reserves of power in time to exploit a market breakthrough.

Review. We need a periodic review of the plans in order to examine the variances to see where they may have cross-over effects in other departments. We also need to up-date the information on which the plan is based; particularly is this true of research and development forecasts and the fitting in of successful tests. We need a periodic review of the plan in order continuously to motivate management to achieve the aims upon which the plan is based.

The more frequent the reviews, the greater the management motivation to watch performance, but the more cursory the attention paid. In most plans there are critical stages; if these are not right, then the remainder of the plan may go askew. It is better to identify these critical times and plan the Review Meetings for the time when the data becomes available.

The Marketing Audit

In investigating marketing operations, to identify the practices used, and the problems faced, in order to make appropriate changes, it is not unusual to carry out what is known as a marketing audit.[4] This usually falls into two categories.

The first is the 'marketing mix' audit which comprehensively examines all the elements which go into the whole marketing operation and the relative importance laid on each. The second is the 'functional' audit which takes an aspect of the marketing operation, such as sales, and subjects it to a thorough, searching study and evaluation.

Very few companies are ever managed with such skill and wisdom that there is no room for improvement. And marketing being what it is, and in large part based on subjective judgement, it is in the nature of general management to question marketing more frequently than other functions.

It is traditional to use an auditing technique, either through outside consultants or through some assessor who is independent of the function being surveyed, when a company's marketing operation falls into obvious disrepair. But a new move is developing which uses the marketing audit technique periodically rather than only in a crisis. The periodic audit is concerned with marketing strategy, in that it examines the basic framework in which marketing action takes place as well as the action itself. And it appraises all the elements of the operation, not just the problem-strewn ones.

A marketing audit will investigate the company's success in identifying, influencing and controlling the following factors:

---

[4] P. Kotler, *Marketing Management, Analysis, Planning and Control*; Prentice Hall, New Jersey, 1967. pp. 594–607.

The demand variables. These include the numbers of buyers in the market and their structure in terms of demographic classification, motives, needs, attitudes and purchasing habits.

This includes environmental variables such as economic activity, the weather, government action, and so on. And the competitive factors, including the identification of the closest direct and indirect competition and its performance relative to the company.

Marketing decision variables. Company sales are affected by product, quality, price, promotion and distribution. A marketing decision variable is a factor under the control of the company which may be used to stimulate the company sales. These could include the product mix, the distribution mix, and the communications mix.

Marketing mix. This refers to the amount and kinds of marketing variables that the company is using at any particular time.

The marketing effort. This refers both to the level of marketing effort and to its overall effectiveness. The first is usually measured in terms of cash; the second is measured by how ably the funds are employed.

Marketing allocation. This describes the division of the company's marketing expenditures between products, customer segments and sales areas.

Market response. This refers to the behaviour of sales in response to alternative levels of expenditure, allocations and mixes of marketing effort.

Procedures. The marketing audit is concerned with the procedure for making marketing decisions of varying kinds. It also examines procedures for developing marketing information, say, on sales or costs, or competitive intelligence, or forecasting.

Organisation. It examines the marketing organisation structure, the formal lines of authority and responsibility, the informal power and knowledge centres, the adequacy of personnel as groups and as individuals.

The marketing audit is a very sizeable task. At the start of a corporate planning system, with little historical experience of planning, it is usual to have someone take as comprehensive an audit as time and funds will allow. Commonly, the head of the operation may be asked to undertake a self-audit, but the limitations of the method are obvious and powerful, and it misses the point about having an independent auditor. Alternatively, a company can prepare an audit using someone from a separate function. Apart from the problem that technical marketing knowledge may be lacking, the obvious political handicap of having one executive be seen apparently to be checking up on another's performance is highly undesirable, to say the least. A company task force, comprising several executives from different functions can work, if the brief is widened beyond marketing, and if they investigate other functions also. But it can be costly and the executives may not be skilled enough, nor independent enough, to carry out the task .

So outside consultants are often used, having the skill and the independence of judgement required. With care, they can often avoid the implication that marketing is being examined because it is not performing properly. The major disadvantage is that they are expensive and they have to overcome the 'learning curve'. It may take them some time to become acquainted with the details and circumstances of the company and its markets. But to institute a marketing planning system for the first time requires a detailed appraisal of all the elements of the operation. Laborious as it may be, it must be done by the operating heads of the marketing functions or by an outsider.

The only alternative is to implement the planning procedure piecemeal. The organic approach to planning has already been described, and providing that the company faces no immediate threat it may be wise to build up the planning procedure bit by bit as problems occur, and cutting the analysis of the subject wider than the problem itself demands, in order to build up a data bank of information.

The real difference between the traditional style of marketing planning and that used today is that marketing men recognise that organisations have many objectives, only some of which fall into the marketing area. These may be the most important ones, but they are not the only ones. Secondly, it is recognised that objectives need to be set for varying lengths of time. This is why no distinct time-scale for planning is recommended here—the time to sort out each problem will vary with the problem and the resources available. And thirdly, companies now recognise that they need many levels of objectives and that a hierarchy of subplans to meet specific functional objectives is required.

This is harder than the old style of marketing plan,[5] described as follows:

Step one

In the traditional manner companies used to set themselves market share objectives by adding something to their present share of the market, depending upon how ambitious they were.

Step two

Then they added up the estimates for all brands in the market for the following year; and multiplied step one by step two. This gave them a cash turnover figure.

Step three

They subtracted factory cost, including materials and labour, fixed and general management overheads, their required net profit, and what was left was their 'planned' marketing expenditure.

[5] L. Winer, 'Are You Really Planning Your Marketing?'; *U.S. Jnl. of Marketing*, Vol. 29, Jan. 1965, pp. 1–8.

Step four

Was to compose a marketing mix of all their activities which just used up the funds, and hopefully would give them the forecasted sales volume. If only it were so easy!

Example: A Simple Marketing Plan and its application

Background

All Precision Engineering Ltd. is a small engineering company in Sussex, which produces, amongst other products, a height gauge. This has been on the market for ten years.

The product is technically very sound, with several distinct advantages over competition. Yet it has not achieved the market penetration of some of the leading competitors. Partly this is due to competitors having a wider and complementary range of products.

The technical basis of the product is different from that of competitors, giving it a substantial and obvious differentiating feature. The product offers advantages in price and ease of use. The product is branded and is called the 'Microball Height Gauge'.

The Problem

The company was selling 600 units per annum and wished to expand sales by a further 600 units. The price was raised by 30 per cent in September 1970. Instead of increasing, sales dropped.

The company held little data about the total size of the market, but believed that the share they held was very small. No accurate data existed on the structure of the market, the nature of the leading competitors, their size and strength.

The company also wondered whether the market was large enough to attract another competitor with an identical product, once the patent rights on Microball expired.

The evident need was for a marketing plan which would recognise the limited resources of the company and one which would improve sales.

Method

The company employed a consultant to carry out a short industrial market research assignment, through a mailed questionnaire backed up with personal calls.

The study used existing sources of published information on the market so far as they were available, and attempted to estimate roughly the size of the total market in the u.k. for height gauges. The competitive structure of the market was examined, and share of the market estimates obtained.

The study showed that the total market was smaller than was originally believed by the company. The Microball product had a fair penetration into the market, and was liked by those who used it.

The fact is that few users of height gauges had ever heard of the Microball, or if they had, they had little idea from where to buy it. The need for extra advertising and sales pressure was clear.

The marketing plan for the product called for the maintenance of the current price levels, and for no product modifications.

Within the market two journals offer great power and coverage, *Tooling*, and *Machinery*. A year's campaign was booked into these publications, with the twin objective of seeking sales enquiries and of making the name of Microball better known. The copy stressed the accuracy of the gauge, its legibility, ease of use and accuracy. A press release about the product and its means of use was also circulated to the appropriate magazines.

The number of sales enquiries received each month are used to determine the effectiveness of the media. *Tooling* magazine may be dropped from the schedule owing to a low enquiry rate, and replaced with *Industrial Equipment News*. These are compared with the number of orders finally converted to show the effectiveness of the sales follow-up. The benefits resulting to the company from the study of the market are clear, and further market investigations are planned within the constraints of the company's funds.

4. Marketing Strategy

Marketing strategy answers the basic question of how the company is to reach its objectives. No company has complete freedom of movement in the selection of its marketing strategies. Historically, many companies concentrated on marketing a single product, or a very narrow product range, and selling this to a wide variety of markets for a similarly wide variety of uses.

The original Model T Ford, the Volkswagen 'beetle', Coca Cola, Kiwi Shoe Polish, survived long after their competitors cut up the markets by introducing different product varieties. These companies have all felt the effect of competition and have been driven into product diversification. They have found also that their new range of products is less profitable, that their resources have become stretched, and that management and technical problems have caused them sometimes to long for the good old single product days.

Single product range companies

Many narrow product range companies exist, particularly those serving industrial markets. The companies involved fall into three categories. First, are those firms which have some unique material procurement asset to which others have no access, and which is sold to convertors and processors. Many commodity suppliers fall into this category—sugar, beef, aluminium and so on. Such companies are often concerned in their marketing strategy to attempt some measure of control and influence over the distributive chain. Some move into a policy of vertical integration, where they take on the task of processing the material into different products and the development of new markets and new uses. Du Pont has an outstanding record of achievement in developing new uses for its products. Union International control beef supplies from Argentina, ship them in their own fleets, sell on the open markets and in processed form through the wholesale trade, and, in addition, they own the largest chain of butchers' shops, Dewhursts, in the country.

Narrow product range companies also exist in technically-intensive industries such as computers. These companies will have a policy of market development to widen the range of uses.

In service industries, it is common to find a narrow base of service range, particularly in information-intensive companies. Market research companies for example often specialise in a narrow range of techniques.

The main strategy for such narrow range companies is to design a programme which will appeal to the broadest mass of buyers. Market strategy for them is concerned primarily with developing the total use of the product category, and identifying new potential uses.

Multi-product companies

Most companies, in time, adopt a multi-product system. This is where a firm decides to operate in all the key segments of markets with alternative products, brands, or varieties for each. Multi-product companies usually operate over a wide range of directly competitive markets. They seek to establish a specific buyer's loyalty in one product field, in order to secure his business in a related product area.

Most material processors, with high 'added value' content to their products, operate on a wide product/market range basis. The widest possible range of marketing strategies is employed by these companies, but more emphasis is laid upon the efficiency of the company's existing operation than is laid upon, say, market development.

Such companies typically have a need for continuing product modification and are often concerned about the problems of new products 'cannibalising' sales from other products existing in their range. They are often concerned with the problems of product clutter, and of eliminating poor profit products from their range.

Externally, these companies are often quite sophisticated in their search for new market segments which can be explored. In consumer product markets, such companies are traditionally the highest spenders on sophisticated segmentation analysis techniques. Industrial companies will lay great stress on field intelligence, their salesmen may have a powerful influence in providing new product ideas.

Concentrated marketing

Many companies, particularly those which have limited resources or high specialist skills, and those companies which are new, may opt to go for specialised product marketing in a concentrated area. This involves tying a company's growth to one segment of the market, with its obvious risks. Another theoretical risk is that competitors may identify the same opportunity and enter the same market segment. However, companies operating in this way often secure for themselves a high rate of return, and often a relatively trouble-free existence.

Such companies may be concerned with defensive strategies. They are not likely to boast about their slice of the market, or about the profits they make. They may be concerned even to restrain their market segment from becoming too large if that is possible. Such companies can often trade easily in high price sectors of their market which demand a high reputation and lay great stress on service. They may be strategically secure in this sector because the larger manufacturers of standard products find it difficult to raise their reputation and standards sufficiently to trade in the high price sector.

Even in highly competitive food markets, for example, some small companies find it highly profitable to make small quantities of the kind of delicacies which are sold in, say, Fortnum and Mason. In the soup market, Baxters with their range of game soups and other exotica are the envy of their mass production competitors, notably Heinz, and Crosse and Blackwell.

There are, therefore, six general factors to take into account when selecting marketing strategy.

The first factor relates to the company's resources of money, specialist and management skills, and material accessibility.

The second factor relates to the homogeneity of the product range. Widely differentiated products serving widely differentiated markets will require a set of strategies which will not be useful to the company with a narrow product range selling to a small cluster of buyers.

The third factor, the stage in the product life cycle, will be dealt with more fully in the Chapter 9 on Market Segmentation. The types of strategy required for the beginning of the cycle will be remarkably different from those required for the peak position which, in turn, differ from those required at the declining end of the cycle.

The fourth factor refers to market homogeneity, which is the degree to which customers are alike in their needs, attitudes, and preferences.

The fifth factor refers to competitive marketing strategy. It is hard for a company to move against the general strategies of its closest competitors. Successful marketing strategies, by their nature, tend to polarise in the market as competitors copy.

The sixth factor refers to market position. The biggest supplier within a market will be more concerned with defensive moves to counter competition and secure his position. The smaller competitor may be more aggressive and take more risks—he has less to protect.

Nine different classes of marketing strategy have been identified.[1] These relate not so much to specific market or product situations but more to the

[1] P. Kotler *Marketing Management; Analysis, Planning and Control;* Prentice Hall, New Jersey, 1967. p. 284.

general style of management, or its 'philosophy'. Frequently, such marketing philosophy is determined by the experience of the general management group. Their own careers lead them to take a certain view of business, and their experience of the industry will mould their style.

The nine general classes of marketing strategy are:

Non-adaptive. A strategy where the initial marketing mix is held constant through the product life cycle. Such strategies are common in capital-intensive companies of long standing, serving industrial markets. Indeed, their market movement may be so slow that the concept of a product life cycle is hardly recognised. They set their advertising and sales budgets, for example, as a fixed proportion of their total expenses.

Time-dependent. This strategy provides for pre-scheduled changes to take place in the marketing mix through time.

Oligopolistic companies serving consumer markets plan for their movements at each stage of the product life cycle, even before the product is marketed. A programme of 'planned obsolescence' in products which involve questions of fashion or taste such as cars, or clothes, is clearly an aspect of this technique.

Competitively adaptive. This is a strategy in which the company adjusts its marketing mix according to changes made by a competitor. Traditionally, this happens in price sensitive markets amongst smaller companies who are virtually forced to follow the behaviour of the market leader.

Sales-responsive. This is a strategy in which the company adjusts its marketing mix according to sales in the previous period.

Mail order companies generally follow this system and vary their advertising schedule, copy themes and media on the basis of their immediate responses.

Profit-responsive. This is a strategy in which the firm adjusts its marketing mix according to the profits earned in the previous period.

The big users of sales promotion, such as the detergent companies, use a manœuvre similar to this. Having set their profit objective and attained it, they are concerned to plough back any excess into sales promotion and market forcing techniques. Some companies use up excess profits by increasing their advertising budgets at the tail of their financial year. This avoids taxation and assists market development. The problem occurs when profits fall below target. Then the advertising or promotion budgets are hit and they may be the items required to bring back the profits.

Completely adaptive. This strategy produces monthly changes in the company's marketing mix in response to all the current developments. Many distributors work like this, and the technique is very common among sections of the retail and wholesale trade who take up suppliers' offers of promotions as they come along. This is also the technique used by smaller businessmen who continually 'have ideas'. It is not unknown amongst large company chief executives.

Diagnostic. This strategy produces changes in the marketing mix only after distinguishing among possible causes of current changes and developments. It is used by those with a sound corporate and annual planning system, and where heavy stress is laid upon information-gathering and market research. It is a technique more familiar to brand leaders who have the responsibility for leading the market itself.

Profit-maximising. This strategy seeks to maximise the firm's profits. The more vigorous conglomerates and investment companies have this basic attitude, which frequently leads them into asset stripping take-overs.

Joint profit-maximising. This strategy seeks to maximise total industry profits under collusion. The practice is illegal, but most industries which are other than highly fragmented have some loose arrangement between leading competitors. Government action frequently forces companies to collude, as in the recent national policy on prices and incomes. But this practice provides social and economic commentators with their basic fears of oligopolistic markets.

In the selection of the appropriate marketing strategy there are at least five attitude hurdles to be overcome within an organisation. These have been identified[2] as:

Marketing Foresight. This is the belief that only those people who are already in the field of marketing and of the industry are the ones who understand it best and who know what the customer wants. The only person who really knows what he wants is the customer himself, and many of the greatest developments have originated outside the field of knowledge of those experienced in the industry. For example, jazz was developed outside the halls of classical music; anesthesia and X-rays were discovered outside the field of surgery; and it was an anatomist, Galvani, who discovered electricity.

New market development. One of the greatest weaknesses in long-term market strength is to concentrate on gaining an ever-increasing share of existing markets with existing products. Companies which fail to innovate fail to create new markets and new uses eventually give up the market leadership to others. The biggest single cause of lost market leadership is due to those products which become technically obsolescent and are overtaken by new, superior versions.[3]

Competition. The third weakness in attitude is to assume that competition is a closed system, and that competitors are those making substantially the same products and offering the same services. For example, the makers of rolled gold fountain pens are not just competing in the writing implement market. They are in the luxury gift market. As such they compete with cigarette lighters, men's toiletries, and leather wallets.

Present purchasers. The fourth weakness lies in appealing only to present-day purchasers.

Markets are changing constantly. Individual buyers change their circumstances, become promoted, develop new needs. And new buyers arrive in different directions from the old. Distribution channels are changing; more companies are buying direct and the industrial agent is being squeezed

[2] L. Burnett, 'The Five Fallacies of Marketing'; speech to American Marketing Association, 1966.
[3] 'Marketing Management Overview'; *Nielsen Researcher*, July–Aug. 1968. pp. 3–23.

out. Other distributive channels are polarising into fewer hands. In general, buyers are becoming more knowledgeable, have greater buying power, and are becoming more sophisticated in their needs. Furthermore, new classes of buyers, with totally different motivations, are entering most markets.

Decision making.   Because we live in the age of the specialist we may believe that only qualified experts with specialised skills will be competent in the future to make basic decisions. In fact, the reverse is happening, and there is growing power moving towards the generalist. He is the one who balances the information from the specialists, who synthesises the decision. We need managers who know perhaps one thing well, and many related things fairly well.

Market Situations

In chapter one we described thirteen market situations, each of which cause significantly different attitudes to the subject of marketing. Nowhere is this more apparent than in the lines of approach which each company is likely to adopt when producing the marketing programme designed to achieve its objectives.

Packaged goods: consumer

The packaged goods company selling to consumer markets is likely to have numerous products in its range. Most usually these will use common facilities such as raw materials or processing equipment. It is very likely that although they may serve different markets, they will use the same broad channels of distribution.

In mass marketing, it is the channel of distribution which holds the key to new product development, simply because so much of the company's goodwill, physical distribution and other marketing investment is tied up in the trade.

So such a company will be using a wide variety of different strategies for each product group in its range. And the company will be most closely concerned with any factors which indicate that the product group in general is moving out of the hands of one trading channel and into another. Its strategy may be to develop new sales through growing channels, with a consequent effect upon its branding and packaging policy.

Consumer durables

Companies in these markets may be highly dependent upon a relatively narrow product range for their profitability. Their emphasis may be towards developing the profitability of sales of minor products and defending their key product interest. They are more likely to use a diagnostic approach to changes in their marketing mix since changes in the market behaviour are slower, and they usually have heavy capital at risk, particularly in the form of finished stocks. They will be particularly responsive to competitors' moves in adding new features to their products. Many companies will have a high seasonal bias in their trade, and they will set longer-term objectives for their plans than merely one year. They may be concerned to develop products to offset seasonal fluctuations.

Plant and Equipment

These companies will be among the slowest in responding to market dynamics and will take much longer over their objectives. Their demand forecasting will be carried on in detail for up to three years ahead. Indeed, a sizeable proportion of the following years' business will be known to them when they make their plans and will be already at the 'work in progress' stage. They will be affected by the long lead times between tendering for a contract and receiving the first revenues from it. Their strategies may be concentrated upon the problems of sub-contractors or the problem of securing an adequate pricing base. They will be concerned about the long-term problems of developing new technologies and skills, and of new market development.

Components

These companies will vary widely in their situation—and will be affected by the degree of direct competition. Most of their immediate problems will concern communications, and their strategies may depend upon their ability to 'reach' all those behind the purchasing officers who influence decisions. They approximate to the mass marketing company in that their main concern is about new products and new market development. These companies will concentrate on sales strategy; new account openings in particular.

Materials supply

These companies will focus their attention upon existing products and upon the level of service they offer. In some industries they may attempt policies which will help their customer to make more and better use of their materials and in this way hope to develop new uses. Their policies will be set at rather longer range than others because in most materials markets the changes in purchasing pattern take place fairly slowly and are more predictable. They will make use of indicator statistics to help forecast demand. They are also more likely to use traditional methods of promotional budget setting, perhaps by using a share of forecasted turnover in order to calculate the level of marketing expense they can afford.

Fragmented markets

Small companies in fragmented markets are more likely to use very short-term plans, and alter their strategies in response to movements in sales turnover. Leaders in the market will concentrate upon general problems of the industry, while the smaller companies may look to geographical expansion of their business to gain growth.

Oligopsonistic markets

Companies selling to a narrow range of buyers tend to be weak in marketing planning simply because their destiny is in the hands of such a small cluster of individuals. They may develop strategies to help them 'sell through' the buyers to the end-users, provided that this does not upset the trade. They may also seek to develop their basic skills into manufactured products which are capable of wider distribution.

Undifferentiated products

These companies will be more concerned with sales and promotion strategies, since their livelihood depends upon them. They will seek to 'add value' to the products. They may develop and sell on the basis of their service. Their problem also may be to locate customer prospects. This will throw their emphasis upon methods of personalised screening of prospects such as telephone sales, direct mail and cold calling.

Example: Marketing Strategy

Background

In the U.K. approximately 80 per cent of the paint market is in the hands of about six companies. The remaining 20 per cent is highly fragmented, there being some 500 other producers.

The product, Silexine, now manufactured by Silexine Paints Ltd., is a special form of stone paint. It was rescued from a paint company in liquidation.

Problem

Initially, this company was one of hundreds of producers all vying for a share of the tail-end of the market. Simply, Silexine's problem was how to increase their market share with their limited resources. They encountered great competition at one end of the market, and domination by a few at the other.

Solution

The strategies used in different stages are described below.

Stage 1. The strategy initially used involved the following decisions.
(a) Quality—Continue to sell high quality products.
(b) Distribution—Sell direct to customers. Use no sales force.
(c) Price—Charge a price at such a low level that no competitor could meet it.
(d) Advertising—Advertise directly at the Do-it-Yourself segment.

Direct selling was managed through advertising, and by mailing direct to the handyman. From a half-page advertisement in *Practical Householder* they received over 1000 replies, about a factor of 10 higher than the expected response. The advertisements generally had an initial soft, sexy sell, but with hard copy following.

A low price was needed to encourage people to buy direct from the company. This price level was achieved by manufacturing a single white paint, and hence benefiting from whatever economies of scale could be achieved. A colour range was possible by selling a range of tints that were added to the white paint. Their distribution policy also aided their low price aim, as no discount had to be offered to retailers, and a sales force did not have to be supported.

The competition inevitably responded. Indeed, the Paintmakers Association stressed the usefulness of the advice that could be given by members to customers when deals were done 'over the counter'. However, this had no substantial effect, and Silexine's advertising budget grew from £15,000 to £250,000.

Tactics concerning the product range changed later, the original products being joined by a limited range of gloss paints, some based on polyurathane. Furthermore, their product diversification policy led to a variety of special purpose paints being introduced.

Result of Stage 1

This initial policy proved to be highly successful. However, for some undefined reason, direct selling alone has been found in many industries to lose its effect and impetus after four years. This caused Silexine to review their strategy.

> *Stage 2.* The initial strategies remained basically the same. However, in order to allow for growth, changes were made in the distribution policy, which now favoured some method of selling through retail outlets.

Problem

The company's turnover had grown from £180,000 to nearly £1,000,000. Even so, with 15,000 retail outlets it was impossible to cover them all and compete with the brand leaders. Furthermore, the company did not want their direct sales programme hit by competition from their own retailers. Having these two distribution channels without some inter-reaction, and consequent reduction of individual channels effectiveness, seemed to present a considerable difficulty.

Solution

Silexine decided upon a selective and partly exclusive distribution policy. From a possible 15,000 outlets they selected about 400. The retailers are not expected to sell Silexine paints exclusively, but they are not allowed to stock products competing with their ancillary lines.

The dealers are spaced out geographically so that no Silexine outlet competes with another. Although they are not asked to encourage brand switching, stockists are expected to give the Silexine display material prominence.

With this policy the company needed distributors. Those already in the paint trade were heavily committed to the brand leaders and even if products were accepted, they were unlikely to be pushed. Consequently, Silexine have developed distributors themselves, and have sought others in related fields such as wallpaper, or building merchants.

Result of Stage 2

The stockists benefit by having control over their own particular area. Through the pricing policy they are able to undercut even the supermarkets. The arrangements result in Silexine having a chain of distributors without the complication of owning their own sites. Furthermore, they are probably the only paint company who do not have, or need, a salesforce.

Overall, the strategies adopted by this company have made them very successful. For example, they have obtained a 40 per cent share of the total market for stone paint. This study shows that with an unorthodox strategy companies are able sometimes to take their competitors by surprise and increase their market penetration.

P.M.

5. *Marketing Organisation Structures*

The historical developments of marketing organisations can be traced quite easily since they correspond so closely with basic economic trends. In the days when the demand for products was strong, with limited choice from few suppliers in easy competition with each other, then the traditional organisation structure would be headed by a sales director, with perhaps an advertising or publicity manager either next to him or within his department.

As technology and competition grew, it was recognised that the term 'marketing' meant a set of closely integrated functions. Many sales directors found a marketing manager growing alongside them, taking over the functions of advertising, market research, and having a say in product development. Frequently sales directors saw the trend, switched names, and absorbed the newcomers in a swift takeover bid, calling themselves marketing directors.

Economies moved from a supply-dominated economy to a buyer-oriented economy. Competition grew, it began to be a struggle to move the output, and companies discovered the need to build a separate management structure into their marketing organisation. This, the product management system, cuts across the boundaries of the traditional operational function of sales, and is now held to be responsible for the sales, growth and profitability of groups of products. The transplant of such a management organisation on traditional company structures has often been painful, and it has not always worked, even amongst consumer goods companies. There are still signs of what is apparently 'tissue rejection' by the corporate body in many companies. All marketing organisations, whether sales and marketing are run separately or together, must somehow accommodate five factors affecting the company. These are:

> Various functions: sales, advertising, research.
> Various products: including development.
> Various regions: whether centralised or not.
> Various distributive trade groups: including trade prospects.
> Various markets: purchasers and end-users of the products.

A marketing organisation structure which placed equal weight upon all these factors would be hopelessly uneconomic and would suffer from activity

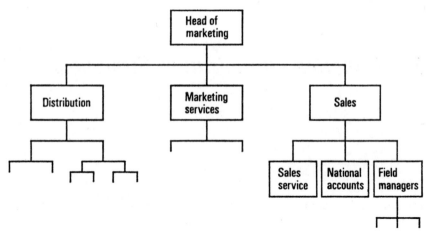

Figure 9A Standard organisation structure.

indigestion. All organisation structures result in a compromise: they will be centred on the predominantly important factor, with parts of the structure taking care, as best they can, of the other factors.

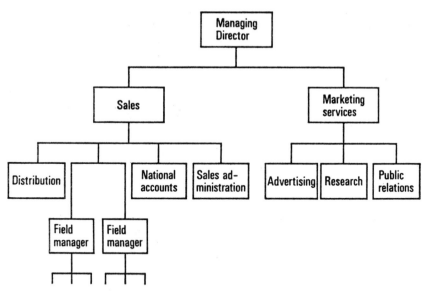

Figure 9B Transitional organisation structure; often used in industrial marketing.

In the most common organisation the head of marketing works through a set of managers who are specialised by function. (*Figure 9A.*) A small research, planning or product unit supplies a basic service of information to the functions.

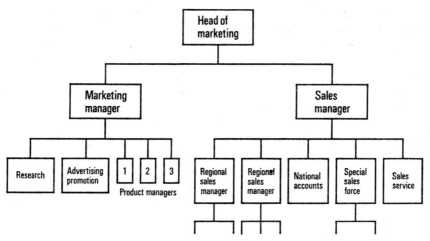

Figure 9C Marketing organisation for a multi-product company.

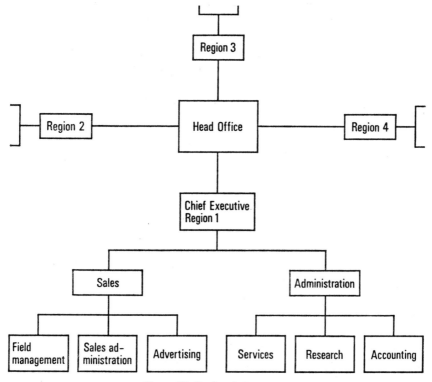

Figure 9D Regional structures.

In the traditional structure, particularly within industrial marketing companies, one would find a sales chief reporting to the chief executive and responsible for handling sales, distribution, and possibly sales promotion. A separate marketing services unit reports to the chief executive handling advertising, public relations, research and product/market planning. (*Figure 9B.*)

In multi-product companies, particularly those serving mass markets, it is more likely that a product or brand management structure has been interposed, crossing the functions. This decision is influenced by the sheer number of products and by their diversity. (*Figure 9C.*)

Companies selling over a wide area, particularly those with a high degree of local service, must decentralise some of their decisions. They may use a Regional Management Structure. This may use local marketing services, and have local promotion funds, and it may move ultimately to a properly decentralised structure, with a managing director and executive management in each area. (*Figure 9D.*)

Where customers fall into distinctly different groups in terms of buying practice, or product interest, then the marketing organisation may have to be clustered around market managers, instead of product managers. In most cases where this happens, the companies are highly technical in their activity often with a very narrow product range. And in these cases it is usual to find that the sales force is highly specialised, that it needs strong technical back-up, and that it reports to the market manager. This situation causes several sales forces in one company. (*Figure 10.*)

Such sales structures are always cumbersome, and companies are often helplessly trying to juggle with the structure to achieve the most economic use of their manpower.

Marketing systems management

Today, all types of organisation structure can be found even within the same industry. But there are signs that marketing organisations are moving towards a 'marketing system' approach and away from a simplified marketing orientation structure. An unpublished study by O. W. Palmer of the City of London Polytechnic[1] shows that some companies, notably in the drug industry, are moving towards a structure where a small group of high calibre marketing executives work on new markets, new products and new services only. This group works alongside the corporate planners and with research and development sections.

This group is effective in areas of decision theory, network analysis and long-range planning. It works in the behavioural science area, data processing and marketing model building. The structure is useful particularly where

[1] O. W. Palmer, *Management Structures in Modern Marketing Management Systems*; City of London Polytechnic, January 1971.

A. Market manager in staff capacity only . . .

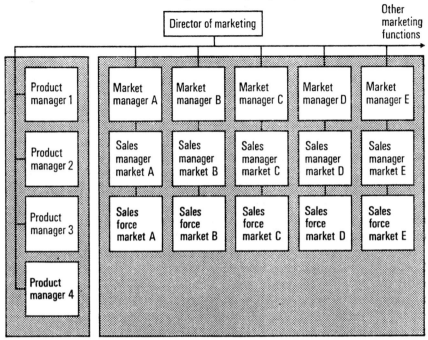

B. . . . and with combined line and staff responsibility.

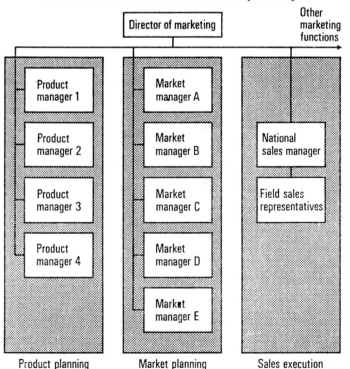

Figure 10 Two approaches to meet the needs of the marketplace.

(*Source:* B. Charles Ames, 'Dilemma of product/market management'; *Harvard Business Review*, April 1971, p.72)

research and development are considered essential key factors in the company's survival.

In many companies, management pressures have built up in the handling of new product development and in the imposition of new management and marketing techniques upon unwilling, older, management structures.

In addition to the effective handling of established revenue earning products, every company has to develop new generation products, but there is usually not sufficient planning time spent on these new products and services. Often, the product manager handles both established and development lines, but in times of intensive competition pressure the current profit earners must take executive priority. Palmer established in his survey a major gap in the standard organisation structure: too often, no one has overall responsibility for new products.

The active executive, who often is promoted when a company moves from a sales to a marketing orientated stage of development, is not necessarily equipped for the more advanced analytical and numerate approach to management and marketing. Decision theory, network analysis, management by objectives, application of the product life cycle are just a few of the areas which are difficult for the promoted operations executive to handle.

Therefore, with the pressures of present product considerations and the required development of a more sophisticated management a new organisation structure has begun to develop, called a marketing systems orientated organisation. This type of organisation has all or most of the following profile characteristics, some of which duplicate with marketing-orientated organisations (*Figure 11.*):

Research and development is the essential key factor in relation to a company's survival and is directed to profitable fields through corporate and marketing planning data.

Research and development is well founded in relation to company turnover and profitability and is used to promote company *long-term* growth. The structure recognises R & D as part of the marketing function.

Management and planning. Marketing planning is linked closely with long-term corporate planning.

'Future Products' group works within the framework of the company's Corporate Plan, which, depending on the type of market, operates within a time span of five to ten years.

The 'Future Products' group is concerned solely with new markets, products and services for these markets. At a certain point in development the operational plan will be taken over by the 'Present Products' group.

Market research. A fully developed marketing information system uses a wide range of market research services, statistics and data banks for management.

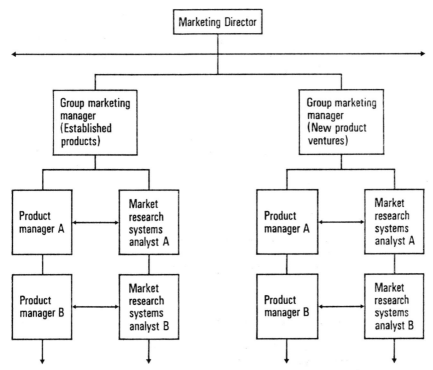

Figure 11 One example of a marketing system orientated organisation is illustrated conceptually in the above flow diagram of part of a pharmaceutical company organisation. The two key factors which distinguish a marketing system orientated organisation are shown on the flow diagram; the separate groups for new and established products are the 'systems' approach through the use of market research systems analysts. In some companies they go as far as setting up a separate subsidiary for new product development as the only way to develop new ventures in a large international operation.

(*Source:* O. W. Palmer, City of London College, 1971)

Product planning. The fundamental need is for new product ranges for new markets, new product ranges for established markets, and replaced ranges of current lines for established markets.

A sound commercial and financial policy is related to product withdrawal. There is a close interlink between corporate and marketing objectives in relation to the requirements of product planning.

Finance. The financial director has an advisory role, but customer considerations are paramount within the requirements of return on investment and the allocation of resources.

Financial planning is closely related to corporate/marketing planning and the Financial Director appreciates the customer's strategic position as the determinant of the company's survival and growth. There is sound understanding between the financial and marketing spheres of management

Project management

Every organisation structure hits a barrier from time to time when activity which is non-routine, or is alien to its normal operation, has to be developed. Frequently, this activity will involve co-operation between different operational functions, will require special funds to be voted and will need the acquiescence of different levels of management. It may necessitate the bringing together of specialist personnel. Such an activity may involve the setting up of a project team to plan and manage its development.

Before establishing a project organisation, a company must define the nature of the job and its requirements. Typically, a project organisation is responsible for completing a defined task on time, within cost and profit goals, and to established standards.

The project approach can be applied to an undertaking which is:

(a) Definable, in terms of a specific aim.
(b) Infrequent, unique or unfamiliar to the company.
(c) Complex and interdependent between tasks.
(d) Critical to the company.

A project organisation for a product development or design move is normally provided with responsibility for:

Product definition, including performance standards.
Work assignment, and control of funds.
Make-or-buy decisions; co-ordinating the company's capabilities.
Scheduling; and producing network analyses.
Problem analysis: all problems in the project area.
Functional liaison.

In any project organisation great stress is laid upon the abilities of the project manager; it is he who must produce the result on time, he who has the responsibility for the ultimate success, and he who must mould together into a team personnel from different, frequently specialised, functions.

The span of planning

Corporate plans work best if they are produced 'from the bottom up'; that is, when they emerge as a series of calculations and relatively short-range planning efforts produced by second-line and junior management upwards, with the appropriate meshing and compromising of objectives on the way. They are also most accurate when they are tied in closely with budgeting systems.

Different levels of management are capable of planning the future according to different time-scales. To take an extreme example; the Chairman of a large public company can personally exercise little short-term effect on its performance. Certainly he can guide his colleagues into endeavours which, if successful, may pay off handsomely in three or more years' time.

The field salesman, however, has the power to affect his own area of performance almost daily. Certainly he will be affecting only a minute part of the company's operation, but it is the sum of all the tiny parts which make up the total performance. In contrast, he finds it difficult to predict and plan for his activity months ahead, let alone three years ahead.

The hierarchy of marketing planning and budgeting systems should normally work as follows. For week to week and month to month performance, the lowest levels of line management and field salesmen can usually be involved. The more they set their own objectives the greater their involvement in reaching the goals, provided that information about their performance is fed back to them.

At junior management level, perhaps regional managers and product managers, the first contributions to the annual plan will be made; although the main emphasis is on the shorter-term actions required to achieve quarterly and monthly budgeted results. Changes in the marketing plans made necessary by the review procedure can be operated through this level of management.

From a build-up of the short-term plans, senior management can then assess the annual plan objectively. One of the measures used in personnel evaluation, particularly in establishing job status, is to identify a manager's 'time span of control'. In general, the longer it takes for his decision to affect the company's performance then usually the more senior he is.

There is one great human problem in all planning work. It affects the field salesman preparing his next journey cycle; it affects the ambitious project manager; it affects corporate planners and chief executives. It is called Gresham's Law of Planning. This states that there is a tendency for easy problems to be preoccupying and to drive the harder ones away from resolution.

Example: Marketing Organisation Structures

CASE 1—U.K.

Background

Massey-Ferguson is the world's largest manufacturer of tractors, self-propelled combines and diesel engines. In the U.K., which is the world's leading producer of tractors, this company is dominant. The company's headquarters are in Canada and the worldwide organisation is sub-divided into eleven geographical operations units; the U.K. unit being the largest outside the U.S.A. The group's export company is also based in the U.K.

Their products are grouped into three divisions:

(1) Farm machinery, which accounts for a major proportion of sales.
(2) Engines (Perkins).
(3) Industrial and construction machinery.

Initial Marketing Organisation Structure in the United Kingdom

During the 50's, Massey-Ferguson was volume-orientated and met problems of mounting stocks. The merger between Massey-Harris and Harry Ferguson was taking longer than anticipated. A consultant was called in during the early 60's, and by 1964 a new marketing structure had been established. (*See Figure A.*)

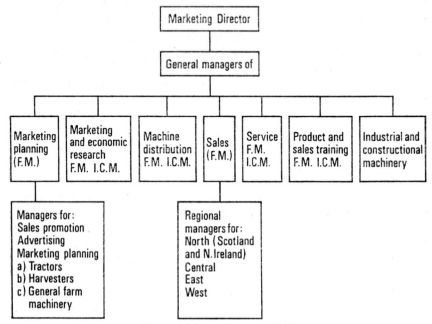

Figure A Massey-Ferguson U.K.

(*Source: Marketing,* August, 1968)

Results

This organisation structure was basically sound, and the decisions made caused turnover to rise by 70 per cent in the 1964–1968 period. Massey-Ferguson then accounted for about 40 per cent of U.K. tractor sales.

Problem

All markets change, putting greater emphasis on various marketing aspects at different times. Consequently, a company's marketing structure may prove too inflexible for changing conditions, although initially sound. This, together with increased competition and changing agricultural trends in the U.K., made revision necessary in Massey-Ferguson.

The farming trend is towards larger, more expensive machines which are more sophisticated. The market has become a replacement one rather than a growth one.

Solution

A general reorganisation of the marketing function was required. The trouble was diagnosed as being the disproportionate numbers at general manager level. The answer was a reduction in the number of general managers from seven to five. The most noticeable change was the abolition of the general manager (sales) position and the consequent upgrading of the field managers, who obtained further autonomy. *(See Figure B.)*

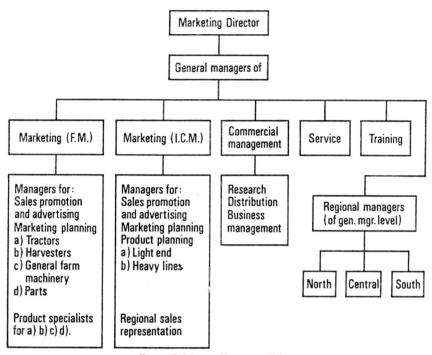

Figure B Massey-Ferguson U.K.

(Source: Marketing, August. 1968)

CASE II—EXPORT

Background

Massey-Ferguson (Export) Ltd. is purely a marketing organisation. It sells the products produced in British factories as well as those from other countries. It sells to all territories apart from those served by other (national) Massey-Ferguson Operations Units having their own factories and marketing departments.

Initial Marketing Organisation Structure

The former marketing organisation, headed by the Managing Director, consisted of two service divisions concerned with finance, and planning and supply. There was also a single line division under a marketing director dealing with the marketing of all products to all territories. *(See Figure C.)*

Problem

It became evident that the two classes of products, i.e. farm machinery, and industrial and construction machinery, required different marketing approaches. Furthermore, the markets which were served by this organisation separated

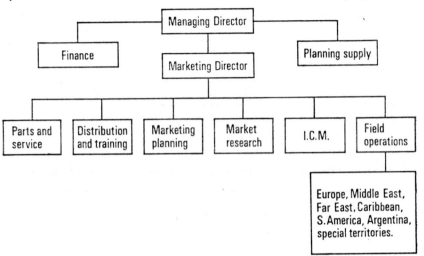

Figure C Massey-Ferguson (Export).
(*Source: Marketing,* August, 1968)

into two groups. One group consisted of the developed countries of Europe, and the other of the less saturated markets outside Europe.

Solution

Under the reorganisation (*see Figure D*), the single marketing division has been split into four line divisions. A director, responsible to the managing

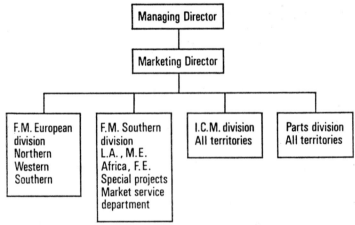

Figure D Massey-Ferguson (Export).
(*Source: Marketing,* August, 1968)

director, heads each division. The two staff divisions remain, but have been modified to serve four line divisions instead of one.

Result

The effect is to bring top management into closer contact with the field plans and problems in the different territories, and in the segments of the markets.

At the same time, the divisional directors have been given a larger share of authority within their particular sphere. Distribution has also been reorganised. Together with the restructuring described, this has allowed Massey-Ferguson (Export) to move closer to its markets.

(*Note*: In 1971 a further reorganisation took place merging the u.k. and the Export operations under a single managing director. The two legal entities remain, but the new operations unit is known internally as 'United Kingdom & World Export Operations'.)

6. Resource Allocation and Control

Most marketing men have a basic attitude towards business, which looks for growth rather than productivity. They seek to widen the range of activities; widen the range of products and of markets. They overcome marketing problems by the use of sometimes expensive forcing techniques, such as sales promotion. Their allocation of financial resources is usually based upon the need to develop growth areas.

They may be profit conscious in all this activity. But the nature of their work, involving as it does the committal of assets from all parts of the business towards a marketing growth strategy, requires careful control and analysis. Particularly is this true of financial controls. In many companies this leads to what can be described as an uneasy relationship between the financial and the marketing teams.

Financial accounting has so far played too small a part in the management decision making process owing to its historical nature, which involves a time lag between cause and effect. Balance sheet information does not cluster around management decision areas.

So the marketing control function generally makes use of a standard costing system linked to budgetary control. The most effective form of control is by budget centres, these being the points at which expenditure is planned, authorised and applied. Codes are used to identify budget centres, to trace the expenditure as it is incurred. Additional analyses either by the nature of the expense, or by the 'cost centre', can also be coded. The cost centre is the ultimate destination of the expenditure.

Statements are prepared for each budget centre, and for each related group of centres for periods in time, usually monthly, quarterly and cumulatively. The contrasts between budgeted and actual expenditure are then highlighted as variances.

Product profit analysis. In addition to budgetary control, a number of profit analyses can also be used on a recurring basis. The most usual analysis is by product line profit. This calculates at least the variable material costs, together with the direct labour costs, if these can be measured. A multi-product organisation producing a cluster of products from one batch of machines requires work study to identify the direct labour involved in manufacture.

Any other variable or semi-variable costs associated with, and traceable to, the individual product are deducted and an allocation of supervision and factory overhead may be made across a range of products. This will provide, at one level, a gross margin, or 'working profit' figure. But at this stage the net profit on the product is still unknown.

If the analysis is taken further, then the rest of the management costs, marketing and sales expenses, fixed costs of rent, rates and so on are apportioned across the entire product range, in order to arrive at a net profit estimate for the product.

Here lies the first difficulty. If the sales do not run true to forecast, and they so seldom do, then the fixed cost allocations will be wrong. This leads to the next difficulty; that the higher the element of fixed cost and other overheads, the more difficult it is to rely on the product profit figures. In multi-product companies, the management accountants are involved in a multitude of separate judgement decisions in spreading the overheads.

As the total cost of marketing gets higher, and in many companies it exceeds more than half the total price of the product to the buyer, then the cost apportionments become increasingly inaccurate. In multi-product companies there is a strong tendency to over-estimate the net profits of small selling lines through using the standard costing procedure, because the total of the company 'activity' is a much higher proportion of the turnover of these products than is the average for the business as a whole. This is one reason why having too many products in a range acts as a drain on the resources of the company, without anyone ever being able to prove it.

Other sources of error which do not show up easily in analysis of multi-product ranges is that the standard costs assumed for the procurement of materials are varied through changes in buying decisions, and in suppliers' price offers. The same problem occurs in costing even direct labour when turnover excesses push factory staff into overtime.

Despite these limitations, there is no other way for marketing executives to plan for the profitable running of the business unless they know of the product profit estimates. However, marketing planners often take such figures as being 'perfect' analyses, and subject only to minor day-to-day flaws. In fact, such analyses in all companies which are operating on a high gross margin base of more than 45 per cent can be capable of wild distortions and great swings. Compare this with the fact that few marketing men are happy that they have a very accurate reading on the total market size and of their own proportionate share of the market. They do not necessarily qualify every statement they make on the subject. Neither do management accountants qualify their statements on every occasion.

Market profit analysis. In a narrow product range company, servicing different markets through several distribution channels and using different sales forces, it is usual to provide an analysis of the profits obtained from each market. This is handled in the same way as the method for calculating product profits. That is, the contribution to overheads and profit is arrived at after charging the variable costs and others which are identifiable with each market.

The difficulty is met when a widely different 'product mix' is sold to each market, and on which there are varying rates of gross profit. The computations then are very complex.

Distribution profit analysis. In some companies, particularly those which have several versions of the same product sold through distinctly different channels of trade, for example through 'mail order', through wholesalers and retailers, and through distribution agents, it may be necessary to take a profit analysis through the various channels.

Order profit analysis. Companies selling in oligopsonistic markets frequently take profit analyses by individual customers or by groups of customers. Companies selling high price equipment frequently take a check on the profitability of individual orders. This is particularly true of companies involved in tendering for contracts. In this way, the actual profits resulting from the completed production can be compared to the profit estimate made when setting the tender price. The accumulation of these figures over time provides a better guide for pricing decision in the future. The snag is that the original estimate must show all the assumptions involved in allocating fixed and semi-fixed costs so that the variances at each level of cost can be explained.

Financial control ratios. A large number of control ratios can be calculated, but the ones of prime importance to the general run of companies, and their desirable safety levels, are:[1]

Current assets/current liabilities	:	should not be less than 2:1
liquid assets/current liabilities	:	should not be less than 1:1
current liabilities/tangible net worth	:	should not be greater than 3:4
total liabilities/tangible net worth	:	should not be greater than 1:1
funded debt/nett working assets	:	should not be greater than 1:1
fixed assets tangible net worth	:	should not be greater than 3:4
nett sales/inventory	:	should not be less than 3:1
inventory/nett working assets	:	should not be greater than 1:1
nett sales/tangible nett worth	:	should not be greater than 8:1 for manufacturing companies;
nett sales/net working assets	:	should not be less than 12:1 for manufacturing companies.

[1] D. W. Foster, 'Marketing and Financial Planning for Small Companies'; seminar, Business Intelligence Services, 1969.

If the values of the last five ratios are more than double these norms the company is overtrading.

Figure 12 A Resource Allocation Problem.

£'000 Project	A	B	C	D	E	F	G	H	I	J	K
Turn over/ Price	10	11	12	13	14	15	16	17	18	19	20
Raw material cost	3	4	5	6	4	5	6	3	4	5	7
Labour cost	1	2	3	1	1	2	3	4	5	3	5
Gross margin	6	5	4	6	9	8	7	10	9	11	8

Maximum Capacity

Raw material available	35 units
Labour available	10 units
Overheads	30 units

Q. Select projects within the availability of raw materials and labour that will provide overhead cover and the best profit return.

Problems such as this will show the practical value of using ratios in allocating resources. The problem is difficult to calculate unless the gross margin return on labour, and the gross margin return on raw materials is calculated for each project. Then it is clear that the best projects are E A D F J B, in that order, which add up to a full labour utilisation of 10 without straining the raw material capacity.

	E	A	D	F	J	B	TOTAL
Return on labour	9	6	6	4	$3\frac{2}{3}$	$2\frac{1}{2}$	
Units of labour	1	1	1	2	3	2	10
Raw material units	4	3	6	5	5	4	27
Overhead and profit contribution	9	6	6	8	11	5	45
					Less overhead cost:		30
					Net profit:		15

There are two other kinds of static analysis which are useful to marketing men. These are the cash flow graph, (*Figure 13*) shows a payback analysis of three investment projects, and the more familiar break-even analysis which can be used as a guide for short-term decision making. This is particularly useful for evaluating short-term market forcing techniques where the investment, for example in a sales promotion scheme, is expected to be paid for out of the revenue earned during the period of the scheme. (*Figure 14*.)

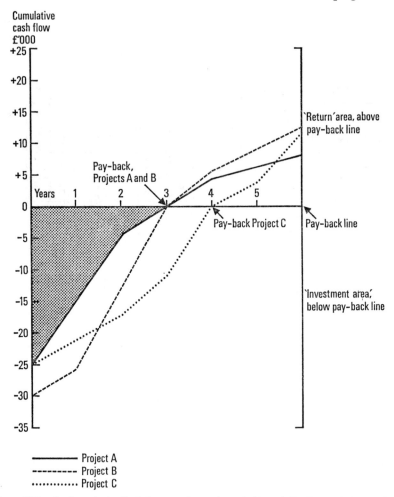

Figure 13 Pay back analysis. Cash flow graph; projects A, B, and C. The shaded area shows the amount, duration and rate of withdrawal of the original investment in Project A.

(*Source:* A. S. Johnson, *Marketing and Financial Control*, p. 158, Pergamon Press, 1967)

Information flow

Elaborate and unnecessary control systems are often installed in a mood of insecurity following mistakes or errors of judgement.[2]

The basic requirement of management information[3] is that it should provide each executive with the information which is relevant to his needs, and to enable him to check his progress.

One basic procedure is to link orders and invoices; but advance indications

[2] A. S. Johnson, *Marketing and Financial Control*; Pergamon Press, 1967.
[3] R. M. S. Wilson, 'The Role of the Accountant in Marketing'; *Marketing Forum*, May–June 1971, pp. 21–30.

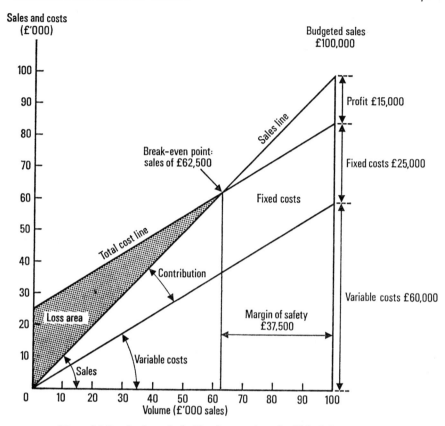

Figure 14 Pay back analysis. Break-even chart for X Ltd. 1st quarter.
(*Source:* A. S. Johnson, *Marketing and Financial Control*, p. 117, Pergamon Press, 1967)

will be more helpful for control purposes. These could be based on enquiries linked to quotations.

In marketing high cost products to industry, particularly those with long delivery lead times, it is critical to relate marketing decisions to the company's liquidity. Many a company has gone into liquidation while it was trading at a profit. Rapid expansion causes a strain on a company's credit and cash resources. It is part of the purpose of planning to make a company recognise the limitations of its resources and to avoid over-trading. Cash flow reports can enable a manager to predict and control liquidity.

This is a particularly aggravating problem in a company which has a marked difference in time between its income generation and its expense incurring activity. For example, farmers traditionally face the problem of laying out cash for materials which will only be converted into income months later. And with long purchasing cycle products, expenditure on promotion may not be recovered from extra sales for up to five years.

Figure 15 shows a typical profitability report for a company making a relatively narrow range of products. For this analysis, most of the data is traceable from distinct activities, such as delivery, to particular products. Those activities which are not traceable, say service costs, or sales call costs. must be allocated by judgement.

There are several problems which emerge when using such analyses. First, the *percentage* figures of profit often provide a distortion. It is perfectly possible to show a product with a high rate of net profit, and one would normally promote it harder: but it may be a small seller in the range, or its sales may be strongly related to another product; or it may be receiving favourable treatment in the fixed cost allocations. Any decision to promote it, oblivious of these factors, may therefore be wrong.

There is an inherent dislike of net profit figures by managements when applied to individual products, owing to doubts about the fixed and semi-fixed cost allocations. Many managers prefer to judge questions of resource allocation by gross margin figures instead. But even this can be difficult. For example, a product showing a high gross margin rate would normally be promoted to the exclusion of a low gross margin product. But the product with the high gross margin may require very high marketing costs to sustain it. For instance, high promotional and delivery costs will drag up expenditure more or less in proportion to the total number of customers and deliveries. However, a low gross margin product may be sold to one customer, without sales or advertising backing, and with relatively infrequent delivery. An increase in the sales of such a product may be absorbed by the existing resources quite easily. Most of the gross margin on extra sales may flow through direct to net profit as a result. Problems of this kind are dealt with more fully in the chapter on Product Planning.

Figure 16 shows a Marketing-Oriented Profit Statement. The item 'cost of sales' can be difficult to calculate since it takes into account all the costs incurred up to the point of the products leaving the factory. But it varies according to the 'product mix' being sold, and it will also vary according to the seasonal sales factors.

Even the figure for 'cash discounts', which usually comes under the executive responsibility of marketing, can vary considerably according to the 'distribution channel mix'. A few very large orders, placed at high discount levels, perhaps collected from the factory, can distort this cost easily—and this may, in turn, show up the distribution cost favourably as a result.

The control of expenditures based only upon percentage calculations is dangerous. It is better to take the comparisons with the *actual* cash sums involved and compare them period to period. The length of these periods cannot be too short, otherwise the distortions will be wilder.

When using management accounting figures, it is best to control the larger items first; to recognise the variability of the figures; and to understand that if an activity is to be cut off because it is losing money, this will not save

For the month ending	Total	Product A	Product B	Product C	Product D
1. Sales Volume					
2. Market potential					
3. Sales per cent of potential					
4. Total Marketing costs					
5. Total call costs					
6. Total service costs					
7. Total delivery costs					
8. Total advertising and promotion costs					
9. Total marketing research costs					
10. Total marketing administration costs					
11. Marketing cost % of sales					
12. Gross margin					
13. Profit contribution (volume less V.C.)[1]					
14. Profit contribution rate (% of volume)					
15. Product net profit					
16. Volume % of total					
17. Gross margin % of total					
18. Profit contribution % of total					
19. Profit % of total					
20. Number of customers					
21. Volume/customers					
22. Call + Service + Delivery/Customer					
23. New profit/customer					
24. Inventory					
25. Cost of goods sold/investment					
26. Total investment					
27. Net profit/sales					
28. Sales/investment					
29. Return on investment (27×28)					
30. Break-even point (B.E.)					
31. Safety factors (Volume—B.E.)					
‾‾‾ B.E.					

Figure 15 Profitability report.

(*Source:* R. M. S. Wilson, *The Role of the Accountant in Marketing*; Marketing Forum, May–June 1971, p. 26)

[1] V.C. = variable costs.

		£	£
GROSS SALES:		0,000	
Less:	Cash Discounts	00	
NET SALES:			0,000
	Cost of Sales		000
GROSS PROFIT:			0,000
Less:	MARKETING COSTS		
	Advertising	00	
	Promotion	00	
	Field Selling	00	
	Distribution	00	
	Product Management	00	
	Marketing Management	00	
	Marketing Research	00	
	Sales Research	00	
	Total		0,000
MERCHANDISING PROFIT:			000
Less:	Administrative Expense	00	
	General Expense	00	
	Research & Development	00	
	Total		000
PROFIT BEFORE TAX:			0,000

Figure 16 Marketing-orientated profit statement.

(*Source:* R. M. S. Wilson, 'The Role of the Accountant in Marketing'; *Marketing Forum*, May–June 1971, p. 27)

all the losses. It will add something to the costs of the remaining activities, however marginally.

Marketing budgets

The normal procedure for the build up of budgets is to take each budget or centre in the marketing operation and to allow for an increase or decrease in activity during the budget period. This is compared with the current year. The total cost of all the company budgets is subtracted from the forecasted revenue and the resulting net profit figure judged as being acceptable or not. Usually it is not acceptable. This is because human factors creep into budgeting considerations. In particular, managers tend to hedge the risk of something going wrong by building in as generous an allowance for their activity as they think they might need, and one as good as their debating skills can win for them.

This procedure is what can be termed 'loose budgeting' practice. It is a contributory factor to what Galbraith called in *The New Industrial State* the 'technostructure' where the managers run the company for their own ends. It results in mediocre levels of management performance being accepted. And, at its worst, it can stifle a company's initiative and attack. One of the most interesting aspects of successful take-overs, as witnessed by those taken over, is the way that the previous budgeting sequence is radically altered by the new managers, and a totally different pattern of decisions relating to costs is adopted, often to the incredulity of the original managers.

It is not at all unusual for new owners of a business to work substantially greater profit out of the operation without touching the assets of the company, and without bringing any other specialist skills to bear, except those of making money.

Tight budgeting.   The first principle for making more profit out of current marketing operations is to recognise that the budgeting problem is a human one, and does not lend itself totally to a measurement process. It is a behavioural problem.

The tight budgeting sequence proposed here recognises three simple factors:

(1) That marginal opportunities for cost-saving exist in any cost centre or budget.
(2) That marginal opportunities for increasing turnover, at low additional cost, exist in the sales budget.
(3) That managers are constantly striving to be improving their performance; which means their getting greater output from lower inputs.

During periods of inflation, companies have noticed that their sales forecasts have often failed to be met, despite allowing for future price increases; their expense budgets have been exceeded even after allowing for rises due to the effects of inflation; and their planned price increases have not kept in line with inflationary costs, all with consequent pressure on net profit. As a result, management becomes frightened, allows even greater estimates of inflationary effects, leading to longer planned price increases. The cumulative sum of these effects upon our economy is to cause the rate of inflation to accelerate. This acceleration could be eased by tight budgeting for the short-term.

Reducing costs.   There are, in essence, two questions to be asked of any manager preparing his budget. The first relates to costs. 'How can the effectiveness of your work be maintained if you were to absorb . . . per cent for inflation during the period?' The point can be sharper, with a higher loading factor for cost reduction, if this is required. The manager is then forced to identify and list those activities which are central to his job and

which require basic resources. He is forced also to list those activities which
he must drop or alter if his effective budget is to be lower. These are ranked
by size of cost reduction. These activities will fall into three areas:

(1) Activities which are dependant upon decisions made in another part of
the organisation. For example, if sales department agree to allow an
increase in the delivery lead time for customer service, then route planning
can be altered, journeys extended, and fewer drivers and vehicles will be
required in the transport budget.
(2) Activities which the manager judges to be of high risk if dropped. The risk
would be measured in terms of his ability to perform the task adequately
with smaller resources, or in terms of those activities which he regards as
central to the company operation.
(3) Those expenses for which he is nominally responsible, but which are
incurred at lower levels of management within his department.

The technique for dealing with his first problem, that of interacting
diseconomies between departments, is to cluster the interacting costs together,
make responsible managers meet and decide ways of saving such expenses.
They are forced to propose such savings in ranking order of cost and feasibility. They may have to set up a project team with the help of management
accounts to find the economies. They can add whatever qualifications and
riders they judge to the proposals and, as a result, the proposals may not
go through senior management. But at least they are examined for what
they are—high cost and peripheral areas of activity.

The second problem relates to risk. Through the tight budgeting process
management is, after all, asking its departments to take some risk with their
performance and efficiency. The heads of the spending departments are not
the people to judge what level of risk is acceptable to management; and each
will be concerned to protect his current performance. The economies must
be ranked, as before, each with its statement as to feasibility and the degree
of risk attached. A decision is taken on each after appropriate consultation
with senior management—and not all the economies necessarily will be
accepted.

The important thing is that a contingency factor must be built into the
central budget, in order to allow for the fact that some of the savings cannot
be achieved, and that the expenses may have to be replaced in the budget.
General management cannot use the tight budgeting procedure as a yardstick
for performance. Managements frequently praise managers who 'beat'
their budgets and 'punish' those who fail to meet them. If the budgeting
procedure is properly handled, management cannot work in this way. It
should be equally reprehensible for a manager to be so poor in his estimates
of cost or sales that his performance is significantly 'better' than budget,
as it is for one which is 'worse' than budget. However, the tight budgeting
technique involves money being taken out of a budget, so that managers
are forced to stretch their performance. Any high-risk economy move which

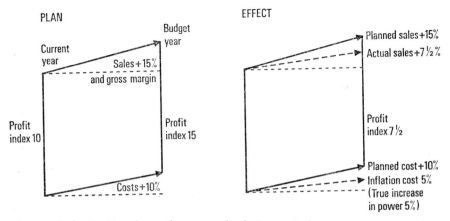

1. *Loose Budgeting.* Here the starting assumption is that marketing management argues for an increase in budget of, say, 10 per cent. This is based upon the estimate that it will bring an increase in sales and gross margin of 15 per cent. There is no allowance for inflation. We can see that inflation has absorbed one half of the total 'power' of the additional marketing expense. As a result sales have grown by only 7½ per cent (assuming that the relationship between changes in marketing expense and sales is linear). The profit index therefore has actually gone down instead of up.

2. *Tight Budgeting.* The two questions to be asked are: (a) How can the effectiveness of the marketing operation be increased to absorb the 5 per cent inflation? This will flush out all the short-term budget savings since it reduces, in effect, the amount of cash available at current costs.

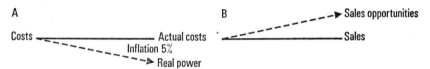

(b) The second question is: 'where do opportunities lie within the existing budget?' This identifies all the smaller sales opportunities which exist at the margin of the current operation.

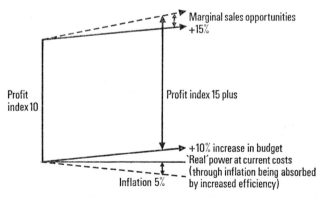

We can now see from a combination of the two sets of figures, that not only has inflation been contained, but the profitability of the operation has probably been improved. If there is, subsequently, an agreed 10 per cent addition to the total marketing expense it can be expected to operate at full 'power' achieving its planned profit index of 15 or more, since (1) the productivity of the existing expenditures has been increased; (2) marginal sales opportunities have been identified; (3) the budget increase is a true increase of marketing power.

Figure 17 The advantage of tight budgeting.

fails to mature is replaced from the central contingency fund without pena-
lising the responsible manager.

The third problem faced by cost cutting managers is that a heavy part of
the costs, and the associated decisions, must be handled by lower or specialist
levels of management. This means that the general technique of tight budgeting must be passed through the organisation as part of the normal management procedure. Every level of expense must be questioned in the same way,
and the resulting decisions judged by the level of management immediately
above.

Budgeting becomes a two-stage process, therefore. The first stage is a
directive for forced economy allowing sufficient time for judgement and
consideration at all levels. This results in a series of analyses of economic
opportunities. At the second stage, the opportunities are taken up, or not,
and the expense budgets drafted.

Increasing marginal sales. The second question can now be asked of the
sales and marketing function of the business. This relates to marginal sales
opportunities. 'If the total expense budget remains the same, but if you
allocate sales resources differently, how much can sales increase, and where?'

However well-motivated and controlled a sales force, it always suffers from
the human problem that it could do just a bit more if it tried. The men can
convert more calls; they can take more of the right kind of orders; they can
stretch their day to include more pioneering work; they can search harder for
new sales leads. The total organisation needs only a marginal increase in
performance from each man, in order to result in an overall increase in
business performance.

The questions again resolve into three:

(1) Opportunities which occur at each level of management.
(2) Opportunities which result from different amounts of energy applied.
(3) The direction of the effort.

From the sales director down, in each man's area, there is always one good
account which could be developed or opened. The problem is to identify
these marginal customer prospects, and to motivate men towards them.
The assumption is that each man has had one year's more experience than
last year, that he had completed his main sales priorities and is now looking
for the next, and so on. The fact that sales organisations change, that men
are replaced and promoted, should not alter this basic management attitude.
The object is to flush out all the lower priority activities which are lying
dormant.

Marketing managers can be pushed to identify the smaller markets which
have not been attacked so far. Regional managers can be forced to identify
those areas which can be held defensively for a while, in which the company
is strong, so that more men can be pushed into a campaign to develop a
weaker area with potential. A host of low-cost low-risk opportunities can

be developed from most sales and marketing operations which require a motivational starter mechanism to get them going. A tight budgeting procedure can provide this, and can set up many short-term objectives for all levels of management.

Adding the growth. At this stage of the tight budgeting procedure, we have all the economic opportunities identified and analysed, together with the marginal sales goals. Draft budgets are now prepared.

But the company requires expansion and additional investment. Growth areas can now be analysed separately and the necessary funds voted to them. They can more easily be seen for what they really are—investment opportunities. It will be easier to identify the associated costs and profits resulting from expansion moves than it would otherwise be in budgets which are allowed to drift into expansion.

Of course the expansion costs subsequently must be added to the global budget figures concerned with keeping the business running. Managers may be surprised to find they have been voted additional funds after they have taken pains to cut their costs. At least they know three things. First, they know the short-term objectives to achieve from the current business. Second, they know clearly what the extra funds are for, and that these funds must be made to work as hard as their normal budgets. Third, they know more about the interacting effect of their decisions on the costs of other departments in the business.

Top management has one additional and priceless asset through the tight budgeting sequence. They now know the 'soft' areas of the business where, in the views of their managers, additional savings can be made, at some risk. These are the economic opportunities which have not been taken up by management. If external factors put pressure on the company's profitability, then top management has two lines of defence. There is, first, a contingency budget, which is written down to profit as the year continues. Secondly, they know there is a series of cost cutting actions which they could take, if circumstances dictate that they must.

Marketing controls

Figure 18 shows a control information checklist. All companies vary in their attitude towards control data. The decisions on company information relate to the frequency with which the information should be supplied, the personnel who should receive it, the standard against which it is to be measured, the method of reporting variances from standard, whether it should be shown cumulatively and for the reporting period.

Information relating to the control process, however, falls into four stages, each akin to the planning process itself. The objectives and standards need to be specified and written down. The results of the programme to meet these goals need to be shown against the aims, in short time periods, with a cumu-

Marketing Management Control Information Checklist

Managers receiving reports
C = For control purposes
I = for information purposes

Performance information	Report frequency	Year-to-date	Standard	Variance shown by:	Marketing mgr.	Sales mgr.	Advertising mgr.	Marketing research mgr.	Product mgrs.	Marketing services mgr.
1. Sales										
(a) Total sterling	Daily or weekly	Yes	Forecast	Sterling and %	C	C	C	I	C	I
(b) Units and sterling:	Weekly or monthly	,,	,,	Units, sterling, and %	C	C	C	I	C	I
(1) By product line	,,	,,	,,	,,	C	C	C	I	C	I
(2) By region	,,	,,	,,	,,	C	C	C	I	C	I
(3) By district	,,	,,	,,	,,		C		I	C	I
(4) By territory	,,	,,	,,	,,		C		I	C	I
(5) By major accounts	Monthly	,,	,,	,,	C	C		I	I	I
2. Profits										
(a) Net for company	Quarterly	,,	,,	Sterling and %	C	I		I	C	I
(b) Company return on investment	,,	,,	,,	,,	C	C		I	C	I
(c) Gross profit or marginal return:*	Monthly	,,	,,	,,	C	C	I	I	C	I
(1) By product line	,,	,,	,,	,,	C	C	I	I	C	I
(2) By region	,,	,,	,,	,,	C	C	I	I	C	I
(3) By district	,,	,,	,,	,,	C	C		I	I	I
(4) By territory	,,	,,	,,	,,	C	C		I	I	I
(5) By major accounts	,,	,,	,,	,,	C	C		I	I	I
3. Expenses										
(a) Total marketing	,,	,,	Budget	Sterling and %	C	C		I	C	I
(b) Each department	,,	,,	,,	,,	C	C		I	C	I
(c) By region, district, and territory	,,	,,	,,	,,		C		I		
(d) Administrative and rental for each branch office	,,	,,	,,	,,		C		I		
(e) Operating expenses by field warehouse	,,	,,	,,	,,	C			I		C
(f) Cars and vans	,,	,,	,,	,,	C			I		C
(g) Product transportation	,,	,,	,,	,,	C			I	C	C
4. Production costs										
By product	,,	,,	Plan	,,	I			I	I	I
5. Customer accounts										
(a) Number added by region	,,	,,	,,	Number	I	C	I	I	I	I
(b) Number lost by region	,,	,,	,,	,,	I	C	I	I	I	I
(c) Net change by region and total										

Note (Sales mgr., Expenses section): For control—receive report for own department only

	Frequency	Yes/No	Plan	Sterling and %							
6. Pricing Amount of variance from planned prices by product, region, and district					C	C		I	I	I	C	I
7. Inventory of finished goods												
(a) By product:												
(1) Units	Weekly	No	"	Units and %	C	C		C			C	C
(2) Number of days of supply	"	"	"	Number	C	C		C			C	C
(b) By plant and warehouse:												
(1) Product by units	"	"	"	Units and %	C	C		C			C	C
(2) Product by number of days of supply	"	"	"	Number	C	C		C			C	C
8. Order backlog by product												
(a) Number of orders in excess of standard time allowed to fill:												
(1) By plant	"	"	0	—	I	I		I			I	I
(2) By distribution point	"	"	0	—	C	I		I			I	C
(b) Anticipated date will become current:												
(1) By plant	"	"	—	—	I	I		I			I	I
(2) By distribution point	"	"	—	—	C	I		I			I	C
9. Customer service												
(a) Number of complaints by product and by type of complaint	Monthly	Yes	Acceptable ratio to units delivered	%	C	I	I	I	I	I	C	I
(b) Number of claims and adjustments	"	"	"	"	C	I		I			I	C
(c) Number of exchanges and refunds	"	"	"	"	I	I		I			I	I
(d) Number of technical service calls	"	"	Plan	Number and %	C	I		I			I	C
10. Credit												
(a) Number of accounts and cash amounts outstanding:												
(1) Over 10 days	"	No	Goal	Number, £, and %	C	C		C			I	C
(2) Over 30 days	"	"	"	"	C	C		C			I	C
(3) Over 60 days	"	"	"	"	C	C		C			I	C
(b) Names of accounts with amounts over 60 days	"	"	—	—	C	C		C			I	C
11. Advertising												
(a) Expenditure by:												
(1) Media	"	Yes	Budget	Sterling and %	C	I	C	I			I	
(2) Sales promotion	"	"	"	"	C	I	C	I			I	
(3) Co-op	"	"	Plan	"	C	I	C	I			I	
(b) Exceptions to schedules	"	No	"	—	C	I	C	I			I	
(c) Status report on degree of readiness for trade shows and exhibits	"	"	"	—	C	I	C	I			I	C
(d) Status report on scheduled functions such as label design, signs, bulletins, product literature	"	"	"	—	C	I		C			I	
(e) Market awareness of, and preference for, company and products	Semi-annually	No	Goal	%	C	I	C	I	I	I	I	C

Performance information	Report frequency	Year-to-date	Standard	Variance shown by:	Marketing mgr.	Sales mgr.	Advertising mgr.	Marketing research mgr.	Product mgr.	Marketing services mgr.
					Managers receiving reports C = For control purposes I = For information purposes					
12. Marketing research										
(a) Projects completed and projects pending, with expected completion dates	Monthly	No	Plan	Projects and % complete	C			C	I	
(b) Share of market:										
(1) By product line	Quarterly	„	Goal	„	C	C	C	I	C	I
(2) By region and district	„	„	„	„	C	C	C	I	C	I
13. Product planning										
(a) Status of each product and packaging with estimated completion date; new projects begun or scheduled	Monthly	„	Plan	Number of weeks	C	I	I	I	C	I
(b) Schedule of each project showing assignments for each department and estimated completion dates for each	„	„	„	„	C				C	
14. Marketing personnel										
(a) Manning: Number of unfilled positions by type, number of weeks unfilled; and those for which candidates are being sought	„	„	—	—	C	For control—receive report for own department only				
(b) Training:										
(1) Number and type of courses in process and completed	Quarterly	Yes	Plan	Statement of variance	C	„	„	„		
(2) Number and classification of personnel attending and completed	„	„	„	„	C	„	„	„		

Figure 18 Marketing management control information checklist.

(*Source:* V. Bluell, *Marketing Management in Action*, p. 222–227, McGraw-Hill, 1966

lative build-up. The significant variances from the aims need to be highlighted so that the final stage can take place. This is to adjust the aims, or the programme, or both.

Example: Adapting Military Planning Processes to Business

Background

In March–April, 1966, the *Harvard Business Review* ran a feature called, 'Six Business Lessons from the Pentagon' by D. Smalter and R. Ruggles Jr. This showed how one business, the International Minerals and Chemicals Corporation, has applied six concepts of the u.s. defence planning process to its own business. What follows briefly summarises the six lessons.

The Summary

In 1961, the u.s. Secretary of Defence, Robert McNamara, found the Army, the Navy and the Air Force budgeting rather independently, hardly co-ordinating with each other's programmes. He brought into existence what was called 'the planning-programming-budgeting process' which is used in conjunction with cost-benefit analysis. By 1965, owing to its success, this system was being applied to other non-defence departments of the u.s. Government.

Six lessons can be learned from this process of general application to business planning problems.

(1) *Top management's primary job in any enterprise is the allocation of limited resources—for selected mission purposes, in proper dimensions of time—for the furtherance of specified objectives*

Central to this is the idea of the 'mission'. In this the motives and purpose of the business operation are examined from the viewpoint of its service to customers. In military terms, the idea of budgeting for 'mission' purposes led the three u.s. service arms to consider jointly the alternatives for action, for example should they be faced with the air-lifting of a police-type force somewhere in the world; or perhaps a nuclear retaliation mission.

(2) *Management should integrate one-year budgeting with long-range planning in an annual cycle*

Previously, there had been a distinct tendency for the head of each u.s. service arm to allot sums for the continuation of present commitments without a proper analysis of changing circumstances. By integrating the budgeting process with a long-range plan, the sales and profit forecasts have already been established before the work on detailed budgeting commences. All the strategic aspects are already analysed and long-term decisions have been taken.

(3) *Management should apply operations-research or systems-analysis principles of mathematical analysis to complex strategy questions*

In 1961, McNamara found there was relatively poor co-ordination between the u.s. services. He found that service chiefs often did not know fully the supporting costs of some of their weapons systems; there was no procedure to look for alternative ways of reaching the same objective with lower funds. The result led to cost-benefit analysis of varying alternatives. This can best be described as a continuing dialogue between the policymaker and the systems analyst, in which the former asks for alternative solutions to his problems, while the analyst attempts to define alternative possible objectives, and to explore each alternative in terms of cost and effectiveness.

(4) *Systematic programme analysis and planning can best be accomplished through use of logical, sequenced steps of action*

Ten years ago, the financial implications of u.s. defence decisions were poorly determined. For example, the u.s. Chiefs of Staff authorised the development of major weapons systems, yet did not project the development costs beyond a year. And they often did not determine how much it would cost to run these weapons over time. The setting of a list of basic questions and staging them in sequence, eliminated many otherwise wasteful projects.

(5) *Logic- or task-sequence network should be used in planning, implementing, and monitoring complex projects.*

The PERT technique and other network planning systems was developed by the u.s. Navy, together with commercial firms. Through the use of it, many hundreds of contractors and subcontractors running into thousands were co-ordinated so effectively that the Polaris missile was operational two years ahead of the original schedule.

(6) *Decision making centres are useful devices for reviewing or approving programmes in complex organisations*

Originally there was an excessive number of committee meetings in the Department of Defence. Consequently, a specially designed strategy decision room was created. Full use was made of visual display to increase the effectiveness of presentations. Pertinent data was made available quickly and in visual form. A sophisticated information system and document retrieval was available to the decision makers who man these rooms. The idea of a decision-centre in business goes beyond merely having a conference room as a place in which to argue proposals and plans.

The company used as an illustration, IMC, applied these ideas with great financial success. It established a Corporate Planning and Development Division, and in doing so, management said they wanted its past methods of decision making challenged. They wanted proposals evaluated by a disinterested team of specialists, their strategic moves made in the light of penetrating environment 'intelligence', and their alternative courses of action systematically identified and weighed.

A measure of uncertainty will always remain in business, but the prize will go to the one who plans and leaves the least to chance.

J.W.

Controlling the Market Variables

7. The Information System

Marketing executives are at the mercy of their information. They get too much information of the wrong sort and too little of the right kind, too late. The information is decentralised—it exists somewhere in the organisation but it is too difficult to locate. Sometimes the information is suppressed. Sometimes it goes to the wrong person. Sometimes it is incorrect; and sometimes it is unverified. Executives then do not know whether it is right or wrong.

These are the common complaints. They will be heard decades from now, just as in the past, in organisations which should know better. The overwhelming of industry by the computer will multiply the problems and the complaints, not resolve them.

Information in marketing can be classified either as situational or dynamic. Situational information is such that describes the outline and nature of a subject leading to its analysis. A market survey or a product specification fits this description.

Dynamic information describes the ebbs and flows of changes in a situation. This is of two kinds; (a) trend information, such as the rate of market growth, or (b) variance information, such as a comparison of performance against a control.

Situational information has, as its main function, an improvement of the executive's comprehension, reducing areas of ignorance to known factors. Dynamic information, as its prime function, provides cues and signals for action, leading to a better timing of decisions.

Information relating to tests and experiments has both a situational and a dynamic quality. To run a test, the situation must be known beforehand, reaction predicted and controls set up. The dynamic information relates to the performance of the test itself against the controls.

There is an evolution in the marketing information function as it develops within companies.[1] The route starts with basic studies of market size and structure. It moves through studies of product and distribution mix, and

[1] F. T. Pearce, 'Marketing Research for Optimum Profit'; *Management Accounting*, Nov. 1968.

related questions of product development and competition. Then it moves into the areas of administration and promotion, covering questions such as return on advertising investment and sales force size. It continues through feasibility and investment studies such as test marketing operations, and grows finally into a completely integrated information routine for the purpose of forecasting and planning. (*Figure 19.*) The study of departmental activities develops from the general to the specific; from 'appreciations' to investigations, and moves on to association with other management services.

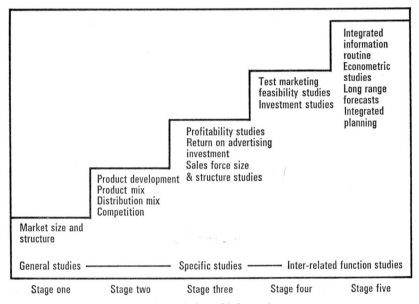

Figure 19 The evolution of information systems.

Companies are providing themselves more than ever with formal marketing information systems.[2] They recognise that accurate situational information is usually expensive to collect, and time consuming. Expensive information should be treated as an item of short-term capital expenditure, subject to decay. Updating this information in order to locate underlying fundamental changes can be made more simple if the basic data is collected as part of a standard procedure with a known method. In this way the subsequent monitoring process may be relatively simple. (*Figure 20.*)

A marketing information system provides for continuous study of the marketing factors which are important to an enterprise. We have moved a long way from intermittent examination of markets. A system uses far more information sources of all kinds, both internal and external, in order to build

[2] C. Berenson, 'Marketing Information Systems'; *U.S. Jnl. of Marketing*, Vol. 33, Oct. 1969, pp. 16–23.

up data banks. And we now recognise that the decay rate of information varies from very rapid to relatively slow; following the dynamics of the subject.

The basic requirement of a system is that information must be presented in a form which management can use. Furthermore operating management must participate in creating the outline of the system, because they will be the ones using it. The information must be aggregated with previous inputs in such a way as to enable the data still to be retrieved and used even should the system itself be changed. Finally, the system itself must alter in time to fit the changing needs of the organisation.

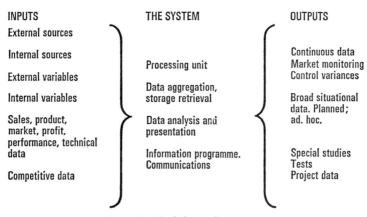

Figure 20 The information system.

A system requires the setting up, aggregation and storage of all the relevant information as a series of 'inputs'. The system includes not only any data processing unit, but also the human resources and the programme to meet the marketing information needs of the company. It does not need a computer to set up an adequate information system, but it helps.

The first output to consider is the provision of continuous key data—the variances and trends compared to any control data or forecasts. This provides action signals to management. The second is the intermittent provision of broad data, as it becomes available. This would include, for example, analyses of the latest government figures on the trend in the industry, or the reporting of competitors' annual results. Finally the provision of special analyses and data is prompted in two ways. Either it comes from the information system itself, after, say, the publication of an important piece of technical research which has a bearing on the industry. Alternatively it is in response to demand from the operating management.

The information unit has four main responsibilities:

> *Search.* The unit goes inside and outside the company in search of appropriate information, and is responsible for the control of the market research budget;

but probably not the product testing budget. It is better to allocate this responsibility to product management, or to product development.

Filtering.   The unit validates the information, reduces it to its essentials and prepares it in suitable form for different levels of management, and for different functions.

Dissemination.   It passes the information to the operating managers, holding personal briefings when appropriate.

Storage.   It codifies the information for storage, updating, and later retrieval.

The problems which concern marketing information systems usually relate to the integration of the system with the rest of the organisation. It is, after all, only part of the total management information process, the other parts including finance and production. There is often a problem concerning the relationship between the systems' designers and the users of the information. The designers must provide relevant information, and not an indigestible mass. The users must allow the system to help them make decisions. And the system must itself be changed as the company changes its organisation, documents and operating personnel. Some larger organisations promote the information system into a corporate planning unit.[3] In this way it becomes bound up with the long-range planning and short-range budgeting tasks of the company, and is integrated with other company information. This may leave the system too far removed from the needs of operating management. It also focuses upon the information requirements of top management, who are not responsible for day-to-day operations, and away from middle and lower managements who are in the thick of the fight.

There are at least three basic misconceptions about marketing information.

Market size: Most companies do not know the total size of the markets they serve, either in units or in volume, with any degree of accuracy.[4] Even in the large continuously researched consumer goods markets the total market size estimates will vary considerably from one company to the next. This is partly due to the definitions of the product field being different as between one company and the next. It is partly due to different research techniques being used. And it is partly due to methodological problems such as sampling error. This is not true of some industries which are well recorded —but it is true that most companies in the same market differ in their estimates of the market size.

It does not matter too much if the company's share of the market is 21 per cent or 23 per cent. What does matter is that the company is a leader or a follower, or has a special distinction in one aspect of the market in comparison with competitors. However, the bias, if not too strong, should

[3] F. W. McFarlan, 'Problems in Planning the Information System'; *Harvard Business Review*, March–April 1971, pp. 75–89.
[4] R. V. Brown, 'Just How Credible are Your Marketing Estimates?'; *U.S. Jnl. of Marketing*, Vol. 33, July 1969, pp. 46–50.

remain constant whenever the research is repeated. The same product field definitions, the same sampling frame, the same technique should be used, whenever the market is measured. Consequently the control remains constant and the performance can be meaningfully compared to it.

The second misconception is that market size and structure measurements must involve the use of formal market research studies. In fact, in measuring the markets for industrial products it is usual to search every information source for the data, and only in the last resort to commission a market research study. This search procedure will include the normal sources of library information, government statistics and other published data. It may also include searching through company sales records, checking with key customers and the use of other 'expert' opinion. The limitations of this procedure are obvious and must be recognised; but for all practical purposes this is what most companies can afford on a continuous basis, and no more.

It pays not to lend too much credence even to government-based information. In 1968, an American Professor of Marketing checked the British Census of Distribution for accuracy. He took an area of the country and checked the Census against other desk information, and finally used a personal field check. He found that the government had effectively 'lost' over 27 per cent of all the retail shops in the country.[5]

The other misconception is that expenditure on information should be constant and level. This is not so. At one time in the history of an enterprise it will have a great need for external information which is expensive to collect. As this information is translated into management decisions, it needs only monitoring to evaluate trends plus small studies to counter the decay factor. The emphasis at this time will be on internal information, which is easier to collect and much less expensive. Then, as the organisation expands into new markets, it requires more external information again, and so the process is repeated. (*Figure 21.*)

In the last five years, there has been an expansion in the demand for continuous market measurement.[6] This is particularly true of consumer markets where a range of standard measurement services is sold to many clients at the same time. This operating method has pushed one company, Audits of Great Britain Ltd., into one of the two largest research companies outside the United States. There are signs that similar trends are occurring in certain industrial markets where companies such as Industrial Market Research Ltd. are developing monitoring services.

Industrial market information

More than its consumer counterpart, the industrial marketing company relies for its existence upon a relatively few key purchasing decisions. Mass

[5] W. E. Cox, 'The Census of Distribution: A Critique'; *Jnl. of the Market Research Society*, Vol. 10. No. 4, Oct. 1968. pp. 225–233.
[6] R. I. Haley and R. Gatty, 'Monitor Your Market Continuously'; *Marketing*, Sept. 1968.

consumer markets are generally easier to measure; they are more stable in their behaviour than minority markets, usually because there are more repetitive events and people involved. The purchasing behaviour patterns are discrete and fairly repetitive.

Industrial purchasing decisions are much less standardised. There are more random influences at work. With the exception of materials purchasing and some small component parts, the buying decisions are not as repetitive as in the consumer market. This affects market study methods in a number of significant ways.

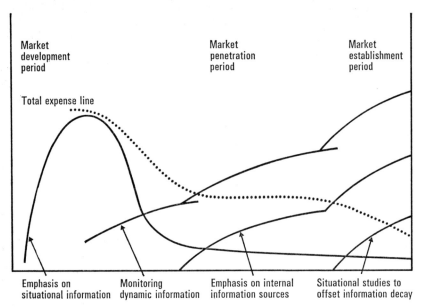

Figure 21 The information life-cycle.

The salesman. For example, the industrial salesman is an important source of information. He reports back information about his customers' plans and organisation. He reports new technical developments which are relevant to his own enterprise. And he reports on product use, competitors' actions, and so on. What is lacking in all of this is a systematic review of the sort of information which the salesman should report, and a method of sorting and classifying this data, so that it can be used within the marketing information system. One company, Bakelite-Xylonite Ltd., goes so far as to have a military-style 'debriefing' session with its salesmen after every journey cycle is completed.

The use of postal survey and telephone survey techniques will develop more in the industrial field, particularly to update market information. In carefully designed industrial studies, response to mail questionnaires can be as high as 75 per cent or more; and 40 per cent response is fairly common.

Media information. Next, the standard of industrial media information in this country lags sadly behind what is available in the United States. The circulations of British trade and technical magazines are small by comparison, but more market research will be carried out by industrial companies in future, relating trade press readership and other industrial media such as exhibition attendance to the target audiences for their own particular products.

Product testing. One of the biggest differences in standards between consumer and industrial research concerns product testing. The attitude of most industrial managements to the qualities of the products they make is still unbelievably production-oriented. Having great technical experience in manufacture may be the most inhibiting factor to developing customer-satisfying products. The basic attitudes are wrong. The very term 'quality' to an engineer is associated with the quality and performance of the ingredients of the product, or the complexity of the manufacturing process. These factors are not at all in the customer's mind when he describes 'quality'. Only through product testing can we discover how satisfactorily our products meet customers' requirements, as opposed to how well we believe or assume them to be satisfactory.

The blatantly inadequate products are shown up quickly through customer complaints; but these are not the difficult problems. There can be a large area of faint customer satisfaction where products are not quite right, but they are not sufficiently wrong to receive criticism. A competitor, detecting the weakness, can move in having a product without these deficiencies. Moves towards the setting-up of customer test panels and selected depth interviews will continue to expand. This is in direct contrast to the usual system of judging customer preferences through a jury panel composed of the sales chief and his engineering colleagues.

The decision influencers. The multiple 'buying influences' within the industrial company pose the biggest communications problem for industrial marketing companies. There are two problems: to whom should we communicate and attempt to sell; and whom should we interview in our market research? The nature of the buying influences changes with the type of product, and whether the decision is a first purchase or repeat. Many different individuals are concerned before an order is placed. The company which concentrates its attention solely on the purchasing officer is likely to be missing opportunities.

A survey[7] published in 1967 showed that, in Britain, when materials are being bought by industry, the influence of the purchasing officer is at its greatest. Yet, only 37 per cent of them select the suppliers from whom to

[7] Industrial Market Research Ltd., *How Industry Buys*; Institute of Marketing, 1967.

invite bids, and only 31 per cent decide who gets the order. So in two companies out of three someone other than the man nominally responsible for
purchasing materials actually makes the decision.

The situation is worse when selling plant equipment. Here, the purchasing
officer hardly rates. Most tenders are put out by design and development
staff, and the Board of Management takes the final decision in more than
half the cases. The Board is also responsible for deciding who gets the order
when most components are bought.

More investigation is needed on the question of the primary and secondary
purchasing influences for a company's specific product range. It is in this
area that the salesman and service engineers can provide the most useful
data. The salesman may be able to reach three personnel—yet there can be
up to a dozen people involved in the decision. This is a strong argument for
the use of industrial advertising and promotion to supplement the personal
selling effort.

Sales forecasting

Accurate sales forecasting is essential but impossible, so the saying goes.
Techniques vary in their costs, as well as in their scope and accuracy. Managers using sales forecastng methods must fix the level of inaccuracy they can
tolerate in the forecast through asking the question, 'For what purpose is
the forecast required?' If, for example, a go/no go decision is required on a
particular course of action, then a relatively wide tolerance in forecasting
accuracy may be acceptable. However, suppose the forecast is for the purpose
of shifting a wide inventory of expensive stock through a pipeline to the
end-users. Then the cost savings in having the right stock at the right place
at the right time must be set against the on-cost of using a more sophisticated
forecasting technique. *Figure 22* shows how the cost and accuracy of various
forecasting techniques increase with sophistication.

The choice of forecasting technique relates to the dynamics and components of the system for which the forecast is made. It is necessary for the
industrial marketing organisation to show the relative positions and inter-
actions between the company sales system, the distribution pipeline, and the
establishment levels of the product within markets. Also the replacement
rates, new user rates and the trends of the ultimate end-users from which the
product demand is derived must be considered. All of these are primary
influences. Secondary factors such as credit conditions and other environmental influences will distort the forecast.

Then there is the degree of importance of past history in estimating the
future. For the short-term, the immediate past history may be a sufficient
guide to the future but its predictive powers decay with time.

Forecasting methods.   There are three types of basic forecasting method.
Qualitative systems use judgement and experience to provide the forecast.

This system is used whenever a company's forecasts are made up from a synthesis of sales force opinion. In strongly repetitive circumstances it may be perfectly acceptable. It may also be the only system available in circumstances approaching great ignorance, when data is scarce.

The second system is based upon time series analysis. When sufficient historical data is available, a fair reading of the future can be gained by

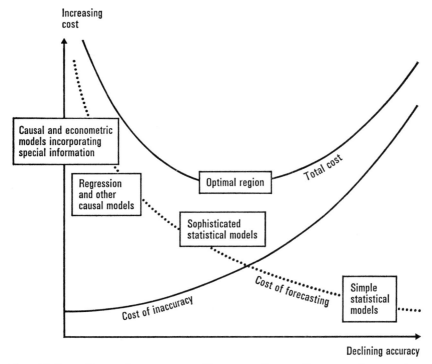

Figure 22 Cost of forecasting versus cost of inaccuracy for a medium-range forecast, given data availability.

(*Source:* T. Chambers, S. Hullick and D. Smith, 'How to choose the right forecasting technique'; *Harvard Business Review*, July–August 1971, p. 47)

a statistical analysis of the past. Using raw data, a series of trends can be built up. Changes in past data can be correlated to new product entries, or price changes, or seasonal market fluctuations. The problem is that industry demand runs in cycles, and it is difficult to separate the trends of growth and decline from cyclical movements. Another problem with the technique is that it is difficult to predict when a trend will alter significantly. It is a common phenomenon amongst forecasters that companies operating in markets with a history of slow growth tend to be conservative in their forecasting; and companies in high growth markets tend to optimism.

The most sophisticated kind of forecasting tool is the causal model. It expresses mathematically the relevant causal relationship. It takes into account everything known about the dynamics of the system, including pipeline stocks; it uses time series analysis; and where information is lacking it makes assumptions about the relationships and then backtracks these to the data to see if they are true. The equations are then solved to provide a forecast.

Forecasting through the life cycle. A series of forecasting systems will be used as a product progresses through the life cycle.[8] At the earliest stage, a manager will want to have a situational analysis of the proposed market. For well defined markets, the estimate of a new product's likely performance can be produced in a number of ways.

First, a comparison of the product with competitors' present products will show the essential differences. Comparison with other competitive factors such as distribution and sales systems and market penetration may provide a broad yardstick of likely performance.

This is followed by separating off different segments of a complex market into areas, types of use, or customer cluster. By making certain assumptions, some estimates of demand may be produced. These assumptions would include the likely penetration rate in each segment, the opening of new accounts, and the replacement rates allowing for fall-out and for pipeline stocks.

The resulting forecast can then be set against the performance of previous company products with similar characteristics.

Frequently the market for a new product is undefined, the company's experience of it is weak, or the proposed market may be fluid and history seems irrelevant. Under these circumstances, studies of expert opinion plus some attempt at input-output analysis may be the only method.

The test marketing phase is designed primarily to check the marketing and production assumptions behind the product launch. It is a poor device for forecasting sales. Even in repeat purchase consumer markets, where the results could be expected to form a most reliable base upon which to forecast national sales, the test marketing procedure is notoriously unreliable as a predictive mechanism.[9] Error ratios of $\pm$ 50 per cent are not uncommon even in these standardised markets. Testing new industrial products may be totally impossible anyway, for technical reasons—but where it is possible the error factor will be even higher.

Once the product is moving, however, the company's knowledge is vastly improved, and the sales forecasting process should then be used to provide three points of information: the date when rapid sales might begin, the rate of market penetration during this period; and the ultimate level of sales in

[8] J. Chambers, S. Mullick, D. Smith: 'How to Choose the Right Forecasting Technique'; *Harvard Business Review,* July–Aug. 1971.
[9] J. A. Gold, 'Testing Test Market Predictions'; *U.S. Jnl. of Market Research,* Aug. 1964. pp. 8–16.

the market when it steadies. This usually involves the use of statistical tracking and control measures.

At the steady stage in the life cycle, forecasting is more inclined to relate to the setting of performance standards. Against these standards are checked the effectiveness of marketing operations, and projections which are designed to aid profit planning. At this time, econometric models may be developed.

Econometric models are forecasting models which take into account relevant economic factors. These factors include the leading economic variables that change before the industry itself reacts.

Over a long period of time, changes in general economic and technical conditions will account for a significant part of the change in a product's growth rate. The econometric model does, however, require sufficient stable data, so that relationships can be established.

With durable products, for the consumer and for the industrial markets, there are three measures to take into account. The first is the level of 'establishment' of the product. That is the total number of users times the numbers of products they own. The second is the rate of growth of these users together with quantity levels. This is called the rate of new user penetration. The third is the replacement rate—that is, the average time it takes for a user to replace the product. A computation of these factors can provide a surprisingly accurate forecast for the future.[10] But if the distribution and pipeline system is complex, perhaps with wastage, and users, occurring at each point of the chain, then it is probably better to build a series of input-output models.

The Effect of Different Market Situations

Most companies will conform to the general principles of information gathering, assessment and dissemination. But there will be differences in emphasis, depending upon the market circumstances.

Package Goods: Consumer

Here the main emphasis will be on information which relates to the specific market segments in which the company operates. The companies may be considerable users of market research measurements, particularly from continuous audit panels of the syndicated kind. The company will be keenly interested in competitors' activities, particularly advertising and promotions.

Consumer Durables

There will be a stronger emphasis on evaluating long-term trends in the market, and relating these to other external influences. Continuous market information is less accessible to the companies in these markets, so a fair amount of *ad hoc* research work has to be done.

[10] J. Treasure, *Forecasting the Demand for Durables*; J. Walter Thompson, booklet 19.

Plant and Equipment

In these companies the econometricians have most influence. A long-term view is taken and the day-to-day information process usually relates to key customers and their behaviour. Day to day, the company seeks tendering opportunities, and makes estimates of competitors' bids.

Components

The main emphasis will be on obtaining information relating to the trends in the immediate markets served. However, for the long-term, the trends in the end-user industries, from which demand is derived, are also required.

Fragmented Markets

Companies operating in these fields exert the most frenetic activity in relating their information to the behaviour of distribution channels. They will be most closely concerned about a few key competitors who operate in their own direct markets; and much emphasis will be laid upon competitors' price and discount activities.

Oligopolistic and concentrated markets

As the market supply becomes more concentrated, then the emphasis moves towards the factors which will affect the market as a whole. Technical innovations will be watched; as will political movements, particularly those connected with the consumer protection movement.

Distribution

The mass distributor is concerned with many interacting parts of the chain. He will be concerned to measure the different pressures which are acting on every part of the distribution network. Distribution methods which move more towards oligopsony find less need for data concerning the market as a whole. The suppliers will be much more concerned with trends which will affect the behaviour of their individual customers. There will be an emphasis on the exchange of such information between various levels in the supplying and in the buying company.

Example: Marketing Information Systems

Background

Electric Power Storage Ltd. is a company that has absorbed several small firms into an international company. In September 1966 a Market Research Department was set up to provide information on consumer surveys, product and package tests, in order to resolve specific marketing problems.

Problem

Management found that although the department provided the required data, it was not the only source. In fact several departments each submitted overlapping information.

Through these many channels flowed a great deal of information which was not directly relevant to the problem in hand. All the information received had to be sifted to produce the small amount of data that was relevant to the problem.

Approach adopted

The flow of information to the marketing function, and within it, was studied. The objectives of this exercise were to determine:

(1) The various operations concerning data assimilation that were being carried out in the Marketing Division. The operations included market and marketing research, statistical and economic analyses.
(2) The extent to which the result of these operations met the needs of management.

Solution

The outcome of the study was the decision that management required a coordinated and integrated information system. Consequently a centralised Marketing Information Department was set up.

A Marketing Information Manager was appointed to coordinate a small but professional complex of 3 sections:

An Information Officer who defines management information profiles, controls the information centre and is responsible for the development of information, indexing, and retrieval systems. He liaises with management. An Industrial Research Officer carries out marketings research needed by the Industrial Marketing Division. A Consumer Research Officer carries out the same function for the Automotive Marketing Division.

Each office provides external data directly to the approprate divisions and to the information centre. A marketing statistics officer deals with the internal input factors of statistics, economic data and forecasting.

Result

On introducing this system, management set certain objectives and the benefits expected to result. These are:

Objectives	Benefits
(1) To be more productive than a fragmented information system.	Increased return on money invested in key staff.
(2) To ensure that information is put to work.	Assist marketing to take decisions based on facts, not opinion.
(3) Provide detailed and continuously updated information, market by market.	Make more reliable one, three, five and 10-year forecasts—better analysis of opportunities.
(4) Provide a single source of company marketing knowledge (Information Centre).	Known location for immediate access to information, plus the avoidance of duplication.
(5) Provide information to seek potential customers and study their needs.	More ability to recognise and exploit opportunities.
(6) Provide an information feed-back to monitor marketing policies.	Finer control by marketing management. Better use of time.

Furthermore, all marketing information known to the company is expected to be presented in summary within one hour from the time of the request. It should be from one source only, containing only data relevant to the topic. This data is expected to be integrated with any data collected or bought outside the company.

The information system provides management with the data required for decision making to help realise the company's objectives. It also analyses the company performance by comparing the results produced with the objectives set. This allows management either to alter its plans to meet the objectives; or, with updated information, may result in management setting new objectives compatible with the changed position.

P.M.

8. Marketing Models

One of the things given to us by the military of World War II was operations research. Many non-numerative marketing executives wish they would take it back.

Teams of researchers, primarily mathematicians, sought solutions to the wartime problems of supply, communications, bombing, defensive and offensive strategy. Afterwards, they adapted their techniques neatly to the business problems of production and inventory control. This area had a close parallel to the wartime problems; there are tidy quantitative properties surrounding problems of, say, physical distribution. And managements accepted the techniques as a logical development of work study.

Even today, the major contribution within the marketing function made by operations research is still in the area of site location, transport, and inventory control.[1]

Marketing was left by the operations researchers until the 1960's. It was thought to involve too much judgement; marketing was seen as a kind of 'art' form. And, to be fair, the marketing measurement systems in use at the time left much to be desired. This was the age of trying a bit of research here and there, to see if it helped.

Then, in the late 50's, a series of studies began to be published relating to specific parts of the marketing function which seemed suitable for statistical analysis. These works included studies on advertising budgets, sales force size, and pricing strategy. This last is still regarded as being the preserve of the mathematician, the economist and the accountant, despite the fact that it properly belongs to behavioural theory. Now, as computers become more fashionable and companies are served increasingly by specialists in data analysis, model building is beginning to operate at all levels of the marketing function. It ranges from macro studies of entire market systems to micro studies involving salesman's journey planning. The effect of model building in marketing is patchy. One of the most inhibiting factors is the resistance of some operating managers who still believe that marketing is a

[1] R. Jackson, 'Operational Research—Your Competitors Secret Weapon?'; *Business Administration*, Sept. 1969, pp. 53–55.

function that calls primarily for creative flair, rather than scientific analysis. In truth it calls for both: either way model builders have a contribution to make. (*Figure 23.*)

The building of a model appears deceptively easy, and it often appears capable of making only a small contribution. Experienced marketing executives carry very good implicit models of marketing processes in their heads. Sometimes, these are written down, as in a marketing plan. This is in itself an explicit model showing the allocation and direction of marketing inputs.

A salesman calling upon a buyer for the first time carries a model in his head of various offers he will make, in response to the buyer's moves. This leads to his ultimate perception of the appropriate 'deal'. He starts with a descriptive model of the buyer's needs matched with his offers, and leads on to a decision model when he attempts to close the sale.

A 'descriptive' model shows things the way they are, and is concerned only with describing the operation of the system (*Figure 24.1*). A 'decision' model shows how things should be, and is intended to help to evaluate the merits of different actions. (*Figure 24.2*).

Steps in model building. The model builder, whether he is about to make calculations on the back of an envelope, or about to process a mass of data through a computer, starts by defining his problem and his objectives with as much clarity as he can muster.

He identifies, if he can, the core of the problem; those factors upon which the problem really turns. He selects what he believes to be the 'independent variables'. The other factors, the 'dependent variables', are affected by these.

He then attempts to show the relationships between them. He constructs what is called a 'means/ends' chain. Selecting one of the important dependant variables to be explained, he works through a list of all the important variables which affect it. For example, the familiar demand curve shows the elasticity of demand according to various pricing levels. This is a simple descriptive model which rests upon the assumption that demand (the dependant variable) changes only according to price (the independent variable). This is too crude a simplification for marketing men who apply themselves all the time to the problem of forcing demand by means other than price. Therefore they require a more elaborate model to be built. They need one which would show, for instance, the various effects of distribution upon demand, of product features, and of advertising pressure, for example.

So the model builder might show them a more complex pattern of relationships, and in such a form as could answer the question, 'What would happen if...'

Suppose a sales test is set up, offering products at different prices and with varying levels of marketing effort behind each. The resulting equations would be expressed as a model—perhaps by a series of charts, or mathematical formulae. All of this is a descriptive model process.

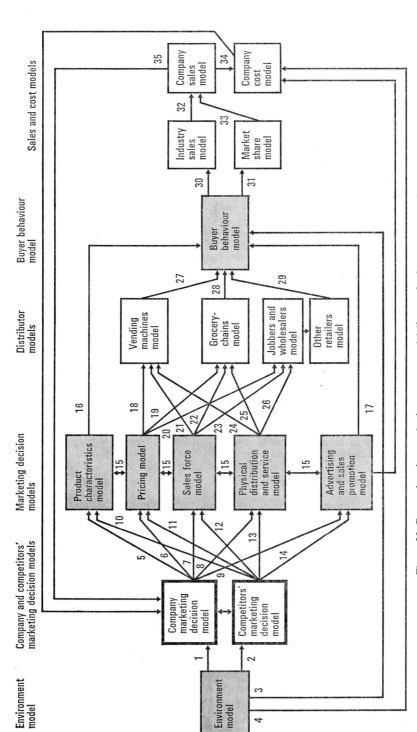

Figure 23 Comprehensive marketing system model (for confectionery company).

(*Source*: P. Kotler, 'Corporate models: better marketing plans'; *Harvard Business Review*, July–August 1970, p. 135–149)

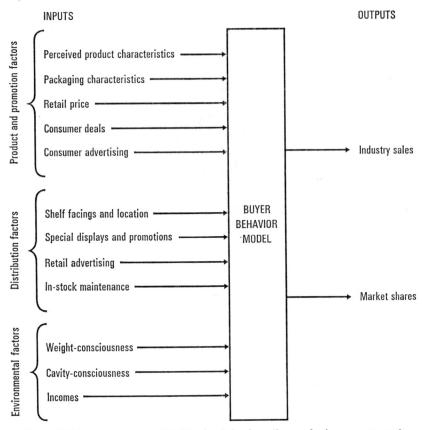

Figure 24.1 Input-output model of buying behaviour (for confectionery company).
(*Source:* P. Kotler, 'Corporate models: better marketing plans'; *Harvard Business Review*, July–August 1970, p. 135–149)

For decision making purposes, a decision model might be needed however. It may surprise marketing men to know that they have been using some for years. They are familiar with break-even charts and payoff cash flow diagrams which are two of the simplest decision models ever made. Occasionally these are too simple, as marketing men may know from faintly bitter experience.

Many different modelling systems exist, most of which have little relevance to marketing problems. Kotler identifies five of the most practical types for marketing.[2]

Allocation models. An allocation model helps the decision maker allocate scarce resources so as to maximise some given objective. These models use forms of programming, by setting the objectives in a mathematical form,

[2] P. Kotler, *Marketing Management; Analysis, Planning and Control;* Prentice-Hall, New Jersey, 1967. pp. 220–245.

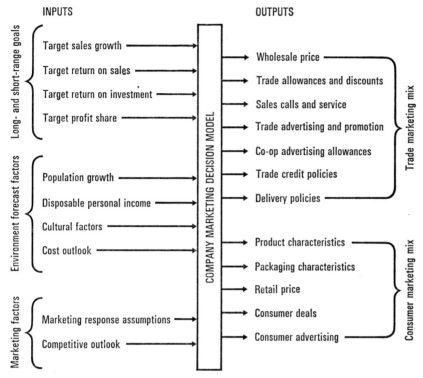

INPUTS   OUTPUTS

Long- and short-range goals
{
Target sales growth
Target return on sales
Target return on investment
Target profit share
}

Environment forecast factors
{
Population growth
Disposable personal income
Cultural factors
Cost outlook
}

Marketing factors
{
Marketing response assumptions
Competitive outlook
}

COMPANY MARKETING DECISION MODEL

Wholesale price
Trade allowances and discounts
Sales calls and service
Trade advertising and promotion
Co-op advertising allowances
Trade credit policies
Delivery policies
} Trade marketing mix

Product characteristics
Packaging characteristics
Retail price
Consumer deals
Consumer advertising
} Consumer marketing mix

Figure 24.2 Input-output model of company marketing decisions (for confectionery company).

building in constraints to reduce the number of variables, and using a standard procedure for searching among the alternatives for the best one. Linear programming is part of such modelling systems.

Game models. Game theory is the systematic investigation of decision making where uncertainty concerning competitors' likely moves exists. For example, before a leading petrol company makes a price reduction for their own brand without a general market move, their management will consider all the possible effects. What will happen to their market share? Will competitors respond? How will distributors react? Will there be political implications? Is it likely to start a price war? Can disgruntled competitors damage their supplies? Are they likely to? These are questions which lend themselves to game modelling.

Game theory should be distinguished from operational gaming used mostly for management training. In this, teams of players compete around a realistic situation and make decisions which are then reported by computer and which become the data inputs for the next round.

Brand Switching models. A brand's share of the market is made up of those buyers who normally repeat purchase the brand (from one period to the next), added to those buyers who have switched their purchase from another brand, minus the previous buyers who have changed over to another brand. The role of the marketing man is to increase the 'switch-in' rate and to decrease the 'switch-out' rate. For mass markets, in repeat purchase fields, capable of being measured continuously through consumer panels, this is likely to be the most significant modelling technique of the 70's.

Early brand-switching models suffered from the problem that they could only describe changes in the form of 'switches' from brand to brand. They could not translate these in terms of quantity, or size of pack, or money value. But a breakthrough in measurement technique called 'preference analysis' developed by Audits of Great Britain Ltd. has resolved most of this problem.[3]

The technique is most useful for describing the effect of sales promotion, price changes, or short advertising bursts. It also shows which brands offer the strongest competition in terms of resistance to attacks, and it shows those that are vulnerable to the marketing moves of the company brand.

Waiting-line models. Waiting-line problems occur in many aspects of marketing. Customers place sales enquiries and wait for proposals; companies wait for bids to be accepted; customers wait for deliveries; and for after-sales service; companies wait to be paid—and so on. The decision problem concerns the cost of providing faster service against the cost of lost sales. In accounting, the cost of chasing overdue accounts at certain levels of debt may be above the financing charge for the extra credit.

The cost of the additional facilities is not difficult to measure. However, the amount of lost sales, traceable to the level of facility provided, is usually very difficult to ascertain. Queueing theory is part of the waiting-line model technique and can handle two questions. First, what amount of waiting time may be expected in a particular system? Secondly, how will this change as a result of additional facilities being provided?

The technique has most application in production planning, particularly in the field of material utilisation and call-off. It is familiar in marketing when dealing with inventory, storage, depot location, transport and other aspects of service.

Simulation models. Many marketing situations are too complicated and changeable to be represented adequately by a mathematical formula. Simulation is becoming slowly more popular as a method of dealing with complex processes.

Within this system are; enterprise models which show how the existing

[3] Audits of Great Britain Ltd., 'The Mapping of Markets'; *Audit Magazine*, Jan. 1971. pp. 2–4.

process within an enterprise affects the flow of men, materials, machines and money. An experimental model is devised to investigate arrangements that appear to improve the flows.

Marketing mix models can be incorporated into business games and used as a research tool. Such simulation studies may help to show what are the productivity levels of various marketing inputs; and what is their elasticity. Is there a threshold of market response and at what level of total inputs is it arrived at? It might be expected to show the time lag in market response, any economies of scale in production or distribution; and the decay rate of marketing inputs.[4]

Market-models: a hypothetical sample of customers is selected and the effect of alternative marketing mixes upon this sample can be tried. Competitor's response models: these are designed to explore the likely reaction of competitors to each other's moves. Distribution channel models: these show the differences which occur in price and purchasing behaviour across various trading channels.

There is little doubt that models will be more frequently used in future. The biggest drawbacks to their use is that the models usually take a long time to prepare, a characteristic of much operations research work. They are usually expensive and they carry the danger of over-simplifying market situations because they often lack valid and reliable data. The fact that they are produced by highly technical numerative specialists is an inhibiting factor in their acceptance. Senior management, who usually must vote the funds, are particularly reticent about their use, but models do have their uses. They make for a clearer understanding of all the interacting variable factors in a given situation. And they can usually state the priorities. They frequently provide a flash of insight in which a new solution, a creative answer, can be found to an old problem. But, like many decision aids, they often tell you to go just where you were planning to go in any case.

At corporate planning level, models can be of real assistance. A model has been developed and published[5] which shows managements what they have wanted to know for many years—how to deal with inflation. It is based on four strategies to counter inflation which are available to management. The first, and most usual, strategy is to raise prices. The second is to re-arrange both suppliers and markets, locally and abroad. The third is to adapt the production processes to minimise the inflation of its costs. Lastly, management can modify the product mix. Since these are also the same strategies which are required for increasing net profit, whether facing inflation or not, then this model could be of real assistance.

[4] R. P. Willett, 'A Model for Marketing Programming'; *U.S. Jnl. of Marketing*, Vol. 27, Jan. 1963, pp. 40–45.
[5] B. A. Lietaer, 'Prepare Your Company for Inflation'; *Harvard Business Review*, Sept.–Oct. 1970, pp. 113–125.

The Effect of Different Market Situations

If companies go in for formal model building and decision systems at all (and very few actually do), they will naturally select those systems which have greatest relevance for their own market situation.

Package Goods: Consumer

These companies could use models almost anywhere—in distribution, for market development or analysis, or to resolve operational problems in sales or advertising. A mathematical model for product planning may be used in multi-product companies. These companies might also use brand-switching models.

Consumer Durables

Companies of this kind often make descriptive models of their markets, and use allocation models to resolve problems of the right levels of marketing energy to use in the mix. Models to solve problems of sales force size; or waiting-line models to resolve after sales service problems are likely.

Plant and Equipment

Gaming models to assist tendering price decisions; and waiting-line models to assist work-flow and service might be used by these companies. Many of the problems in these businesses concern the efficiency of work-flow. Most attention will be paid, therefore, to the work-in-progress.

Components

No one particular model is used by this industry, as each company having its separate varied problems will derive its own.

Materials Supply

A model of the total material availability, or of world prices, or total demand might be used by the bigger companies in materials supply. These companies will also be affected by problems of transportation and storage; waiting-line models being frequently used in such organisations. This is particularly true of companies supplying perishable materials, where much of the emphasis will be on route planning.

Oligopolistic, Concentrated and Mass Distribution Markets

The oligopolist might be concerned to predict competitors' reaction to his various moves and may set up a game, or a simulation model to help. The oligopsonistic supplier may set up a model for his market as a whole, showing the pressures bearing on it. The mass distributor will be concerned primarily with the efficient flow of goods from manufacture to user, and will concentrate his model building in the physical distribution area.

Example: Brand-Switching: Model Building

General introduction

With the preference analysis technique, each household can be thought of as having some idea of relative preference for each brand it purchases in the product field. This is estimated by the pattern of household purchases. For example, there may be a strong overall preference for one brand, but occasionally the household makes a purchase of another brand—and even more occasionally of a third brand.

In this case the household is generally loyal to the first brand but has an important subpreference for the second brand, and a less impoitant subpreference for the third brand.

Using consumer panel data, a matrix is produced similar to that for a brand-switching model. Each household is measured for what it spends on the various brands, and this is multiplied by the preference factor. When all the figures are grossed up, the tables provide an accurate index of the way the market behaves. The model shows the relative magnitude of consumers' preferences for a brand or pack size compared against other brands and over time. The measurements respond to any significant boost in the product field such as a new product entry or a sales promotion scheme, or a price change.

It is the changes in the subpreferences which provide the clue to the model. Most households have a dominant brand preference but, for many reasons, they will also have important subpreferences within a product field.

The analysis is useful for some types of segmentation work. For example, in many toiletry fields there exists an important *second buyer* market segment. In this case the household contains two buyers, each with differing brand preferences and subpreferences. In other fields, it is clear that there is only one main buyer in the household, but there may be different types of products within the same product field bought by the one person. In this case, such as occurs in the biscuit market, a *second choice* segment is revealed.

Background

A company which had a major brand *D*, in the packaged toiletry goods market launched a new product, brand *A*. The other brands in the market included a premium brand *B*, a brand with a declining share *C*, a heavily promoted brand *E*, together with economy brand *F*, plus the rest of the market *AO*.

What the company wanted to avoid was the situation where the new brand *A* took the part of the market currently held by brand *D*, its sister brand. Brand *A* was subsequently launched on to the market.

Problem

The problem was one of determining whether or not the situation described above had been avoided. The company also wanted to know the brand-switching relationship between the various products.

Solution

This solution included the use of Audits of Great Britain's preference analysis in brand switching.

This technique takes normal brand-switching analysis a stage further. It shows changes in customer preference and choice between rival brands which can be traced to the effect of price, promotions, new product entries and so on.

It showed that the company was successful in its aim, and that the new brand had won most of its sales from brands *C*, *E*, and *AO*. The new brand *A*, had little effect on the premium brand *B*, or on the economy brand *F*.

The new brand *A* and established brand *D* took shares from the market held by *C*, whose market was, in any case, on the decline. There was little evidence of appreciable switching between brands *A* and *B*.

Brand *A*, which was sold at a lower price than the average for the market, was shown to be sensitive to the activity of the heavily promoted brand *E*, to which it lost some sales. Further analysis shows that its brand share is affected by a large number of volatile buyers who have a tendency to switch according to promotion activity.

J.W.

9. Market Segmentation and Development

Products start to die the minute they are born. During their life they will be chopped and changed; pushed and pulled; and probably end up where no one intended them to go in the first place. The market just took them there.

Some successful products last only a year before they expire. In that time they may have done all that management required of them; they made money. Fashion clothes selling to women fall into this category. Other products seem to have been with us for many years, and making steady progress all that time, often without much basic change in their formulation. Raw materials come into this category. The market for rice, the staple diet of the majority of the world's population, is growing as never before, even though the product is thousands of years old.

Despite these divergent time-scales, an examination of the product life cycle and of its effect upon planning strategies is, nevertheless, necessary. This is because the idea of the product life cycle is a necessary preliminary to the understanding of market segmentation. No one in his right mind would segment a market if he does not have to. It is the effect of the life cycle pressure on him and on his competitors which makes him do so.

In the early 60's two theoretical papers were published on the concept of the life cycle. Since then researchers have tried to validate the original ideas—without, incidentally, a great deal of success in terms of measurement. Most product fields selected for measurement in order to 'prove' the life cycle idea of rise, decline and fall, have had an uncanny knack of continuing to grow.

Since the first two papers, one by A. Patton, a McKinsey & Co. principal in New York, and the other by G. Mickwitz, a Finnish economist, the original model has been refined by the addition of a 'recycle' phase identified by the A. C. Nielsen company. Also, a series of exploitation techniques have evolved. These have included 'market stretching' proposed by T. Levitt of the Harvard Business School. He also suggested certain market segmentation techniques which have now been adopted by market researchers and model builders in all advanced economies.

Patton identified[1] four phases in the life cycle which have now become familiar. These are the introductory phase, where the skill lies in the development of the product and of the market at the same time. The critical skill lies in the timing of the two together. Company records are full of the results of good product ideas which were developed and introduced, only to fail because they were 'before their time'. They will be marketed successfully one day—probably by different companies. In the U.K. instant tea is a good example. It will happen one day but two attempts by excellent companies, Nestlés and Brooke Bond, failed. Perhaps the researchers could work on this problem of timing, and save us all a great deal of money and worry.

Patton's next phase was called the growth phase. The problem here lies in getting sufficient volume moving into the market to encourage mass production and to hold off competition. Patton showed how many innovators failed to secure the market for themselves by not moving it fast enough, and allowing competition to copy. This is the period of high and rising profits for manufacturers and distributors.

The next stage he called the 'maturity' phase. This is where market forcing techniques begin to take over, as the market becomes saturated. There is now less to choose between competitive products; few new users to be obtained, and the emphasis begins to lie with product development, creative selling techniques, and pricing manœuvres.

Finally, there is the unhappy decline phase. As market demand drops, usually through switching to new and attractive alternative products, the pressures on costs are very heavy. Labour-intensive companies switch out of production and over to other markets; capital-intensive companies begin to go for high volume at any price which will leave them a profit contribution after direct costs. Price wars break out, product quality drops, outdated plant is not replaced, and marginal producers leave the market. A series of mergers may help to concentrate the industry once again and to re-introduce a degree of stability. This has happened in the market for men's hats in Britain; the market having stabilised after its declining and lean period over the past ten years.

Mickwitz[2] went further in his analysis and indicated the types of marketing strategy which feature strongly at these various stages.

At the earliest stages of introduction and growth, he suggests that the levels of quality offered in the various products have the greatest impact on sales. Early products are often poor in their performance, but better quality products take over even if their price is higher. The next most important influence at this stage is advertising for consumer products or personal selling for industrial products, in order to secure purchases by the early

[1] A. Patton, 'Top Managements Stake in the Product Life Cycle'; *The Management Review*, Vol. 48, June 1959, pp. 9–14, 67–71, 76–79.
[2] G. Mickwitz, *Marketing and Competition*; Centraltry-cheriet, Helsingfors, Finland, p. 88.

adopters of the product. As the sampling process turns into repeat sales, buyer resistance becomes greater and the emphasis on advertising and personal selling becomes stronger still.

At the stage of maturity, competition becomes much stronger. Some make an effort to draw in the price sensitive parts of the market by lowering their prices. This is often the first sign of market segmentation. In some markets, the product life cycles are so short and competition responds so quickly, that product innovations are copied immediately at a price level which is usually pitched just below that of the original product.

At the next stage, market saturation, Mickwitz indicated that suppliers should now try to increase the product differentiation between themselves and competition. There is stronger emphasis on service; whilst advertising and selling remain amongst the most potent instruments of marketing.

In the declining phase, Mickwitz points out that price reductions will have little impact on the total market. But this is where price competition breaks out, and where sales promotion schemes proliferate. In this way, companies try to 'add value' to their offerings, disconnected with the quality of the product itself.

Levitt proposed strategies along four avenues.[3] The first is by promoting more frequent usage of the product by existing users. The second is by developing more varied usage of the product among current users. The third is by creating new users of the product by expanding the market. And the fourth is by finding new applications and uses for the basic product which appeal to completely new markets.

In 1967 a study was published covering 454 grocery products showing their life cycle movements over the period 1961–1966.[4] This covered British and American markets. The term 'recycle phase' was used to denote the phenomenon that companies often improve their share of the market significantly at a late stage in the life cycle. This is a result of planned changes in their marketing activity. The same study also noted that the primary cycles lasted for only two years or less, in more than half the cases; and that the recycle phase lasted for less than a year.

The total length of life cycles was found to be shortening rapidly; that competition was responding more quickly; that new product entries were escalating in number. All of this happened in only the five years of the study period. And this, furthermore, was before advanced market segmentation techniques were developed. Consequently the position could be expected to be worse today.

Figure 25 illustrates the life cycle concept and indicates where the main marketing emphasis exists at any time. It also indicates that the management style for innovative marketing at the introduction of the product should be

[3] T. Levitt, 'Exploit the Product Life Cycle'; *Marketing*, May–June, 1966.
[4] *Identifying Phases in an Average Product Life Cycle*; Nielsen Researcher, May–June 1967, pp. 3–7.

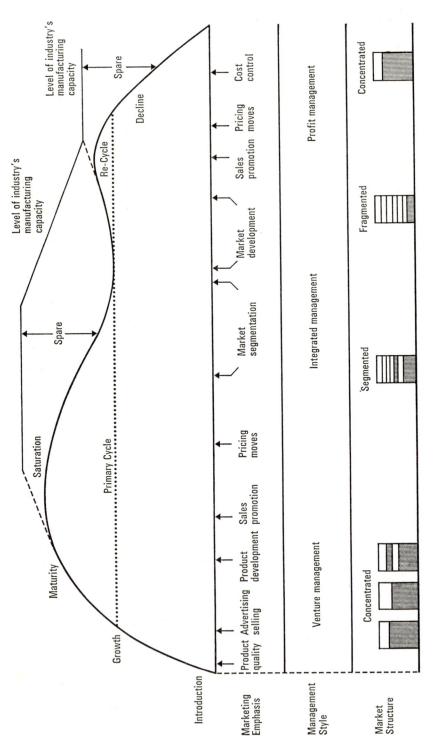

Figure 25 The life cycle.

fairly venturesome, capable of taking risks, and skilled at exploitation. This is when the market is in its concentrated phase with only a few producers.

However, as the market fills up with competition the various techniques of integrated marketing management take over as the full range of the marketing mix is deployed. This is where the planning process will benefit a company which is capable of predicting this situation in advance.

In the later stage, as the market is thoroughly fragmented with all manner of product varieties, buyers are most cost-conscious, and the industry has spare capacity. Then the management process is more defensive in nature. It attempts to avoid the worst excesses of competition; low price, discount wars, and so on. In this period the onus is on profit management, and cutting back on resources.

Notice the two periods, at the top of the primary cycle and of the recycle, when the industry, through using normal extrapolation techniques for sales forecasting, will have too much spare production capacity. When this happens, someone will always cut prices and go for sales volume, even where markets are demonstrably not price-sensitive.

Market segmentation

Companies have been segmenting their markets for years, even before the word was coined. Industrial marketing companies, in particular, take note of various classes of customers and modify their products to suit each class.

In industrial markets, customers' groupings can be identified in a number of ways:

(1) By the *type of industry* in which they are concentrated.
   The makers of slide rules, for example, sell to a wide range of industries, and no doubt some models could be developed which would suit specific industries.
(2) By *type of use* for the product.
   The same industrial product can be used often in a number of ways. Special versions of slide rules are already marketed for particular types of use.
(3) By *job function* of the user.
   A slide rule for accountants might be different from one for engineers.
(4) By *usage rate*.
   Some companies making slide rules will want to sell them only in bulk to the big buyers ('heavy users'). Others will add a service element, price up the product, and go for small customers.
(5) By *geographical variables*.
   Some slide rule manufacturers just concentrate their sales in a part of the United Kingdom, say, in the south-east.
(6) By *company loyalty*.
   Some companies will make and sell slide rules simply because they already do good business in a related product area, and believe that buyers will be 'loyal' to their range of products.
(7) By *buyer's motives*.
   Some companies may select a market segment because of a particular

need or character of the buyer. These could include status-seeking (say, in office furniture) or economy (say, low priced products). It may be that when a young process engineer has just qualified and has been promoted, it is the done thing for him to be seen with a small slide rule protruding from his top pocket.

In consumer markets.   In consumer markets the same circumstances apply, but the segments may be more difficult to isolate and measure. Market segmentation is one of the few areas where industrial marketing companies have an easier time than consumer goods companies.

Consumer markets are not generally divisible into a series of discrete and homogeneous segments of behaviour. Instead, companies are faced in a mass market with, at most, some recognised areas of 'local density' super-imposed. Even then the members of such a segment are not totally different from the mass. In general, they will do all the things which are done by the mass, but they may do some of them more—such as brand-switch—or buy more frequently. The difference is only one of degree.[5]

For most brands the bulk of the sales will be to the mass market. But smaller brands do operate in smaller segments, which may or may not be isolatable. There are two reasons why it may be necessary to isolate them. The first is to provide areas for new product development, producing products with features which have distinct appeal for a particular segment. The second, however, is for more subtle reasons. It may be for the purpose of developing advertising appeals to reach specific attitude sectors of the markets. The more sophisticated models of segmentation analysis, based on attitude studies, are for this second purpose. They help direct the creative sales appeals of brands which already exist on the market.

Consumer markets for years have been segmented by socio-economic variables such as class, age, sex, income, and so on. These standard classifications have been promoted primarily by media researchers to measure the circulations and readership of publications in such a way as to describe the 'quality' of their audience. Based as they originally were on governmental standards, these standard classifications have spilled over into market research work generally. Particularly is this true in the formulation of sampling frames.

This is why the earliest attempts at market segmentation were in the direction of producing separate versions of products which would appeal to certain age groups, or classes. They were produced for one simple reason—that the facts were known and established. These market sectors could be identified, and they could be reached.

Unfortunately, companies often found that the existence of these distinctions between people did not necessarily reflect their buying behaviour towards individual products. Most product fields cross these boundaries

[5] M. Collins, 'Market Segmentation—The Realities of Buyer Behaviour'; *Jnl. of the Market Research Society*, Vol. 13, No. 3, July 1971, pp. 146–157.

rather sharply, although it is true they may have a higher penetration in one sector than in another.

So consumer marketing men moved towards other types of segmentation analysis. Personality variables, for example, have been used as the basis for segmenting many sugar confectionary markets. Advertising men, in particular, believe that personality differences between people lie at the root of many brand choices particularly in food, cigarettes and personal products. Such. variables are often used where there is a high emotive content in advertising.

Consumer products have been directed at heavy user market segments. This technique can work well, provided that this sector can be classified as a distinct group and, what is more, is capable of being 'reached' by the communications process.

Brand loyalty has formed the basis for many segmentation strategies; products have been sold to appeal to a small cluster of loyal buyers. Consumer panel data, and brand-switching analysis are needed to locate these groups. And again, they have to be capable of being reached.

Many products with a planned short life make a deliberately transient appeal to the 'experimenters'. Typically, these are younger people who take up fads and novelties, and drop them quickly.

The family life cycle. Two sociologists, Lansing and Kish, first reported the pattern of the family life cycle and its effect on purchasing behaviour in a paper published in 1957.[6] Since then some further studies have been made, notably by the Market Research Society. There are seven stages identified in the family life cycle.

(1) This theory assumes that at the early adult age, spending is directed towards certain channels while the boys and girls are unmarried, and at work. They spend heavily on social and leisure activities, and on personal products.

(2) The pattern of spending alters considerably when a couple marries, but have no children. They begin to buy things for their future home; they start saving, they buy insurance, and so on. This may be the first time that the new housewife has to shop for food, or choose between gas and electricity for cooking. The couple will rent a flat, or buy a house.

(3) When the family has a child at home under the age of five, this affects their living pattern remarkably. So long as the child is at home and not at school, the mother is pinned to the house; the family are constrained on holidays and leisure activities; spending rises on toys and educational activities; expenditure on children's clothes rises, and perhaps drops where clothes for parents are concerned. There is less income to dispose; second-hand purchases are strong. This is the age of make-and-mend, and do-it-yourself.

(4) When all the children are at school, the family life style is freed a little. Mother may take a part-time job, releasing some of the pressure on the household income. She is more free to shop at greater distances. Leisure pursuits are developed. The husband has often been promoted in his job

[6] J. B. Lansing, L. Kish, 'Family Life Cycle as an Independent Variable'; *American Sociological Review*, Vol. 22, Oct. 1957, pp. 512–518.

by this time, and this produces more spending money. Notice that the effects of these changing life styles are virtually independent of class factors, except at the top and bottom reaches of the scale. They will affect families which are used to a high income as well as families which are used to low incomes. The changes in their patterns of expenditure, which are relevant to their particular stage in the life cycle, remain constant.

(5) When the children leave school and go to work, but still live at home, the mother's focus of interest is still on the family group. But there is extra income moving into the household, and spending patterns become more personalised. The youngsters ultimately split from home and form their own life cycle patterns.

(6) When the children have left, a different pattern of spending breaks out again. The equipment in the house which has lasted through the family's growth may now be replaced. The parents may move into a smaller house or flat. They have plenty of disposable income, and little to save it for. Holidays will move into the exotic area (relative to their experience). Leisure pursuits will be passive rather than participative.

(7) Finally, when one partner dies, the life style of the other naturally changes dramatically. At this stage, the income may be very low indeed. A high proportion of the *E* classes, the poor, are one-person households living in retirement on pensions.

One of the most significant predictors of consumer behaviour is the household situation of the family. Particularly is this true for consumer durables, household products, baby and children's products, toys, personal products of all kinds, educational products and leisure activities. This is also one of the least researched areas of consumer market segmentation analysis.

The process of segmentation

Segmenting the market is the process of grouping individuals whose expected reactions to the producers' marketing efforts will be similar in a specified period of time.[7]

There are three basic conditions for segmentation strategy to be effective.[8]

Measurement. This is the degree to which information exists or can be found on various buyers' characteristics. Many otherwise sophisticated segmentation concepts fail because the groups cannot be accurately identified and counted.

Access. This is the degree to which the company is able to focus and direct its marketing activity on the segment. Not only advertising is involved here, but the other communications vehicles which may be used—personal selling, packaging, and word of mouth communication. For example, the segmentation strategy may call for an approach to 'opinion leaders'. In industrial marketing these can often be identified by job function and ap-

[7] S. C. Brandt, 'Dissecting the Segmentation Syndrome'; *U.S. Jnl. of Marketing*, Vol. 30, Oct. 1966, pp. 22–27.
[8] P. Kotler *Marketing Management, Analysis, Planning and Control*; Prentice Hall, New Jersey, 1967, p. 35.

proached selectively. But in consumer markets, the reading habits of these people may not be distinct from the opinion followers, and cannot be reached in isolation.

Substance. This is the degree to which the segments are large enough to be worth considering by the supplier. Many small companies can exist profitably on a sector of the market which would not be worthwhile for the large company to tailor a special marketing programme.

The latest developments in segmentation analysis use model building. It has been noted that any one set of variables cannot be the cause of all consumer behaviour in a market. It is unlikely that one set will strongly correlate with behaviour since the effect of many personal circumstances and pressures will be acting upon the purchaser.[9] Consequently a method of showing the interrelated variables has been developed using various kinds of models.

The model building process for market segmentation uses three stages.[10]

The first step is to construct what is called a 'product space'. This is a geometric representation of consumer perceptions of products and brands within a particular product field. This involves using attitudinal and prefer-ence research. The next stage is to show the density of these preference distributions by positioning consumers' ideal choices in the same space. Finally, a model is constructed, often in three dimensions, which shows the relationships of these preferences. With it, attempts are made to predict the reaction of consumers towards new or modified products.

Market development

There are three broad methods employed for allocating marketing funds to different area markets. The first recognises markets of different total size and allocates the resources basically in accordance to the sizes. The benefit of this method is that it provides more funds for larger markets, and corre-spondingly smaller funds for small markets, so that the overall level of marketing effort is consistent. However, it takes no account of market poten-tial for growth, nor of existing company shares of the market, nor of company share potential.

The second method is to allocate funds according to the shares of the area markets which are held by company brands. This does have the internal benefit of reflecting company strengths and weaknesses, but it suffers from not being sensitive to competitive spending power, and company potential in each market. Furthermore, it may violate the 'marginal' principle whereby money may be spent without an increase in effectiveness being gained.

Figure 26 shows four different types of market situation. To allocate

[9] A. B. Cowling and E. Nelson, 'Predicting the Effects of Change'; Marketing Research Society Conference, 1969.
[10] R. M. Johnson, 'Market Segmentation: A Strategic Management Tool'; *U.S. Jnl. of Marketing Research,* Vol. VIII, Feb. 1971, pp. 13–18.

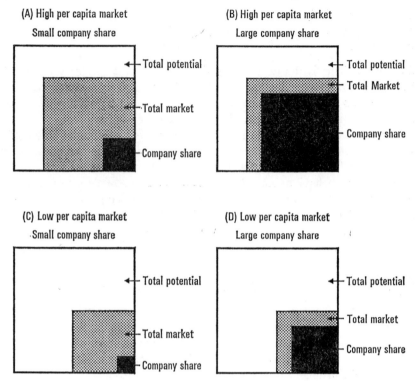

(A) High per capita market

Small company share

Total potential

Total market

Company share

(B) High per capita market

Large company share

Total potential

Total Market

Company share

(C) Low per capita market

Small company share

Total potential

Total market

Company share

(D) Low per capita market

Large company share

Total potential

Total market

Company share

Figure 26 The allocation of marketing effort. All variations of market penetration can be described by the above four basic modules. The problem is how to allocate marketing funds between them.
The decision to allocate marketing funds in each of these cases (whether by market size split or by company share of the market split) should be governed by four considerations which will vary in each case: (1) potential for market growth in each area; (2) potential for company growth in each area; (3) competitive levels of marketing power in each area; and (4) company objective; whether defence or aggression.

marketing funds in each of these basic situations, four considerations will govern the decision:

(1) The potential for market growth up to its saturation point in each area and the relevance and ability of the company's activities to influence that growth. In the market situation *D* the company has a high share of an existing market which has considerable growth potential. In this case the company will be interested in assisting the total market to grow.

(2) The potential for growth in company share of the existing market. This calls for the winning of business from competition. This is required in market situations *A* and *C*; but the manœuvre will be easier in market *C*, because the market can be expected to grow and this will disguise the fact from competition that they are steadily losing their share of the market. Competition could be expected to react strongly in market *A*, which is already approaching its maximum potential.

(3) Competitive levels of spending power. Holding a share of the existing

market requires, in logic, the expenditure of the same share of marketing energy. To win business from competition requires an increase in the share of total spending in comparison to market share. The best guess is that competition has the same skills and abilities as ourselves, and that the business will respond primarily to a difference in levels of energy applied.

(4) Whether the company's object is defence, as it clearly must be in market situation *B*, or aggression. As a rough rule of thumb, backed by some slender evidence of research in consumer markets, it appears that a policy of aggression requires a spending level of twice the normal proportion for a defensive policy. Each share point to be gained in the total market, requires an increase in two share points of the total spending.

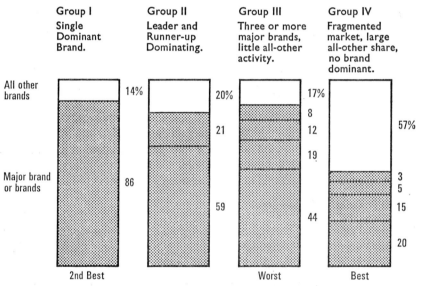

Figure 27 For a new brand . . . Which field offers the best chance of success?

A study has been reported[11] related to the types of markets which offer the best opportunities for new product entry. Researchers examined four different types of competitive market structures in the U.K., based on foods, toiletries and household products in eighty-nine product fields. Four classes and market structure were defined. (*Figure 27.*)

Concentrated markets. It was demonstrated that the rate of success for new products entering fields which are dominated by one large supplier is surprisingly high. Seldom do these new products take over the leader's role, but they fill a useful 'runners-up' position. Seldom can one product satisfy all the various sectors of the market. A new product entry showing a distinctive appeal to a sector of the market has a relatively high chance of success, when compared to the average success rates of new product entries.

[11] 'Which Field Offers the Best Chance of Success?'; *Nielsen Researcher*, Jan.–Feb. 1966, pp. 3–5.

This success rate is now accepted to be about 50 per cent of new consumer products launched.[12]

Duopolistic markets.   This market contains two strong supplying companies and it would appear that the chances of success for a new product entering markets shaped like this would be slender. However, the study demonstrated a fair success rate for new products entering markets of this kind.

Oligopolistic markets.   These markets are so strongly competitive that only limited opportunities exist for new products to enter from outside the existing suppliers. The companies involved are skilled at countering competitive moves and the only time they unite in harmony is when there is a threat of a new supplier entering their market. The market shows a higher rate of new product failure than any other type of structure.

Fragmented markets.   In these markets there may be perhaps three or four brand leaders, but the market is really controlled by many small competitors. The chances for short-term new product success in a market such as this are fairly good, but the innovators' advantage, if it is a good one, does not last for long. A characteristic of these markets is that they are often labour intensive in manufacture. As soon as a new product appears, competitors copy it, often offering a price advantage. Competition polarises quickly, and profits are often difficult to retain at a high level.[13]

Trends in Industrial Markets

A regional study was carried out relating to the purchasing behaviour in industrial companies.[14] Distinct and growing trends were identified which have important implications for industrial marketing policies.

Reciprocity.   Most of the companies were involved in some form of reciprocal trading practice. These varied from relatively innocuous sympathies to formal arrangements for exerting pressure by sales departments on buying departments to favour certain suppliers. Sometimes, however, reciprocal action was aimed at not offending any potential customer, so that buying procedures were deliberately allocated across a wide variety of customers.

Centralisation was noticed to be a factor in making reciprocal arrangements easier to apply. A tendency towards centralisation was noted, since buying power is easier to exert at the centre. This means less buying autonomy for the local unit; and more comparative costing and auditing between suppliers, thereby removing local sentiment and buyer goodwill from the process.

[12] 'What are The Odds?'; *Nielsen Researcher*, Jan.–Feb. 1968, p. 7.
[13] J. Winkler, *Marketing for the Developing Company;* Hutchinson, 1969, pp. 24–27.
[14] B. G. J. James, *The Industrial Market—Practices, Motives, and their Marketing Implications*; University of Strathclyde.

Centralisation also leads to industrial companies using their power to buy direct from suppliers, rather than to use agents.

Middlemen weakening. Monopsonistic tendencies in industrial buying, added to reciprocal trading practices is likely to cause the market for distributors, factors and agents to weaken. Very few buying firms were found to have a formal system for the continuous appraisal of suppliers. Any action to change from a regular supplier was likely to be prompted by one of two events, either an increasing pressure on end margins, leading to the requirement to buy from cheaper sources; or disaffection with the supplier for a variety of reasons, such as service. Only in very few cases could there be detected a change in buying habits due to the discovery of a new and better supplier.

Experimental marketing

Experimental marketing is used to reduce the risks which flow from uncertainty about the likely response to marketing actions.

If there is little uncertainty or if there are only small funds at risk, then it is pointless to conduct an elaborate experiment. Most experimental marketing moves concern new product entries—but not all experiments are of this kind.

The procedure for setting out testing operations is to prepare the full plan first, complete with objectives and strategies. From this point, the key areas of uncertainty are analysed and selected for testing.[15]

The uncertainty may relate to the product itself. Product questions normally fall into two areas. First, how do its features meet buyers' needs by comparison with competitive products? This leads to a product testing programme. Secondly, can the product be made according to specifications under regular production conditions? This will lead to a controlled production experiment where the marketing role is simply to move the goods produced in test runs.

The uncertainty may relate to one key aspect of the marketing operation, and its effect upon distribution or competition. This might be the proposed price level. In this case there is little for it but to undergo a test area operation using different price levels in each area, plus a control area.

The uncertainty may rest on the sales method to be employed. Again, a controlled experiment to check on various sales methods might be used. If the problem is about the distribution channel to be selected, then this poses one of the most difficult questions in test marketing. The committal of a product to one distribution channel, even in a test, nearly always leads to its ultimate use on a national basis. To test a change of distribution channels is one of the hardest marketing tasks, because of the disturbance which results from the trade.

[15] B. G. J. James, 'The Current Application and Validity of Test Marketing'; *Marketing Forum*, March–April 1969, pp. 3–9.

Test operations have moved away from a rigid formula of using matched pairs of towns. They have also been criticised for their limited success in projecting national results. Manufacturers are using phased regional launches instead.

For a long time experimental marketing has suffered from suspicion by industrial marketing organisations who find that the practical problems involved in testing new products are too great. For one example, the costs of tooling up for the production of a small run of industrial products for test marketing are often as great as the investment in full-scale production facilities.

However, now that the practice of experimental marketing is concerning itself with means rather than ends, there is more hope for its acceptance within industry. Marketing executives are applying more mini-tests and pilot runs than before. These are not necessarily designed with a scientific, quantified base. They are designed more to iron out difficulties in the distribution flow procedures. These are to make certain that sales stories are correct, for example; or to ensure adequate product protection during carriage. Travel tests are well used by packaging experts, for example.

More emphasis is now being laid on pre-testing. Paired comparisons often are made between different products shown to groups of buyers. Sophisticated research techniques can be, and are, employed in the statistical analysis of these tests.

A survey of test marketing practice[16] has shown that the most common reason for consumer goods companies running test markets is to measure the effectiveness and acceptance of the total marketing mix. This is done to aid the construction of national marketing plans. The same survey also showed that detailed test objectives are seldom set in advance, and that the selection of a test area is based usually on the result of an intuitive cost-effectiveness analysis.

E. J. Davis, a leading British authority, says that experimental marketing methods of the future are more likely to concentrate on pre-testing methods, on model building, on experiments and controls which can be applied in a single area.[17] The heyday of test marketing when everyone rushed into testing procedures based upon pseudo-scientific forecasting equations is over. Too many companies have been disillusioned when they discovered that market dynamics are much too complex to respond significantly to a change in only one or two variables. The heavy constraints laid upon testing operations, such as distribution problems and human bias in sales operations, make the results questionable.

Experimental marketing is now likely to be more practical and to con-

[16] G. Wills, R. Hayhurst, 'Test Marketing: Can We Improve Practice?'; Market Research Society Conference, 1969.
[17] E. J. Davis, *Experimental Marketing*; Thos. Nelson & Sons Ltd., London 1970, pp. 170–182.

centrate on making specific marketing activities efficient, rather than to provide a crystal ball for the future.

Different Market Situations

Package Goods: Consumer

Companies in these fields are finding that product life cycles are becoming extremely short. Their activity concentrates on market segmentation work, often of a very sophisticated kind, primarily to direct their advertising operations. Their products are often used widely, but they direct their appeal to particular segments, say young adults, in the hope that these will 'lead' the rest. These companies are the most sophisticated users of formal test marketing procedures.

Consumer Durables

This type of company is more concerned with the product life cycle, and with the life cycle of the family. Many of these products are bought at distinct times, or for distinct occasions, such as weddings.[18] These companies are concerned very much with the type of market structure and entrenched competition. Brand loyalty remains for a long time, largely because purchasing cycles are so long.

Plant and Equipment

To most of these companies, the concept of the product life cycle is academic theory—the purchasing cycles are so long, and 'repeats' often form the smaller proportion of their total sales, compared with sales to new buyers. These companies may find all of this chapter, including the section on segmentation and on experimental marketing, too far divorced from their day-to-day operations to be practical to them.

Components

Product life cycles may be impossible to distinguish here, because so few of these markets are measured consistently. 'Market stretching' techniques appeal to these companies, and they often search for new types of users. New products which trade upon the company's general reputation and which appeal to 'loyal' buyers are often introduced; and the segmentation practice of developing products for special uses is the most popular.

Materials

'Market stretching' is the most popular technique. The markets for materials last for so long that the basic life cycle concept is irrelevant. Segmentation techniques concentrate on finding new types of customers and new processes

[18] Audits of Great Britain Ltd., 'The Big Give-Away'; *Audit Magazine,* July 1970, pp. 8–10.

in which to use the materials. Many of the most expensive and sophisticated product research departments in the world belong to these companies. Their expenditure on pure research is higher than that of other commercial organisations.

Competitive Structures

A study of the differing attitudes of companies facing alternative competitive structures has already been reported in the chapter under the heading 'Market development'.

Oligopsony and Monopsony

Companies in these situations, selling to relatively few buyers, find the life cycle concept and segmentation strategy of little help in deciding policy. Their plans may be based, however, on the life cycle and segmentation prospects for their customers' markets. They may actively work with their customer groups in developing new end markets for their products. Experimental marketing is almost impossible, except for those occasions when a product may be developed in close harness with one customer. The customer would then carry out most of the testing work on behalf of the supplier.

Example: Segmentation Analysis

Background

Bird's Eye Foods Ltd., the dominant brand leader in quick-frozen foods, decided that it was essential to know what criteria were operating in the crucial area of the mid-week meal time selection. Consequently they embarked on analysis of products designed for this period; use being made of factor analysis. Each product was rated for different factors, such as nourishment, substantiability, etc., so that an overall picture of customers' attitudes to their products could be gained.

We shall deal here with one section of the study; that dealing with the comparison of quick-frozen fish products to their 'natural' counterparts. Six products, fishmonger's plaice, plaice fillets, cod steaks, fish fingers, fish and chips, and crispy cod fries, were rated according:

(a) To the nourishment that they gave.
(b) To how substantial they seemed.

Problem

Table 1 shows that most of the fish products proved to be popular on the nourishment scale. However, as far as the substantiability factor was concerned, these products rated poorly. Only fish and chips had a reasonable rating for this latter factor; presumably that being due to the presence of chips.

There appeared to be a large area on this two-dimensional map that was unfilled by any of their quick-frozen fish products. Of course, not all empty areas indicate a marketing opportunity. However, Bird's Eye believed that in this case the empty area corresponded to a large segment that required quick-frozen fish products of both a nourishing and a satisfying nature.

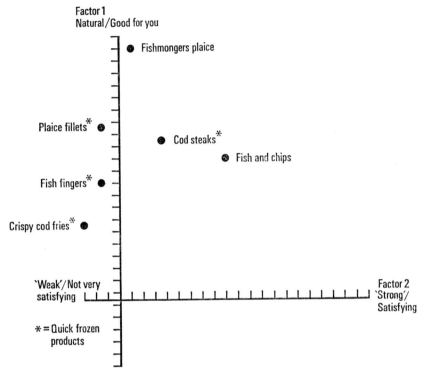

Nourishment × Substantiality.

Solution

The company had developed a system for quick-freezing fish in batter. Consequently a new product was introduced to the market aimed specifically at the segment previously described. This product was known as 'Cod in Batter'. The advertising invited the housewife to make her kitchen the best fish (and chip) shop in the town.

Result

This action turned out to be, in the words of Mr. P. B. Hill, a Bird's Eye executive, 'an extremely successful product with considerable staying power'.

Summary

It can be seen that Bird's Eye segmented the market as follows:

Food Market
    Quick-frozen food market
        Quick-frozen fish food market
            Quick-frozen fish food market for mid-week. Fish being nourishing and substantial.

Having identified this segment of the market, assessing it to be unfilled and having the technical and other resources, Bird's Eye then developed a new and profitable product.

P.M.

The Product Variables

10. Product Planning

A company's product mix sets the upper limit for its potential profitability. The quality of the company's marketing programme determines how far this limit is reached. Therefore there are two factors to adjust constantly in order to optimise profits. One is the product range, and the other is the marketing programme to support the product range. The term 'product planning' embraces both of these factors at the same time. This subject is at the core of company profitability.

The composition of the range of products which a company offers for sale is called the product mix. There are three aspects to this mix, which shall be discussed here. The first is the width of product range, referring to the number of different items offered for sale. The second is the depth of the mix, which relates to the number of products offered within each group of similar products. The third is the consistency of the mix, which refers to the degree to which products within the range are similar to each other in terms of their end use, their distribution channels, or their production requirements.

Products within the range are being modified continuously; more often by managers outside the marketing function. For example, different classes of raw materials are purchased from time to time, yielding different quality levels. Alterations in production systems, or in control, provide different product results. Changes in distribution systems may affect product quality, in terms of freshness, or breakage. Countless pressures are exerted on all products every day and strictly these should result in only marginal changes These changes should be within the levels of tolerance agreed by the marketing function as being acceptable in relation to competitive standards.

Products have intangible characteristics also, which are recognised by the customers as being part of the product's 'personality'. Products are known for their sales appeal, for their colour, for their advertising, for their packaging, for their shape and size, for their after-sales service; and they are known as belonging to the general family of products sold by the organisation. Marketing men change these factors directly, constantly, and usually without knowing the true end result of changes they make.

The truly profit-oriented marketing manager is recognised primarily by his ability to increase the total profitability of the product mix he handles. There are only three points of attack—an attack on costs, an attack on price levels and discounts, and an attack on sales turnover.

New product development, product elimination, and pricing, will be

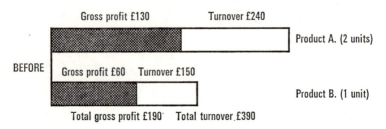

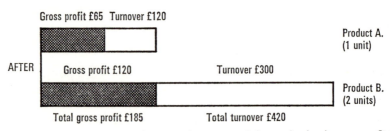

Figure 28 How an increase in your sales may result in a reduction in your profits.

Product A outsells product B by 2 to 1.
Product A sells for £120 and earns a gross profit of £65.
Product B sells for £150 and earns a gross profit of £60.
Product B is easier to sell than product A. A new sales campaign, concentrating on this product increases sales turnover by just over 7½ per cent. At the end of the campaign product B is outselling product A by 2 to 1 having substituted sales of product A.
What happens to gross profit?
As a result of the campaign the turnover has therefore increased but the gross profit margins have been reduced by just over 2½ per cent.
If there are no savings in overheads or marketing costs flowing from the change in product sales mix, then this loss of gross margin must be paid out of *net profit*. There is nowhere else for it to come from.
If the company normally makes a 10 per cent net profit rate, then as a result of these increased sales it could be losing up to one-quarter of its net profits.

dealt with in the following chapters. This text is concerned with product modification and marketing support decisions.

Seven possible alternatives present themselves when modifying products. The use of each technique is dependent upon the circumstances of the product in relation to the buyer, and matched with the product objectives.

Quality improvement. Most managements seek to improve product quality constantly, in the belief that this will strengthen their competitive position. However, the deliberate and sustained effort to build-in extra 'quality' as perceived by the engineer, through the use of, say, higher grade materials, may not achieve the desired effect of increasing 'quality' as perceived by the buyer.

There are four levels of quality improvement in descending order of relevance to the market. The first, and most important, is the quality improvement which is perceived as such by a significant number of buyers, in both the appearance of the product and in its performance.

The second is the improvement which is not visually observable by a significant number of buyers, but is one which they detect in improved product performance once they try it.

The third is the improvement in quality which is aimed at a specialised end use, and only of significance to a proportion of the buyers.

The fourth is the improvement to the product which not only cannot be perceived visually, but cannot be easily detected in the product function; the existence of which the buyers must take for granted. Many proprietary medicines come into this category.

Feature improvement. This aims at increasing the number of real or imagined product benefits. The first cameras were bulky, heavy things. With an improvement in lenses and shutters, a series of alternative speeds was made available, and miniature versions were developed. This led on to built-in range finders: then built-in exposure meters; and flash connections. Such feature improvements are designed to increase the range and scale of the product's use. They can be adapted to appeal to special segments of the market. They are flexible, and here the problem may lie, for it is often fairly easy for a competitor to copy a successful new feature.

Style improvements. This aims at improving the aesthetic appeal of the product, rather than its functional performance. In certain classes of goods, it may be the critical factor governing the buyers' choice, and excellent styling may even outweigh some functional disadvantages. For example, very fine glassware needs to be handled with extreme care (one disadvantage), and it is expensive (another disadvantage). But it appeals to our sense of fashion or taste nevertheless.

Colour, shape and texture are the three most common variables when building style improvements. Style improvements often may be limited to packaging or pack design. Nearly all buyers, including industrial companies, respond to good, clear, presentation. Even when tendering for contracts, companies using glossy presentations have been known to edge out bids from companies which present them poorly.

The importance of having a high level of presentation in marketing products cannot be emphasised strongly enough. The presentation must be appropriate to the market, and to the product function. In competitive situations buyers often make decisions about products which they have never used before, or about products which other people will use. They

W.O.M.P.—F

operate in a situation of ignorance and must therefore rest their judgement of quality upon three factors alone. First, they judge by what the salesman, or other personal information source, tells them about the product. Second, they judge by their regard for the company and its reputation. Third, they judge by the look of the product, the sample, and the literature. The product which looks good will always beat the one which does not inspire confidence.

Style improvements need not be exclusive of other product improvements. And they can often be introduced with little additional expense at the new product stage, provided that thought and care is devoted to the problem.

Value Analysis. This seeks to change the formulation of the product in such a way as to improve the performance, or at the least to hold it constant, while reducing the cost. Value engineering seeks the same end, through the examination of the production process. A series of formal value analysis techniques has been developed, often involving the building of mathematical models, and the creative application of development techniques. The intrinsic worth of each component part of a product and the function it has to perform is questioned and analysed. Many products are made of some materials which are scarce or costly. The replacement of these materials by a lower grade or cheaper alternative, may horrify the engineers or production executives, but if it does not affect the performance of the product in relation to the customers' expectations, then the company has little cause to worry about the change. The value analysis technique has been developed to great lengths in the past few years while inflationary pressures have been felt on company profit margins. A little care needs to be exercised over the continuous application of the technique, since one small modification may not be felt, but the cumulative effect of a series of modifications may be detectable within the product performance over time.

Product degradation. One of the effects of price wars, rapid inflation, and declining markets is to reduce the product quality. In order to stay in business, a company will trim quality from the product, to cheapen it in price, or to maintain its profitability. Bit by bit it goes, until the product performance is affected, and noticed by the buyers. Industry-wide, all the products which are under profit pressure may be produced down to the lowest level of quality that the law allows—and some will go lower than that, through widening their specification tolerances. This is what everyone fears when quality levels are reduced. However, product degradation may be a desirable manœuvre and may not have harmful effects on the market. Most basic quality standards are set by the production function—whatever marketing may say. The production men are the only ones who are expert enough to nominate the alternative levels of quality in a new product from which marketing can choose. They build in quality safety levels. And so products are often made to quality standards which are not desired by the market but are there to shore up production risks.

Therefore, in most products there are wasteful components and materials which are of peripheral interest to the buyer. Packaging often comes into this category. These items can be altered and the products 'degraded' safely.

In consumer product markets, a triangular panel test is usually used to check on the consumer perception of such changes. Two test samples of buyers are drawn—matched in their characteristics. Before each tester is placed three samples of the product; say, two standard products and one modified version. The panel is asked to pick out the odd one of the three. The matched sample is given the reverse order, say, two modified versions and one standard product. If the changes cannot be detected then there will be a more or less even distribution of answers between the two product types across the two samples. A standard preference test can take place after the tester's choice of the odd one out has been made.

Service improvement. A technique of service improvement is often employed by smaller companies competing with large organisations. Service may mean technical advice, more frequent delivery, faster supply, breaking bulk, consultancy help, and after-sales support. The problem with service improvement is that if it works, then competitors tend to copy. It may be expensive to apply. Service improvements usually appeal only to a sector of the market; and work best where the chosen service is the outstanding weakness in competitive organisations. When service standards are already high in a market, it pays to look elsewhere for product improvement.

Promotional benefits. Some companies, particularly those operating in price competitive markets, usually those with undifferentiated products, seek to add value to their products through the addition of promotional benefits. Giveaways, competitions, collector premiums, invitations to the company's sponsored golf competition, all serve primarily as short-term inducements to buy. But some product fields have become so inundated with promotion activities that they have become a regular part of the product offerings. Incentive schemes have a tendency to make buyers switch brands more—and in undifferentiated product fields a significant number of them will often switch primarily for the special offer.

The question of which combination of these seven factors of product improvement to select must be matched against the responsiveness of the market. In order for the selection to be considered successful the buyers must respond in significant numbers. This will largely depend upon the level of the buyers' interest in the product. The greater the risk of the purchase being a bad one, the less likely the buyer is to respond to any product change except that of increased quality. The buyer will perceive his risk as being related to the cost of the product matched against his resources available; or to the importance of the function of the product to him. Material suppliers cannot move far from the basic quality levels of their products simply because materials are usually central to the buyer's need, and they are costly to him. However, low-price consumer durable products can move easily in any direction of product improvement, provided that basic quality standards are met—that is product function, and safety.

The approach to product planning

The general approach to product planning is to identify first those products which are earning the bulk of the company's current profit contribution. Place alongside these the products of the future, which may be unprofitable

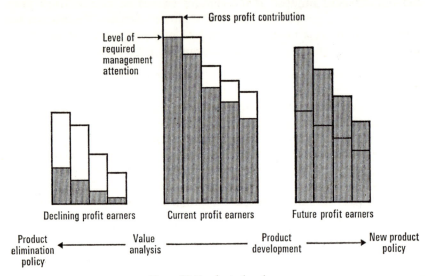

Figure 29 Product planning.

today, but which can be expected to enter the mainstream of profitable products some time. Finally, isolate those products, with their turnover and profit contributions, which are acting as a drain on the company resources.

The main profit earners must be given their due weight of marketing attention, in order to defend the current profits of the business, as shown in *Figure 29*. Tomorrow's profit earners must be given more than their fair share of marketing resources, including time, skill and energy. Development areas of the business are always demanding these resources.

This will only leave a light level of activity to support the weak areas of the business. By weak areas we mean to include those new products which were once produced with great hopes but did not turn out well. We include also those products which used to sell well, but where the market has drifted away; or those products which are becoming steadily more costly to produce and which have pricing constraints applied, and so on. It is logical to provide low support to these areas. After all, a company has only scarce resources to allocate as best it can between every competing demand—and something has to give.

This argument may be logical, but it is rare to find it being applied in practice. Companies actually work in the reverse way. Because these declining product areas represent the 'problems' of the business, they get *more* than their fair share of time, attention and money not less. Most managers worry and meddle with these products to try to 'get them going again'. They also spend a great deal of time and energy on tomorrow's profit caners. This means that the current profit producers within the organisation, those slightly dull products which everyone knows about, but is bored with, receive less than their due share of the resources. Certainly, production departments concentrate their energies here in trying to reduce the cost and increase the productivity of the manufacturing process. But the marketing department often leaves them until they turn into a problem. Even sales forces become bored with pushing the same old products, especially those big ones which are less responsive to sales pressure. Sales forces would rather be faced with a 'challenge' and new products.

Having identified these three groups of products, further analysis is now required in some detail. This will identify specific product problems, starting with the high priority items. A number of quantification techniques may be required at this stage.

Value analysis may be required with those products which appear to be

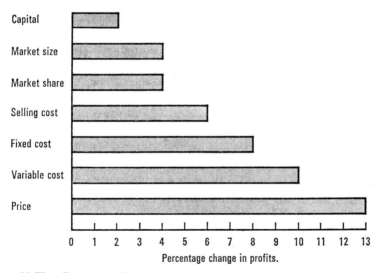

Figure 30 The effects on profits of a one per cent change in various major parameters.
(*Source:* Ivan J. Goldberg, 'Quantification Techniques in Marketing'; *Marketing*, June 1969, p. 37)

capable of cost reductions of some substance, and which will not harm product quality as perceived by the customer. A skew analysis technique may be required to position the profitability of the products in relation to the markets' resources they currently command. This will show the familiar fact that 20 per cent of the products produce 80 per cent of the results, and vice versa. Sensitivity analysis may be used to assist management in assessing those key areas of the product operation which must be carefully controlled. (*Figure 30*.) By the use of consumer attitude studies, it can be seen that some aspects of product quality may affect purchasing habits. Not all the product features are regarded with equal favour by purchasers. How, then, do such features rank, in order of importance? The price/quality/size/style relationship can be investigated in this way.[1]

Signs of an inadequate product mix.

Figure 31 shows, in diagram form, a number of problems which occur constantly in the product mix. Each problem has a distinct character; and most of them require marketing activity of a strategic kind spread over a long time period.

Sales decline. A product group or single line may have been dropping in sales consistently over a period of time. The nature of the problem will often be easy to identify, and this will determine the technique to be adopted. However, when companies are faced with this situation they usually make the initial assumption that the fault is internal, that they are doing something wrong in their advertising, selling, or pricing operation. They often believe that they are not 'pushing' it hard enough. Consequently, the first line of attack is upon the marketing activity. This approach is also the easiest to develop, and should be the quickest in response.

If this does not work, then the problem might lie within the product, and more careful analysis of the cause is required. This may result in a product modification programme, or new variety introduction. This is more expensive, and takes longer.

Beyond this, the market may be topping-out and at the point of maturity. In this case, a marketing segmentation approach is required, leading to new markets and new uses for the product. If the market is in decline, or if some external factor means the product cannot be revived, then it is best to cut the losses as swiftly as possible through a profit-stripping policy, leading to the phasing out of the product. Otherwise an expensive waste of time and money will go on for a long time.

Profits may decline, while sales hold steady. There are three moves to counter this, which may be used together. The first is to raise prices, the second is

[1] I. J. Goldberg, 'Quantification Techniques in Marketing'; *Marketing*, June 1969, pp. 36–38

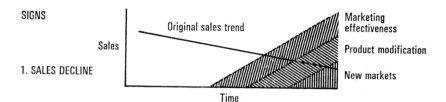

SIGNS

1. SALES DECLINE

Sales

Original sales trend

Marketing effectiveness

Product modification

New markets

Time

2. PROFIT

Profit

Profit trend

Effect of product modification

Effect of value analysis

Effect of price change.

Time

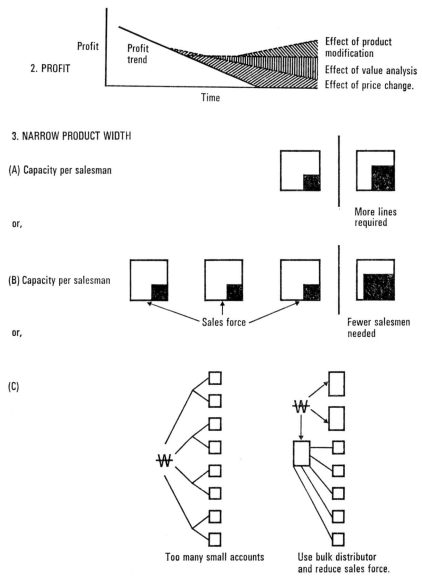

3. NARROW PRODUCT WIDTH

(A) Capacity per salesman

More lines required

or,

(B) Capacity per salesman

Sales force

Fewer salesmen needed

or,

(C)

Too many small accounts

Use bulk distributor and reduce sales force.

Figure 31 Inadequate product mix.

to apply value analysis techniques, and the third is to modify the product, usually by splitting it into varieties—an expensive, large, or high-quality version, and a cheap, small, or low-quality version. Each new variety is designed to operate on a higher gross margin platform than before.

Under-utilising marketing resources. Some companies have marketing resources which they are not fully utilising. A narrow product range company often regrets that its salesmen are not selling more products at each call; that its advertising is expensive. The obvious solution is to have more lines, or fewer salesmen. The problem may lie in distribution with too many small accounts. Here the answer may be to split the system and introduce a distributor for the small customers.

A less obvious solution is to carry 'merchandise' products which may be made by another organisation, possibly packed under the company brand name, and sold to the company's customers. The company will not obtain the prime manufacturing profit from these products, but they will assist the marketing costs. The danger lies in letting this activity form too high a proportion of the total company business. Then capital resources will be applied to it, inevitably, salesmen will be hired essentially because of the demands of the 'merchandise' products, advertising programmes increased, and so on. The company will become a distributor, and will require a distributor's skills and management outlook. This is a danger to any company which is indulging in this activity merely in order to increase its marginal contribution. The long-term strategy may be for the company to engage finally in the manufacture of the bought-in products. In this case the move takes on an experimental marketing role.

High seasonal sales pattern

Figure 31 also shows an annual sales curve for the turkey market. There are three small sales periods for turkeys, Easter, Whitsun and the Bank Holiday—and one enormous sales period at Christmas. Not many companies face the turkey producers' problem that 80 per cent of their annual output is consumed in $1\frac{1}{2}$ hours every year. This is an intractable seasonal sales problem.

The seasonal problem breaks down into two kinds: extending the 'shoulder' of the season, and filling up the off-season slump. The first problem of extending the shoulder often lends itself to some artificial market forcing technique involving sales promotion. By adding value to the purchase, a few marginal users might be encouraged to buy. The sales cost of this approach might be very high, particularly if the offer must be spread across all the normal users of the product at the time. Special price offers sometimes help, but the total cost of the price reduction must be set against the profits earned only on the marginal extra sales. Price deals to clear end of season stocks are also self-defeating in the long run. Buyers begin to realise, after

(D) High seasonal sales pattern.

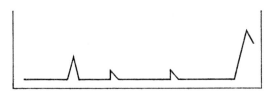

Add lines to offset sales slump while using existing distribution channels.

(4) DISPROPORTIONATE PROFIT RETURN

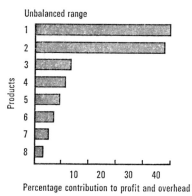

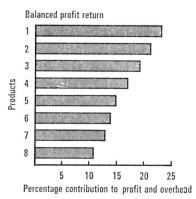

(5) PRODUCT RANGE TOO WIDE:

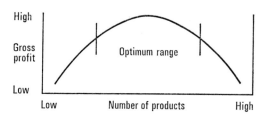

Figure 31 (continued) Inadequate product mix.

a time, that special prices are normally offered at the end of a season, and they hold off some of their main purchases until this time.

To resolve the central problem of lifting sales in the off-season slump can be one of the most difficult tasks in marketing. If the market is not there and does not want to buy, sometimes nothing can shift it. For example, a company making antihistamine products has no market to sell to once the season for hay fever allergies is over. It may move into the development of cough and cold cures to employ its sales force, and to keep its channels of trade busy. But these are major new products operations in their own right.

Filling-in off season sales slumps can be done sometimes—but the successes are rare. The ice cream manufacturers now sell a range of varieties for desserts during the winter, to balance their peak demand in the summer. This meant a major move for them into developing new markets, and required radical new product development.

The problem, if it can be solved at all, needs a product diversification move. The essential characteristics of such a move are that it should use the same marketing skills and resources as the company possess; say, the same sales force and distribution channels. Preferably it should not require the input of heavy development capital, because there is a high risk that the move will not be successful. The more a company attempts to 'educate' the market to a new way of behaviour, the greater needs to be its capital resources, the more dominant it needs to be in its market, and the higher the rate of potential profit return. The real solution may be to acquire a going and profitable concern with the right product range, selling through the same channels, but with an inverse seasonal sales problem. The resources can then be meshed together, particularly the sales forces, economies taken, and the problem partially solved. Strong seasonal sales problems are seldom solved perfectly and always remain a planning difficulty.

Unbalanced product range.   Some companies producing a range of products find that their profits are dependent upon the sales of only one or two lines. This puts them at risk, because all markets change in time, and without these key products the company might not survive. This is the classical product planning problem, because it requires every single development opportunity to be located and exploited. It is also a difficult problem to deal with unless there is a profit squeeze exerted on the company. The reason is that companies in this situation are often very profitable indeed, and find that profit opportunities in the development areas are nowhere near as high. Consequently there is a lack of the necessary corporate stimulus.

There are three lines of approach to the problem. The first is the defence of the existing product markets. This is carried out by splitting the key products, adding new varieties and developing new uses, so far as possible, for the key products. The profit return from these activities will be lower than is earned at present, but it will keep the product markets going, and it will buy the company some time.

The second line of approach is upon those other products in the existing range which might have some future, allied with other new products which can be developed into markets or channels of trade with which the company has experience. This requires product and market segmentation analysis. It may take a considerable time before these new markets can be exploited to their full profit potential. Five years or more is not unusual, from the time of starting development work. The third line of approach requires long-term planning, using the 'gap profit analysis' technique. This will show how far the company needs to go, compared to how far its existing moves can take it. The difference must be made up through merger and acquisition. The acquisition of a profitable organisation with a complementary product range may be the cheapest and fastest way of solving this problem.

Product-clutter. This is one of the most difficult problems to analyse. Theoretically, one can imagine that the total marketing resources represented by salesmen, advertising, promotion funds and the like can be set against too few products, thereby under-utilising some of these resources. Alternatively the marketing operation may have to support too many products, so that the general level of marketing power applied to each product is too small. For example, the salesman with too many products to sell, becomes an order-taker, and can only promote two or three products at each call. There is then going to be a lack of sales drive behind some of the products. Theoretically there is an 'optimal' size of product range. But its precise measurement is difficult. A fuller analysis of this problem is in Chapter 11, under Product Elimination.

Allocating marketing resources to products

The difficulty of assessing product line profits has already been touched on in Chapter 6. The basic choice for allocating resources between the products in the range lies between some notion of incremental profits, and the concept of net profits over full cost.[2]

Incremental profits refer to the difference in the firm's profits with, and without, the addition of the product or activity in question. By adding a new product to existing facilities which are under-utilised, all the cash earned above the cost of materials and other direct costs is treated as a contribution to the company's net profit. As any management accountant will explain, this is a dangerous costing approach to use except in the short-term, and one which will ultimately drive the company out of business, if practised continuously.

This is because these additional products or activities which are designed to mop up overheads will in time produce new overheads. They also incur

[2] J. Dean, 'Product Line Policy'; *U.S. Jnl. of Business*, Oct. 1950, pp. 248–258.

new untraceable costs, such as the drain on management time. The extra gross margin does not all flow through to net profit therefore.

The alternative idea, that of full costing, means that some of the fixed and semi-fixed overheads are loaded on to the new product or new activity, and the cost burdens of existing products are correspondingly lightened. But as any product development executive will explain, the full cost system makes new products look particularly unattractive, because they bear their full burden of overhead charge against low volume production and high manufacturing cost.

The concept of incremental costings and marginal pricing works well under two circumstances. First, it may be useful for short-run activities, such as sales promotion, where the incremental profits are simply the difference between price and the short-term marginal cost. Because the activity will finish distinctly, and because it is run over a short time period, overheads do not have much chance to drift upward. It is fairly safe therefore to treat any returns above material costs and other direct costs, such as discounts, as a contribution to net profit. In this way the existing organisation is squeezed to produce the extra profit.

The second circumstance where it may be useful to use incremental costing is in new product development up to the point at which the product breaks even. The new product forecast will therefore show several levels of break-even. First, there will be a break-even point on materials and other direct costs, which should occur immediately. The second stage allows for breaking-even on semi-variable costs, such as physical distribution, sales and advertising. The third is the break-even on full cost. The fourth is the break-even point allowing for full cost plus required profit objective. This treats the new product fairly, without discouraging the executive team responsible for it. And it still leaves the management accountants secure in the knowledge that the product will pay an increasing share of the running costs of the business.

The most difficult allocation problem in marketing is between existing products with differing rates of profit return and varying degrees of sensitivity to promotion. Take, for example, the question of allocating promotion funds between three different products, *A*, *B*, and *C*. (*Figure 32.*) Assume that the differences in sales response to every unit of promotion from each product can be estimated. (This information is not normally available. Most product ranges are much wider than this, with greater competition for existing resources. Furthermore, there are different types of allocation to make—sales, advertising, promotion and so on. In this example the allocation problem has been reduced to its bare components.)

Some companies will assume that their gross margins on each product are similar, and will allocate the promotion units simply according to the turnover on each product. This is a major error in assumption, but it is often committed by sales-oriented managements, particularly when the accounting

You have three units of promotion funds to allocate across three product groups. You can allocate one on each, but you must support at least two product groups. Product group A outsells product group C by 5 to 1. Its market is sensitive to each unit of promotion by +10 per cent. (For one unit of promotion the sales will go up by 10 per cent, for two units of promotion the sales will go up by 20 per cent.) Product group B outsells product group C by 2 to 1 and its market is sensitive to +20 per cent for each unit of promotion. Product group C is sensitive to +30 per cent for each unit of promotion.

Question. Given only the turnover information above how would you allocate funds?

Answer.

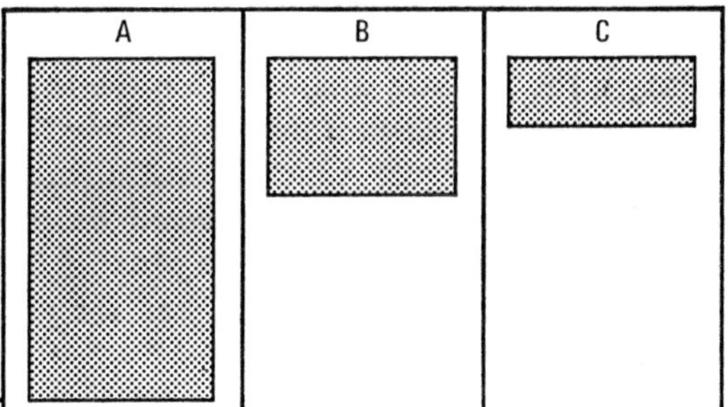

	A	B	C
Original turnover	£500	£200	£100
Percentage increase in turnover per unit of promotion	10%	20%	30%
Actual increase in turnover per unit of promotion	£50	£40	£30
Unit allocation based on turnover	2 units	1 unit	0 units

Question. Given also the following information on gross margins for each group, would you change your decision? If so, how?

> Product group A: 30 per cent gross margin
> Product group B: 40 per cent gross margin
> Product group C: 50 per cent gross margin.

	A	B	C
Original turnover	£500	£200	£100
Gross margin as a % of turnover	30%	40%	50%
Gross margin	£150	£80	£50
Percentage increase in turnover and gross margin per unit of promotion	10%	20%	30%
Actual increase in gross margin	£15	£16	£15
Unit allocation based on gross margin	Either 1 unit	2 units	Or 1 unit

This demonstrates three factors:
1. Allocating funds based on turnover will always be wrong while there are varying rates of gross margin.
2. That using gross margin *percentages* only, as a guide, can be equally mistaken.
3. That the factor which really matters is the total amount of money earned as company contribution to running costs and profit after direct costs have been met.

Figure 32 Allocating funds between products.

information on product line profits is inadequate. Inevitably it will lead to a poor decision. In the case of the problem set, two units will be spent on *A* and one on *B* if allocated in this way.

As soon as the gross margin figures on each product are known the allocation will change. Allocating funds according to the total earning power of the product after direct costs have been met is a standard practice. But mistakes are often made by executives who focus upon the *percentage* return on the product, and not upon the total cash return. It is the total amount of money which is available to pay for the business which matters and not an index figure, which is what a percentage really is.

The answer to the problem if based on gross margin calculations will allocate two units of promotion on product *B* (a change from the previous decision based only on turnover), and the problem of spending the third unit either on *A* or on *C*.

The problem of which product *A* or *C* to allocate this final promotion unit now requires other information before the decision can be made. For example, the attitude of the responsible marketing executive is likely to be concerned with the prospects for products *A* and *C* in the years to come. Which one has the greater growth potential? Which of the two products will help others in the range to sell? These are questions that should be asked. The production executive's view is likely to be concerned with the production planning process; will a higher rate of labour productivity or material utilisation be achieved with one product compared to the other? The attitude of the management accountant is likely to be different again. He will be concerned with the problem of 'scarce' resources. He will ask, at what point will the growth of either product push the company into the provision of extra facilities—say in plant, or in physical distribution?

Alternatively, he may ask for the various levels of capital employed behind each product to be measured, and for the decision to be based upon the product which shows the highest return. The difficulty here, as in most multi-product companies, is to measure the element of capital employed in supporting each product. It is usually only possible to calculate where discrete plant and equipment is used to manufacture each line. Even in this case the total capital employed is often a matter of judgement.

It is not often that allocation problems are as distinct as this, but by reducing this one to its essentials, the natural conflicts in management attitude emerge.

A mathematical model involving linear programming can be developed to solve the problem. But the total of all the allocation problems of this kind are extraordinarily complex, and the factors are changing constantly. The answers turn upon information which is not generally available and which must be guessed at—that is, how responsive are the various products to different levels of promotion?

Allocating the resources according to the gross margins earned from each

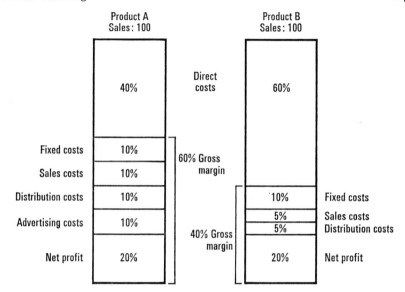

Figure 33 Question. Given equal opportunity for each product, which one do you select for additional marketing resources?

sector of the business will be better than allocating simply according to turnover. But without further thought given to the likely net profits earned from each sector, the allocation will still be wrong. Some products which show a low *gross* margin may still show a high *net profit*. This is a feature which wholesalers and retailers know from their experience, but which is not so evident to manufacturers. Many manufacturers find it very difficult to calculate the net profit returns from different products; and when they do, they often feel reluctant to be guided by them.

Some products may require little investment in sales or distribution; private label products, packed under the customer's brand name and delivered in bulk with no investment in sales or advertising, may show a high net profit despite earning a low gross margin.

Figure 33 describes the difficulty. Product *A* shows a high gross margin (60 per cent) but with high sales, advertising and distribution costs which bring the net profit to 20 per cent. This could be, for instance, the company's brand which it markets itself. Product *B* shows a low gross margin (40 per cent) but with the same net profit of 20 per cent. This could be the private label product, packed especially for the customer.

If both products have an equal opportunity for growth then nearly every manager will allocate extra resources to the high gross margin product. If pressed for a reason, they will probably use an argument based upon marginal profit return. They will assume that if all the fixed costs and over-heads are being borne by the current earnings from sales, then most of the additional gross margin on each extra sale of product *A* will flow through to net profit. Therefore every extra sale of product *A* will earn at the rate of 60 per cent net profit. In the long run this argument is clearly absurd. As the product sells more it will require more sales, distribution and advertising resources. If the marginal profit argument were valid, then we could expect to find products which sell in increasing quantities producing ever-increasing *rates* of net profit. Such economies of scale are very hard to find outside production costs. In fact, most products earn successively *lower* rates of net profit as they sell *more*.

There may be a more substantial case for putting extra marketing resources behind product *B* despite its lower gross profit return. After all, the company can only earn its net profit out of its gross margin. The direct costs are 'dead'. On product *B* a net profit return of 100 per cent is earned for every unit spent in the marketing and overhead area. (20 per cent costs produce 20 per cent net profit.) But product *A* earns a net profit of only 50 per cent for every unit spent on marketing and overhead. (40 per cent costs produce 20 per cent net profit.)

No one is suggesting that companies should promote automatically their low gross margin lines; but gross margin calculations by themselves are not sufficient to resolve allocation problems. An idea of the net profit returns is required, matched with a view of the future growth of the markets and matched with the capacities of the company in terms of sales and physical distribution as well as production resources.

Product planning is one of the most fascinating aspects of marketing. It is also one of the least researched areas, where subjective judgement based upon 'experience' and 'feel' is used in preference to formal techniques. It is an area of marketing where good or bad decisions are seldom traceable in the short run. And the sin of omission, that is, the decision *not* to do something, is never found out.

Market Situation and attitudes to Product Planning

Package Goods: Consumer

The problem in multi-product companies rests exactly upon the question of resource allocation which we have just discussed. One of the primary motivations is the selection of those products which can act as 'leaders' in the range, and which can carry other products with them. This is a critical question for the allocation of advertising support. The greatest doubt exists about the true nature of net profits earned from individual products in the range.

Consumer Durables

Product planning in these companies is often less difficult than it appears. Each product is often discrete in its manufacture and allows for the accountant to calculate the rate of return on capital employed. Each market is often discrete, and the future performance of the product over its 'life cycle' is easier to estimate. Therefore complete profitability analyses over the life of the product can be estimated. Product modification often operates in the area of additional features, or in styling.

Plant and Equipment

Market and customer planning is more the rule in these companies. The capital intensity of the industry makes a long product life cycle inevitable. Short-term incremental costing and pricing practices are common, in order to use up production facilities. Product modification is usually concentrated in the area of quality improvement, and of service development.

Components

Most product modification problems are concerned with quality improvements, but features and styling changes may be effective in some markets. Value analysis is often a feature of this kind of company. The traditional product planning dilemma is whether to allocate all the marketing and sales resources behind a small group of products which are planned to 'lead' the sales of the rest, or whether to promote across the range.

Materials

Material manufacturers concentrate their product modification policy in the product quality and value analysis areas. They often search to find ways in which customers can achieve better utilisation from lower quality grades of material, giving them a price advantage over competition. Advertising resources are often concentrated behind the consumer versions of the products they sell, in order to use the 'carry over' effect of this promotion to influence industrial buyers.

Differentiated Products

These are the companies to whom product planning and the allocation of resources present the greatest difficulties. The problem for them is to get out of the general run of competition supplying the identical product as competition. They search for pockets of markets which will respond to some kind of specialist package of products. Frequently this will drive them into the production of a 'system' or a group of products which, taken together, may form a neat parcel for a particular type of use. In allocating their resources, they will be concerned to support their leading lines. They will also try to develop those products which, having a certain distinction about them, are able to mark the company out from its competitors.

Custom-built Products

Here the planning process will concentrate on separate tenders and will be directed towards making each order profitable. The allocation of advertising resources is more likely to be spent in promoting the general reputation of the company, and the corporate image. The promotion and sales resources will be directed at soliciting enquiries for tender.

Fragmented Markets

Here companies will be quick to copy features and modifications introduced by competitors and which look as if they will be successful. The interest will lie with what the distributive trade will be prepared to buy. Service development often forms a major part of their planning programmes.

Concentrated Markets

The leaders will be concerned with their own performance. They will usually seek to close up parts of the market which might let competitors in, by developing small product modifications. The accent will be on keeping productivity high, and servicing costs low.

Example: Product Planning

Background

Broads Builders' Merchants Ltd. is a private company centred in London. They sell building and decorating materials to the building trade and house-holder. The product lines vary from paints and water taps to manhole covers. Broads specialise in the provision of heavy duty ware, such as bricks and drainage materials for trade users, for example, building contractors.

Initially the company were merchants, but gradual reorganisation of the company and its activities resulted in a holding company (Broad & Co. Ltd.) being formed and two subsidiary companies, thus there were now two branches of the company—manufacturing (Broads Manufacturing Company Ltd.) and merchanting (Broads Builders Merchants Ltd.). It is the latter which is dealt with in this case study.

The Problems

Originally the company had developed in the traditional fashion of builders' merchants, that of having a poor consumer image and uninteresting showrooms other than to builders and architects.

Gradually the company was restructured to place emphasis on the various depots, in this way depots increased their individual buying power and respon-sibility to meeting market needs. By rationalising the stocks over all the depots and tying the whole organisation to a stock-list the advantages in buying and selling gradually gained momentum. During this time the first moves were made by the company towards the establishment of a self-service department and more professional displays in the showrooms.

Whilst the new policies were beginning to work the various departments lacked cohesion and more impetus was required in sales. The R.O.I. was still too low. It was decided, therefore, to appoint a marketing manager.

Solution

With the identification of the new appointment a new division was formed—the Marketing Division.

The division was able to build results on the work that had already been initiated in three main areas.

(a) Stocks were geared to minimum stock turn levels.
(b) The Marketing Division became responsible for overall buying policy —thus the assessment and satisfaction of demand became a continuous process.
(c) The sales force became totally involved with the product range carried by the individual depots.

The traditional market with the builder, lacked immediate growth potential. Expansion was achieved by:

(a) Taking the self-service department that had been started in 1967 and widening its stock range to appeal to the 'do-it-yourself' customer. Colourful decoration and up-to-date merchandising assisted this aim.
(b) Introducing associated products such as fitted bedroom and kitchen furniture, tiles, timber and own-brand products, thereby widening the product range.
(c) The showroom was turned into a 'Bathroom and Kitchen Design Centre' with improved displays. A consultancy service was also added to advise customers of kitchen layout, with a service to design their kitchen, if they wished.

  Advertising was stepped up. This aimed at the Londoner especially, by advertising on the Underground. Direct mail shots became a standard form of publicity to customer and potential customer.

Results

In the eighteen months following the implementation of the new policy the following results have been observed.

(a) For the latter ten months of 1970 'the budgeted figure was beaten by 3 per cent and for 1971 the present trends show that the results will be 19 per cent up on 1970'.

  The average rate of growth since re-organisation is 12 per cent per annum.
(b) They are more marketing orientated.
(c) Personnel are working as a team towards common objectives.
(d) The company is able to recognise and profit from changing demand patterns.

A.J.

11. New Product Development and Elimination

It took 30 years for the common zip fastener to be mass produced, from the time it was invented as a shoe fastening device to the time it was used in clothes, during the first world war.

It took 55 years for television to be marketed commercially from the time it was invented; penicillin took 15 years; the Xerox electrostatic copying machines the same. It took ten years for fluoride toothpaste to be developed.[1]

In a single year, Du Pont now files 800 patent applications. Recently it has taken ten years for nuclear reactors to be developed and applied; only five years for radar, and less than three years for transistors and the solar battery. 90 per cent of the scientists who ever lived are alive today, and the total body of human knowledge is doubling every ten years.

In this frenetic race for material progress, is it any wonder that we are out of control of both its direction and accelerating pace? Can we be surprised that half of all new products fail after the marketing stage, that 58 new product ideas must be screened to find one good one?[2] That product life spans are getting shorter; and that many educated people in advanced societies all over the world are rejecting the entire idea of material progress which is developing independently of progress in the humanities?

In the macro sense, marketing men are not responsible for creating these inventions; but they are responsible for energising the technical development process, for giving it shape, direction and its commercial rationale, and they are responsible for influencing the way people respond. In the micro sense, they may not wish their company to run the great risks of new product failure, nor to engage the tedium of applied development research, but commercial pressures force it upon them.

[1] L. Adler, 'Time Lag in New Product Development'; *U.S. Jnl. of Marketing*, Vol. 30, Jan. 1966, pp. 17–21.
[2] *The Management of New Products*; 4th ed., Booz, Allen and Hamilton Inc., p. 9.

Development problems

Many lists have been made of the reasons for new product failure:

(a) The timing was wrong.
The product was not practical.
Customer needs changed.
Basic assumptions were forgotten.
Goals were not clearly defined.
Product competed with customer sales.[3]

(b) The product/package was wrong.   53 per cent
Price/value was wrong.   20 per cent
Trade acceptance was poor.   18 per cent
The advertising was wrong   9 per cent
All 'main reasons'.   100 per cent

This was an analysis of 44 failures in the packaged goods consumer markets.[4]

(c) Inadequate product/service
Lack of competitive advantage
Bad timing.
Bad pricing.
Lack of trade acceptance
Poor promotion/selling.
Lack of market stability.[5]

Statistics in this area of new product failure rates and of attributable causes have always been contentious, largely because of the problem of definitions. The term 'new product' means a different thing in one company, compared to another; 'failure' and 'success' have a variety of meanings; even the term 'marketed' needs qualifying.

When companies have product failures the reasons are usually attributed by a process of subjective judgement. One authority, Kraushar, has located three management aspects to the problem.[6] He stated that there are a number of problems which occur in the product development area which are more difficult than those which occur in the area of the company's current operations. This leads to flaws of three kinds:

Lack of development policy. Few companies lay down adequate criteria for new products; or the criteria alter with different levels of management. Top management believes that one set of objectives is operating, but these frequently are different from those being worked towards by middle management.

Lack of objectivity. Product development is a traditional area for the

[3] P. Marvin, 'Why New Products Fail'; *Machine Design (U.S.)*, Nov. 23, 1961. Penton Publishing, Ohio.
[4] 'What Are the Odds?'; *Nielsen Researcher*, Jan.–Feb. 1968, p. 7.
[5] P. Kraushar, 'Graveyard for New Products'; *Marketing*, November 1969.
[6] P. Kraushar, *New Products and Diversification*; Business Books Ltd. 1969.

subjective hunch; and for managements to press ahead regardless of poor test results.

Lack of suitable organisation. Companies tend to be organised for the present rather than for the future. New product development requires venturesome management; and it requires an integrated management versed in several types of skill. Most companies handle the development process on a piecemeal basis in various compartments.

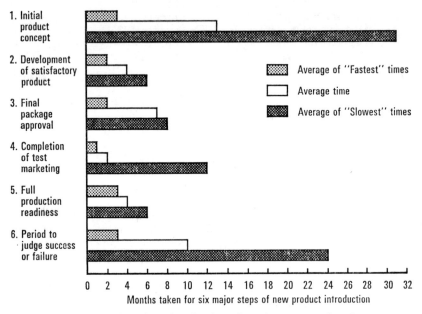

Figure 34 How long does it take to introduce new products?

(*Source:* Dik Warren Twedt, 'How long does it take to introduce new products'; *U.S. Journal of Marketing*, January 1955, p. 72)

The development process

There are six stages which can be identified in the development process. It has been reported as taking $2\frac{1}{2}$ years on average in U.S. grocery products to get new products started. (*Figure 34.*)

Idea generation. This stage ranges from being a highly creative activity to an obvious extension to the company's present range of products. New product ideas can come from anywhere; from customers, from salesmen, scientists, competitors, and from company management.

The screening process. At this stage, the ideas selected for further investigation require to be set against the factors operating in the business, in order to measure their compatibility.

Business analysis stage. Various analyses need to be taken at this stage relating both to the market and its potential as well as to the cost and profitability analysis of the proposed product.

Development stage. Prototypes need to be built and tested; customer tests and preference tests are required. Brand name, advertising and packaging needs to be developed, as well as the product itself.

Pilot marketing. At some stage, whether the product goes into a sales test, a formal test market, or into a regional launch, it needs production in limited

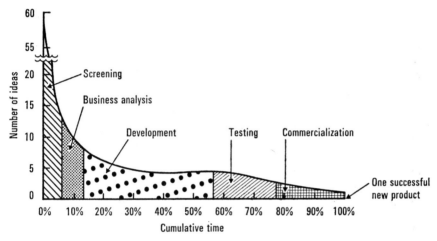

Figure 35 Decay curve of new-product ideas (51 companies).
(*Source: Management of New Products*, 4th ed., New York: Booz, Allen & Hamilton, Inc., 1965)

quantity but under full production controls. This stage eliminates the unexpected difficulties in production and distribution, and helps develop efficient sales approaches.

The launch. The full-scale launch into open market, backed by all the support facilities of promotion and advertising, are brought into operation at the final stage.

Generating ideas

There is seldom a shortage of ideas about the kinds of products which management might possibly market—indeed, there are often too many stray ideas. What is usually lacking is a formal method of ranking these ideas in order of priority and practicability. The starting point for idea generation might be a simple analysis of the company's strengths and weaknesses. From its strengths, the company might search for new product ideas which fit its current resources. (*Figure 35.*)

These ideas would, for example, constitute complementary products, use the same channels of distribution, use the same raw materials, production facilities, technology, marketing or sales resources. The new product might exploit by-products of the existing process.

An examination of the company weaknesses would disclose those areas where there are highly seasonal sales, declining sales, and other signs of an inadequate product mix. This search might push the company outside its own field to look for suitable new products.

Most idea generating systems involve both desk research and various types of management consensus procedures. Common to both is the fact that many different types of specialist experience are called upon to suggest ideas. People always suggest ideas that are close to their existing experience; and it is the contrariness of these many ideas to people exposed to them for the first time which provides the creative spark. A salesman may find some exciting possibilities from technical sources, and he may find slots in his experience in which to locate them. Equally, the technical executive can be exposed to customer ideas which may be new to him. Each searches his library of information—the technical man his latest University research reports, and the salesman his competitors' product lists. The new product ideas are then fertilised at a meeting. The meetings can be organised in a variety of different ways; from a straightforward new products committee to a full-scale Delphi Method or its derivations.[7]

It is critical at the idea-generation stage for marketing to encourage and energise the process. Leadership skills of a particular kind are needed to deal with the very fragile and personal nature of ideas. If a hostile, aggressive, or authoritarian approach is used, then the ideas dry up. People will not suggest anything except the most obvious if they find that they are subjected to faint criticism or if they must fight to get their ideas accepted. The only way to get a brainstorming session moving is to ban the use of the words 'no' and 'not', and no one is allowed to turn down any idea out of hand, however stupid. All the ideas should be listed and then reviewed. At this stage they can then be ranked.

Screening systems

Screening systems fall into two kinds. The first is a simple checklist of all the main company and market features.[8] The new product idea is checked off against these to see how it compares with any alternative. A series of rating scales is used; this is particularly useful when a company has more new product ideas than it knows how to deal with. The second method takes each factor of importance to the product and its market and provides it with a numerical 'weighting'. The new product idea is scored against each factor, and ends up with a final score which can be used to rank the various

[7] J. Chambers, S. Mullick, D. Goodman, 'Catalytic Agent for Effective Planning'; *Harvard Business Review*, Jan.–Feb. 1971, pp. 110–119.
[8] *The Financial Aspects of a New Product Launch*; Marketing Society, 1967.

new product ideas. This final score should not exclude a large element of subjective judgement, but the system makes certain that no key factors involved in new product selection are overlooked in the first flush of enthusiasm for a particular new product idea. (*Figure 36.*)

Business analysis

At this stage the formal construction of a development proposal is required, in business terms. This is then evaluated against the market knowledge as

Sphere of performance	Relative Weight. A.	Product Compatability Values. B.											Rating A x B
		0·0	0·1	0·2	0·3	0·4	0·5	0·6	0·7	0·8	0·9	1·0	
Company personality and goodwill	0·20							0·6					0·120
Marketing	0·20										0·9		0·180
Research and Development	0·20								0·7				0·140
Personnel	0·15							0·6					0·090
Finance	0·10										0·9		0·090
Production	0·05									0·8			0·040
Location and Facilities	0·05				0·3								0·015
Purchasing and Supplies	0·05										0·9		0·045
	1·00												0·720

Rating: 0·00–0·40 poor: 0·41–0·75 fair; 0·76–1·00 good.
Minimum acceptance rate 0·70.

Figure 36 A new product rating scale.

(*Source:* B. Richman, 'A rating scale for product innovation'; *Business Horizons* (U.S.), Summer 1962, pp. 37–44)

it exists. Simple market research studies might be carried out but the emphasis is on low cost and internal analyses, since the chance of failure is still likely to be very high at this stage. This is where a series of break-even analyses is drawn showing the effect of profits of different levels of investment and sales turnover. This stage continues throughout the remainder of the project, continually being re-appraised and modified.

Development phase

At this stage, the development plan is agreed. The product specifications are laid down, and possibly a network analysis chart is drawn up. This familiar technique involves the listing of all the streams of main activity which must be undertaken to get the product to market. At each stage, several streams of 'subactivity' must take place. Estimates of the time required to handle each of these stages is required. The activities which can be handled concurrently with all other activities are shown on parallel lines. Only those activities which are critical to the completion of the project on time are shown on the 'critical' path. A delay on this path will delay the entire operation.

The relationship of all the activities can be drawn, the sequence of jobs is shown. The most important task in the preparation of such an analysis is the estimate of time to be taken for each activity. A close estimate is almost impossible when development tests may keep failing.[9]

At the development stage, every arm of the business will be involved in some way. Purchasing will be asked for cost estimates of raw materials; production will be asked for estimated labour costs—this will involve work study. Process engineers will be asked for machine modifications, or layouts; management accountants will be asked constantly to up-date the costings in the light of new evidence.

Marketing will be handling packaging design, advertising plans and sales promotion schemes. Packs will have to be travel tested, products will be tested in pilot plants, and put into customer preference and placement tests; legal clearances will have to be obtained. The true and hidden cost of development work lies in all this back-up activity. In a new-product sensitive business, key managers can be spending one-third of their total time on products which turn out to be failures. This time is a direct drain on net profit.

Pilot marketing

One of the main handicaps in formal test marketing programmes is that tests take a long time to mature. Customers must be given enough time to sample the product for the first time, and then to repeat the purchase twice more before the results can be relied upon. At least that is the standard rule of thumb operated in the repeat purchase package goods market.[10] It cannot obviously apply to industrial products, or to those with long purchasing cycles. Consequently, researchers have been looking for ways of predicting success or failure from new product tests and launches, from evidence which is available soon after the launch. Two indications present themselves. There appears to be a strong correlation between the early acceptance by distribution channels of a new product and its final acceptance by the user.[10] The exceptions would be those products which do not appear at first sight to have any great advantage until the user tries them out. Otherwise research

[9] P. Baynes, 'Network Analysis as a Marketing Tool'; *Marketing*, Dec. 1968, pp. 34–37.
[10] 'A Solid Base'; *Nielsen Researcher*, Jan.–Feb. 1969, pp. 3–4.

which concentrates on acceptance by the distributive trade gives the earliest indication of success.

In repeat purchase markets, a model produced by the Market Research Corporation of America[11] and developed further in this country[12] looks promising. This shows that from panel data, it is possible to separate those purchasers who are buying for the first time from those who are repeating for the 1st, 2nd, 3rd times, and so on. The size of the market for the new product is predicted on the basis of the number of customers who buy the product, by the frequency with which they re-purchase it, by the amount they buy at a time. Parfitt and Collins have demonstrated that this is a reasonable method of predicting brand share, provided that consumer panel data is available.

One of the most difficult problems in new product development concerns the decay effect of development investment. When a narrow range company starts new product development it is frequently very successful. It may decide to build its future on new products, and so invests more in research. The costs, therefore, begin to mount.

At the same time, its list of new product ideas, which was started with the highest and fastest return products, those with the lowest element of risk, has been reduced to products which are longer-term projects, or lower profit potential projects. Consequently, the returns from development investment begin to reduce very dramatically (*Figure 37*), as more new products are produced.

Properly, development investment should be run in cycles. There is a great need, at one time in a company's situation, for radical new products to be developed. Subsequently, there will be a need for existing product modification; a need for value analysis; and finally a need for product elimination before the cycle starts again. It is very unlikely that all these activities should be run at constant levels in the company life cycle, except in the largest multi-product organisations.

Product elimination

The elimination of sick and dying products can provide a company with one of its major springboards for expansion. Greater power can be generated behind the high profit earners if resources are not tied up with marginal operations. Extra money can be earned from profit-stripping poor performers. The proper and orderly elimination of products from a company range is at least as important as new product development. Given the state of product-clutter which holds in most multi-product companies today, it may be more important. Many companies are suffering from product indigestion.

[11] J. Woodlock, 'A Model for Early Prediction of a New Product's Future'; American Marketing Assn., New York Chapter, Oct. 1963.
[12] J. Parfitt, B. Collins, *The Use of Consumer Panels for Brand Share Prediction*; Attwood Statistics Ltd., 1967. (Private publication.)

NEW PRODUCT SUCCESS RATIOS

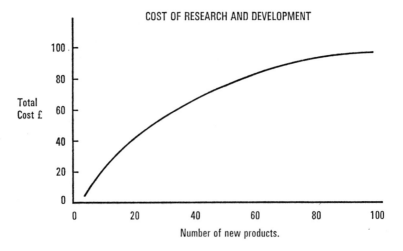

COST OF RESEARCH AND DEVELOPMENT

It is worthwhile examining briefly why new products are started in the first place. When a company has a narrow product range, or when it is small and efficient, it is probably at its highest point of earning power relative to the resources it employs. As it gets larger, although economies of scale are supposed to make it richer, in fact the reverse often happens. It earns progressively less on the extra marginal inputs.

However, the company is safer than it was. Sheer size builds its own protection; a wide product range, covering several markets, may provide only an average return on capital, but at least the product range is protected by its sheer breadth from a disaster in some of its markets.

If the new product development policy is continued with added strength, it may become self-defeating. Not only is there no incremental safety factor

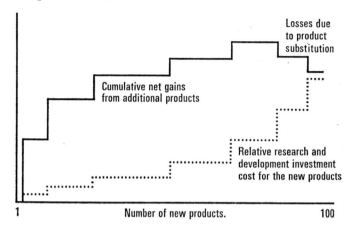

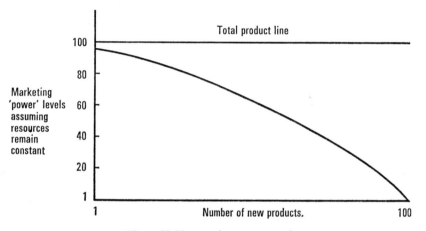

Figure 37 New product success ratios.

but the existing product range becomes more difficult to handle. The data becomes complex to analyse, more decisions are required, so more managers are needed.

The ultimate in new product development is known as product cannibalism. In many multi-product companies, there is considerable doubt about whether apparently successful new products which sell in a fair volume have not, in fact, stolen their sales from some other products in the range. At this point, given equal rates of profit return from the new and the old products, the process becomes ludicrous. It is perfectly feasible for a new product to have great investment cost behind it, and for it to share in the sales and advertising resources of the company. It could add to the production programme, bear its fair share of machine 'down time' and yet not contribute a single unit of additional net profit to the company. It might be apparently 'successful' having met its sales and profit goals. However, its sales and the profits may come mostly from the substitute products in the range.

Surprisingly, only a tiny minority of British companies have any formal procedure for ridding themselves of weak products. This is despite the fact that a formal process can generate a great deal of extra profit in its own right, and from time to time it has been known to turn weak products into such high profit earners that they remain in the product range.

The need for a product elimination system is based upon the fact that weak products tend to consume a disproportionate amount of management time and energy. They represent the 'problems' of the business, so managers at all levels, particularly at the top, keep prodding away, pushing and pulling to try to make them profitable. The actual profit return is probably even worse in small selling lines than the management accounting figures depict. The process of allocating fixed overheads according to the product's share of production facilities, results in the large products shielding the small. This is due to the Gaussian curve factor in human behaviour, which states that only a small proportion of our activities accounts for a large proportion of the results. But the fixed overheads are allocated on a linear machine output or labour utilisation basis, which does not follow the Gaussian curve. This will shield the smaller products.

The smaller products frequently require more price and stock adjustments. Wastage and breakage, often uncosted, usually will be a higher proportion of small product sales than it will of the larger turnover products. Small products often have batch runs, and the machine set up and down time is disproportionately higher. This is seldom costed against them. In all areas of marketing expense, the small product incurs a higher than average proportion—from advertising and sales time, to packaging design costs.

Currently, companies eliminate their weak products in two ways. Either the losses become so conspicuous that it is obvious even to the most entrenched supporter of the product that it must go. There is one certain factor, in this case. The true losses of the product are likely to be very much higher than everyone imagines them to be. The second system is where a financial crisis or persistent decline in sales precipitates the action. It is highly significant that when companies experience a management revolution or a merger, probably the first things to suffer are the small products in the range. They are eliminated very quickly, to enable the others to breathe.

Everyone who wishes to drop existing products finds the world and his corporate army ranged against him. A war of attrition must be waged in the corridors of power over a long period of time by the individual who wants to terminate a product. Contrast this with the way the same man is allowed to behave when he wants to introduce a new product. In the former case he must move slowly and stealthily, carefully examining the politics of the decision and wearing down the opposition. In the latter case he may call a grand meeting. He can invite all the members of management to the great display of the new product idea, complete with all the panoply of packaging and advertising plans, research reports and profit forecasts.

Everyone agrees that dropping products is a good idea, but no one likes doing it. The marketing man finds the production manager against him, using the argument that despite the fact that the product is a small seller, it *is* being worked into the production plan. Any change to this plan, it will be argued, is bound to affect the overall productivity in the short term. Indeed, the dropping of the product may involve re-negotiating labour rates. Consequently the personnel chief may be against it also. Whoever invented the product, or developed it, can be expected to be against the move to drop it. If that person is the company's founder and chief shareholder, then the would-be product eliminator should take care.

The eliminator could normally expect that the financial executives would be on his side using arguments about the utilisation of scarce resources. However, while agreeing in general terms with the spirit of the move, they may deliver one scathing argument which is quite unbeatable and which has defeated many a would-be eliminator in the past, and will do so again. Their argument is: 'Granted that this product does not make as much contribution to our overheads as the average for the entire range, nevertheless it *is* making a contribution, and would you care to explain how that contribution will be replaced on the day this product disappears?'

If the marketing executive has prepared his ground with a nice new product to replace it, on the same day, then the management accountant may argue that he should perhaps put on the new product *and* keep the original for the time being. He is, after all, able to run both, and one extra product in the range will hardly matter.

This argument is almost impossible to defeat by any measurement process. The fact is that by clearing out the low profit items in the range the resources of the organisation will be concentrated on the items which matter. The extra power generated behind these products should more than compensate for the short-term loss of contribution from the eliminated products. But it will be very hard to quantify.

What is needed is a formal product review system operated at least on an annual basis, and in multi-product companies perhaps more frequently. The task of dropping products is too big for one man to take on, unless he is the chief executive. A review committee system was first proposed in 1952[13] and established a system of analysing products only by financial criteria. Financial considerations by themselves are not sufficient for handling complex multi-product decisions.

A small Review Committee should sit in judgement over the product

[13] L. Houfek, 'How to Decide Which Product to Junk'; *Printers Ink*, 1st Aug. 1952, pp. 21–23.

range. The committee should be composed of the key executives whose functions will be most affected by any product elimination. Then they participate in the decisions, and make the calculations, instead of having them imposed. The committee should be charged with dropping a specified number of products from the range. Their task is to identify which products should go, and to calculate the financial effect. In this way the candidate products are flushed out.

Standards should be set for each candidate product. The basic criteria will change from company to company. These could be based on falling sales trends, profit trends, price trends, company substitute products, specialist support required, and so on.[14] Return on capital employed is a difficult calculation to make in most cases, but where possible it should be used.

More practical criteria may relate to market share, or the relevance of the product to the existing range. Its relevance to existing market segments, and its importance to distribution should also be discussed. One of the key questions to be resolved is the significance of the product for existing customers; particularly key customers.

One of the strongest arguments against the dropping of products may be deployed by the sales force. They may claim that the weak product is a 'loss leader' and that they will lose the sales of many other products if it were to be dropped. Examine this case by looking at the customer penetration figure for the product. If it is sold widely amongst a fair spread of customers, particularly to the important ones, then there may be justice in the case. But if, as is often the case, the product has only a few customers taking the bulk of the output, the case fails.

If the product is found to sell as a loss leader, then the management accountants should occasionally charge the profits on the products being 'led' with the losses incurred on this product. This may show that a third product, previously unsupported, could be the most profitable for promotion, since it drags no costly 'tail' with it.

Profit-stripping

Having examined all the candidate products for elimination, and selected a required number—perhaps sufficient in number to balance the range of new items proposed for marketing—then the profit-stripping process can begin.

Once the decision to phase out a product has been taken, then every opportunity must be sought to strip the product of its assets. There have been numerous occasions when this process has been found to be so profitable that the products concerned have not been dropped finally from the range.

Profit-stripping means product degradation. It starts with an analysis

[14] R. S. Alexander, 'The Death and Burial of Sick Products'; *U.S. Jnl. of Marketing*, Vol. 28, April 1964, pp. 1–7.

of those factors which are not central to the product's functional performance. *Figure 38* shows the areas for examination.

Sales. Every aspect of the product in connection with sales cost needs examination. Perhaps it can be taken off the price list and sold only on special order. Salesmen's commission and any special discounts might be eliminated. New customers should not be opened with it, and the samples given out should be reduced.

Advertising and promotion. The product should receive no advertising and promotion support.

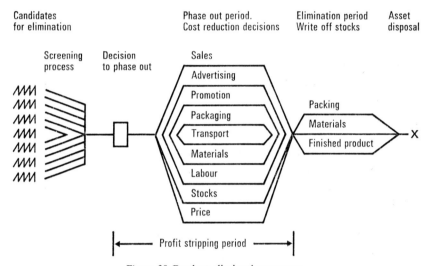

Figure 38 Product elimination process.

Packaging. Here is a marvellous field for profit-stripping. Because packaging decisions on new products are taken by several different departments, few companies are ever aware of the total packaging specifications and cost as a whole.

One company makes a range of powdered soups which were destined to be dropped. An attack on the packaging costs showed that 2 ozs of the powder was contained in a film pouch. This was inserted in a metal foil pack, which was printed in four colours, heat-sealed, and laminated. A dozen of these were packed in a four-colour outer carton, each cut out so as to make a display on the shopkeeper's shelves. These outers were themselves banded together with a paper wrap, then put inside a large cartons, which were then strung together for easy handling on to pallets. They were then loaded on to vehicles for delivery.

The company found its total costs reduced markedly after an attack on its packaging costs, and the product remains on the market today as a very successful seller. The company in fact was selling processed wood in the form of packaging, not powdered soup.

Transport. Costs might be saved in transport and distribution. Perhaps delivery could be made only once per month instead of an 'on call' service; rush supplies could be stopped.

Questions that should be asked include the following:

Materials. Can cheaper materials be used? Are specification tolerances too tight, and can they be relaxed? Can reject standards be loosened?

Labour. Does this product ever drive the company into direct labour overtime? Can it be produced to fill in production gaps, rather than supplied on call to sales?

Stocks. Is it possible for stocks to be reduced by lengthening the delivery lead time? Can fewer sizes and varieties be made to reduce the amount of stock holding? Is it feasible to hold the product at central stores only, instead of in area depots?

Price. Here we come to probably the most significant move of all. The question 'Can the product price be increased. without worrying too much about the effect of competition?' Many a weak product has remained on the market after a substantial price rise, the market being much less price sensitive than management supposed. Indeed, it is not unknown, in markets involving fashion and taste, for a product to increase its sales after the prices have been lifted. This is not the rule; and no one suggests it. However, it is a common enough phenomenon in some markets for it not to be re-markable.

The elimination

Once the final death date is known, then the stock of packing and remainders should be reduced to the minimum.

The cost of finished and part finished products should be very small, and the write-off materials can be minimised. It is possible to save all the write-offs if its withdrawal from the market can be in phased stages, or handled on a region-by-region basis.

When products are not eliminated as a result of a formal procedure, but as a result of a crisis decision, then the write-off costs are often horrific. The costs of disposal of packaging stocks, for example, for a declining sale product can be terrifying. These are assets taken out of the company books. Packaging stocks which were designed to be sufficient for six months' sales can stretch into 18 months' supply, if the product sales decline to one-third of the forecast.

The final stage concerns the disposal of the assets. After a crisis decision, old machinery usually is left idle, with engineers wondering whether to keep it in service to prevent it going rusty. Management is glad to get rid of it at any price. With a planned elimination policy, the preliminary moves for the disposal of the plant can be made a long time in advance. In this way, if a market exists for the machinery, then a better price can be obtained.

Perhaps the prime asset exists in the product itself and in its brand name. Many companies have found products in their range which are weak in relation to their resources but which are highly profitable for other companies to market. Particularly is this true after a merger, when small products are flushed out. Some of these products might be tidied up, put into a fit market position and sold, complete with market. Aspro Nicholas Ltd. did exactly this with the smaller products it inherited from the acquisition of Griffiths Hughes Ltd., in Manchester. They were sold complete to Ashe Laboratories Ltd., who still trade profitably in them.

That is how product elimination can make a great deal of money.

Market Situations

Package Goods: Consumer

These are the companies whose product ranges grow steadily wider. Product development takes its cue from marketing, and is constantly producing a stream of possibilities. These are the companies who suffer most from product clutter, and are in greatest need of a formal product elimination system.

Consumer Durables

There is a greater technical and engineering content with these products, and this often supplies the motivation for development work, particularly on product modifications. Product-clutter may exist amongst small selling items. This is particularly aggravating, since in these companies there may be considerable capital in the form of plant and equipment behind each product, making them difficult to eliminate.

Plant and Equipment

Where development work is undertaken in these companies it is usually a radical move into a completely new market. Development is likely to be a part of the corporate planning process, and operated at Board of Management level.

Components

This is the industrial equivalent of the package goods company in the consumer market. New products are often a constant feature of such companies, but they take their cue from engineering and technical sources, rather than from marketing. Product-clutter exists and can pose a difficult problem because in many of these companies there is no effective substitute product.

The elimination of a single product may mean a withdrawal from a complete market sector, which is a much more serious move.

Materials Supply

The most famous development organisation in the world is Du Pont; which has led entirely new systems of development including Venture Management. Like most material suppliers, Du Pont concentrate on market development, finding new uses for their product. Most materials suppliers, however, find their products less adaptable for development purposes.

Fragmented Markets

Companies in these markets are more likely to copy each other's moves. Their development teams may be quite small, but probably market-oriented. The leaders may search for radical ideas which in the long run may help to lift them out of the general ruck.

Oligopolistic Markets

In these markets, new product development is highly concentrated, and in general these companies are the most skilled. They look for radical ideas, as well as product modification. They are very security conscious; and they are highly skilled at the rapid exploitation of a successful idea.

Concentrated Markets

Companies in these markets often concern themselves with products which will help to stretch their existing markets and to satisfy important segments. They will respond only slowly to new products from outside companies entering their markets. However, they will respond sooner or later, if they find themselves threatened.

Example: The Perils of New-Product Development

'If you make a better mousetrap, the world will beat a path to your door.' All of us have heard this bit of homespun philosophy. But Chester M. Woolworth has probably heard it more than anyone else. Mr. Woolworth is president of the Animal Trade Company of America, of Lititz, Pennsylvania, which makes more mousetraps than any other company.

Beginning in 1928, the Animal Trap Company of America turned out millions of the conventional five cent (now seven cent) mousetraps that have become as familiar as the dustpan. Whenever Mr. Woolworth met business acquaintances at social or business occasions, the conversation frequently produced the familiar question 'How's business?' No matter what Mr. Woolworth responded, he got the inevitable advice, 'Make a better mousetrap, and the world will beat a path to your door.'

So he did, and he has been sorry ever since.[15]

The number of customers that came to his door would never have kept the

[15] Mr. Woolworth told his sad tale in 'So We Made a Better Mousetrap'; *The Presidents' Forum*, Fall, 1962, pp 26–27.

weeds down, let alone beat a path. The better mousetrap became the worst shelf-warmer in the company's history. Although every means of artificial respiration was tried, the 'great new product' gradually expired and had to be removed from the line. Meanwhile the old-fashioned wooden mousetrap went right on selling in the millions, and it still is. What went wrong?

Seemingly nothing could have gone wrong. The Animal Trap Company of America did not embark on its new product rashly. It carefully researched mice habits: eating habits, crawling habits, resting habits, and preferred sizes of holes. After many experimental models, all of which were carefully tested with mice of various shapes and sizes and given to groups of consumers to try out, Mr. Woolworth decided on the mousetrap he would finally offer to the market.

The new trap was a slick-looking little gadget with the appearance of an inverted miniature baby's bathtub with tapered sides and rounded corners. It had a modern, streamlined look and was moulded in black plastic. It had a hole just the right size for the mouse to go in, leaving nothing but perhaps his tail outside. When he nibbled on the easily installed bait, a spring would snap smoothly upward and catch him neatly by the throat, causing almost instant death by strangulation. It then remained only for somebody to press the spring from the top, and the mouse would easily drop out.

The new trap worked like a charm. It never missed. It was clean, noiseless, sanitary, and relatively cheap (12 cents). It was modern. It was simple and safe to operate. A cross section of consumers who pre-tested it said it was splendid. For the first time in his life Mr. Woolworth looked forward to hearing that tired old advice about making a better mousetrap. This time he would not only have an answer, but the profits to prove it.

When the new trap turned out to be a colossal flop, Mr. Woolworth became curious about the source and authority of the ancient advice he had so enthusiastically taken. The adage was attributed to Ralph Waldo Emerson, but nowhere in his works was it to be found. The nearest thing to it was this: 'I trust a good deal to common fame, as we all must. If a man has good corn, or wood, or boards, or pigs, to sell or can make better chairs or knives, crucibles or church organs, than anybody else, you will find a broad hard-beaten road to his house, though it be in the woods.'

Even Emerson's editors, E. W. Emerson and W. E. Forbes, gave up on the mousetrap reference. They couldn't find it. They said only, 'There has been much enquiry in the newspapers recently as to whether Mr. Emerson wrote a sentence very like the above [referring to mousetraps] which has been attributed to him in print. The Editors do not find the latter in his works, but there can be little doubt that it was a memory quotation by some hearer, or, quite probably, correctly reported from one of his lectures, the same image in different words.'

Mr. Woolworth then produced his own eminently quotable quote: 'Fortunately Mr. Emerson made his living as a philosopher, not as a company president.' In short, as a great transcendentalist Emerson did not know much about marketing, which was the subject he chose to comment on in the quotation so loosely attributed to him.

Why was the better mousetrap such a tremendous commercial failure? In spite of the fact that it seemed so perfect and that consumers had liked it so much in the testing stage, subsequent research showed where the advice of Emerson and Mr. Woolworth's friends had gone wrong.

It was learned, first of all, that these days most mousetraps are bought by urban dwellers who have only an occasional mouse or two in the house. The traps are generally bought by the husband. But because of the presence of children who might be injured by playing with a set trap, and because mice tend to roam only when people are not present, the traps are generally set before retiring for the night. Because a trap is a mechanical gadget about which women are supposed to know very little, because men are the traditional 'hunters' in society, and because women are more afraid of injuring their hands on a spring-set trap, the man of the house generally sets it.

If a mouse is caught, there is an eagerness to dispose of it quickly the next morning. But the typical household has a problem in the morning. There is an urgent rush to get the husband off to work on time and the children off to school. The husband seems never to have time to empty the trap he set so carefully the night before. And since the wife doesn't like to have a dead mouse around all day, it falls to her to remove it right after the morning rush subsides.

But she's afraid of both the spring and the mouse, even a dead mouse. Since the mouse that's been caught is probably the only one in the house anyhow, and since the conventional trap costs so little, she doesn't try to remove the mouse. She throws both the trap and the mouse into a paper bag and then into the trash barrel. Quick as a wink the problem is solved.

But the housewives would not do this with the new trap. Even though it cost only 12 cents, it *looked* much too expensive to throw away. Hence it had to be emptied, and that got her entirely too close to and involved with the mouse. Then the trap had to be cleaned. And then stored. Just storing it was unpleasant because every time she saw it on the shelf, it reminded her of the possible awful presence of another crawling and perhaps diseased intruder.

Thus, while husbands bought the new 'better mousetrap' their wives either would not let them use it or would not let them buy it a second time.

Perhaps Mr. Emerson's presumed advice was sound in the days when the mouse was a common and constant household pest, when men did not have to rush off in the mornings to catch a train for work or buck the rush-hour traffic, or when women lived a hardy bucolic existence and mice did not frighten them so much. But by the 1950's, when Emerson's advice was taken, the times, conditions, and people had changed. The result was red ink for the Animal Trap Company of America in spite of seemingly careful product research, in spite of product pre-testing with customers, and in spite of an obviously better mousetrap.

What went wrong becomes painfully obvious. The product was indeed better, but not by the standards, problems, needs and living habits of the urban household in the middle of the twentieth century. The better mousetrap was a commercial flop because, in spite of great care, an incomplete marketing job was done. The company had researched the mouse. It had designed a seemingly perfect trap. It had pre-tested various models with consumers. Everybody agreed that the product was just splendid, and people said they would buy it. But they did not buy it. In retrospect an important reason was that the conditions under which people actually *used* the product involved standards and problems entirely different from those in the pre-tests.

12. Pricing Strategy and Tactics

Seven out of ten company directors in British industrial companies claim that price is amongst the most important factors in their purchasing considerations. Yet two out of ten of them would not change their best supplier for a price change of less than 10 per cent, even though the reduced price product might be identical.[1]

Two hundred of the most successful companies supplying consumer and industrial markets were surveyed to find out what were the key policies and practices which made them successful. One-half of them did not list pricing policy as one of the five key factors.[2] Eight out of ten of them gave answers in the area of product development and research.

The non-price factors in purchasing behaviour are steadily becoming more prominent as consumers slowly become wealthier. Yet in today's economy, supply and production capacity generally exceeds demand. This causes sellers to be completely competitive in their pricing strategy.

The most successful companies find that the only way to freedom in pricing is through product differentiation; hence the suggestion in the study that product development was the most important competitive factor. The company with a successful product variation on its hands finds its pricing strategy relatively easy.

Economists now are finding more difficulty with pricing theory than did their forebears. When the economy was dominated by the suppliers, products were closer to raw material formulation and the key differentiating factor was price. However, in a demand-oriented economy, purchasing behaviour shows signs of irrationality. There is a larger gap than ever between the price theories of the economists and the practical realities of business pricing.[3] Economic models of pricing behaviour normally assume 'perfect' knowledge and 'rational' behaviour on the part of sellers and buyers. Much of this book is devoted to the idea of developing product advantages and marketing

[1] Industrial Market Research Ltd., *How Industry Buys;* Institute of Marketing, 1967 pp. 90–91.
[2] J. Udell, 'How Important is Pricing in Competitive Strategy?'; *U.S. Jnl. of Marketing,* Vol. 28, Jan. 1964, pp. 44–48.
[3] D. S. Leighton, 'Competitive Pricing Strategy—A Behavioural Approach'; Bradford University Seminar, New Developments in Pricing Strategy, 18–19 Jan. 1967.

methods in such a way as will appeal to the emotions as much as to the intellect. Consequently, every time a marketing man succeeds in this, and he succeeds often, he is upsetting the traditional notion of price being the simple product of the supply/demand relationship.

Every market can be described as being 'onion shaped'. Each market has a high-price sector at the top, a competitive middle, and a low-price sector. The degree to which the top range of prices differs from the bottom range is largely dependent upon the degree of product differentiation which exists in the market. Narrow, undifferentiated products, say those in materials supply, will have a very narrow band of distinction between the high-price

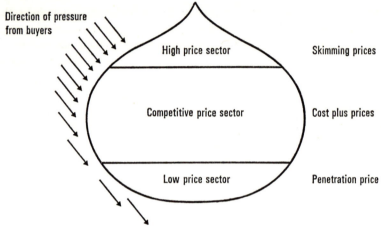

Figure 39 The onion-shaped market.

and the low-price suppliers. It is these markets which are most sensitive to modest changes in price.

Companies operating in differentiated product fields have more freedom on price. Indeed executives in these companies often believe that their markets are more price-sensitive than is the case. This is because the nature of the selling/buying situation is such that even where the buyer is motivated by the non-price factors, he will still attempt to negotiate the price from the platform at which the supplier sets it. Even when a purchasing officer has taken a buying decision, he will still attempt to get the price down; so the debate with the salesman turns on the issue of price. That factor deceives many companies into believing that price is more important than it really is.

Having a high price lends credibility to a selling story about high quality. From a high-price platform, if an excuse to offer a small reduction can be found, the buyer may feel satisfied at his 'bargain'. In contrast, the prices of the cut-price operator are never low enough for the buyer, and the company must fight for its arguments about product quality against a general background of suspicion.

Industrial markets commonly are subject to a feature known as 'derived demand'. The demand for capital goods, for example, is wholly derived from the goods they produce, whether consumer or industrial. Wilson has noted in his 'Assessment of Industrial Markets'[4] that derived demand in general has less price elasticity than direct demand, always assuming the existence of substitutes. This implies that industrial goods manufacturers as a whole are rarely able to expand their total demand substantially through price reductions.

Pricing strategies

A rich variety of pricing strategies are practised, but one authority, Dan Nimer, has found that 80 per cent of companies use only one technique, cost-plus.[5]

Cost-plus. Using this method, the figure for direct costs of materials and labour are added to an allocation of fixed costs and profits through a mark-up system. Nimer describes this as an archaic practice, for four reasons.[6] First, it stresses the cost of production, which is irrelevant to the purchaser, and which can set only the minimum price which is acceptable to the company. Secondly, it leads to incorrect profit projections. Price has an effect on demand; in turn this reacts upon sales turnover and profit. Also, as marketing costs become ever higher as a proportion of the total product cost, then the cost-plus system moves further away from 'cost' and ever deeper into 'plus'. The cost is usually quantifiable; the plus is an estimate. Thirdly, it seldom indicates what the buyer is willing to pay; nor does it reflect market segmentation—particularly price segmentation. Fourthly, it handicaps new product ventures when used by companies who insist on the recovery of the research and development costs within the product price.

However, in material-intensive industries, particularly those having a multi-product range, say, in wholesaling and retailing, it is difficult to suggest any other reasonable form of pricing technique. Where the gross profit margin is 30 per cent or more, then the system should be used only to set minimum acceptable price levels.

Penetration pricing. This is the technique of moving into markets at very low prices in order to buy market share and a large volume of turnover. To succeed, the company must take sales away from competitors or must significantly increase the total size of the market by its move.[7] The dangers involved in not achieving the required volume are obvious. The alternative strategy of moving prices up is seldom available to the cut-price operator

[4] A. Wilson, *The Assessment of Industrial Markets*; Hutchinson, London, 1968, p. 4.
[5] D. Nimer, 'Does Your Pricing Pay?'; *Marketing*, April 1970, pp. 24–27.
[6] D. Nimer, 'Advanced Techniques for More Profitable Pricing'; Incomtec seminar, London, Jan. 1966.
[7] R. Lynn, 'Unit Volume as a Goal for Pricing'; *U.S. Jnl. of Marketing*, Vol. 32, Oct. 1968, pp. 34–39.

because psychological pressures relating to the suspicion about the supplier's quality standards exert themselves on buyers.

The technique can be successful given three provisos. First, the market must be demonstrably price-sensitive. Secondly, the price advantage against competitors must be significant—usually in the order of 10 per cent or more. Thirdly, it is critical that the supplier has some technical or material advantage which allows him a gross profit margin equal to the rest of the industry despite his lower price. If the supplier is price cutting simply because his competition is 'soft' on price, or collusive, then they will copy him immediately and his advantage will be lost. In penetration pricing it is important that competitors find it difficult to copy the reduction.

Skimming price. This is the reverse technique to penetration pricing, where the top price bracket of the market is skimmed off. This is a favourable strategic platform from which to trade. Companies using it recognise that they will not capture the bulk of the market. However, their arguments about high product quality are respected, and they find it easier to counter competitors' price moves. Their high gross margins give them profit protection and a hedge against material cost increases. To sustain their high price, they require a distinctive product or service advantage over the competition.

Target pricing. This technique is used in corporate planning to establish pricing policies, particularly for capital-intensive companies. A required rate of return on the investment is specified, and converted into a trading profit objective. The likely sales volume is estimated, and standard costs based on this estimate are calculated. The profit objective, when added to the standard costs, yields the 'target' price per unit. The flaw is that price is a factor which influences sales volume, and this system ignores it. However, in product differentiated markets and capital-intensive companies, the technique when applied as a long-term policy has its merits. (*Figure 40.*)

Plateau pricing. In price-sensitive markets where costs and prices fluctuate wildly, sometimes prices can be set to stabilise the market. With this technique the rises and falls in the market are borne from net profit returns, rather than flowing through to price changes. This is one of the systems used to stop a price war; perhaps the most difficult exercise in the external marketing operation; for a small company an impossible exercise, however desirable. Its lack of market power leaves it unable to influence industry prices as a whole.

Diversionary pricing. This is where the prices are set in such a way that the true nature of the price to the customer is disguised. For example, ice cream companies supply refrigerators to retail shops at a peppercorn rent. This is sufficient only to ensure that a legal contract exists. In return the retailers agree to stock the cabinet only with the company brand. The higher gross margins earned on the branded ice cream are sufficient to pay for the

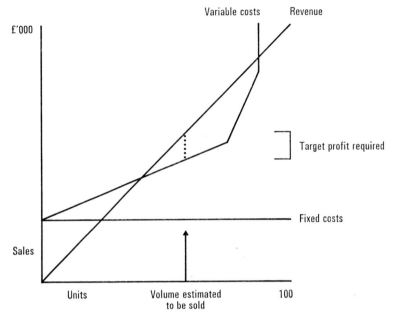

Divide sales revenue by units to arrive at unit price
.which yields the target profit.

Figure 40 Target pricing technique.

refrigerator. The same type of deal operates in the supply of electrostatic copying. The supplying companies agree to provide copying machines at very low rates against a guaranteed order for copy paper. In selling new cars, most of the prices are standard from all dealers. But each dealer will vary the allowance for any trade-in car taken in part exchange. The market looks stable in pricing terms; but the offers vary widely from one dealer to another and are disguised with the trade-in terms.

Prestige pricing. Companies sometimes seek to carve out an exclusive corner of the market and demonstrate their specialisation through very high pricing techniques. This is a useful technique in markets affected by fashion or taste considerations. It has been found that the normal price/demand curve can actually be reversed in some product fields; that is, sales of some products have been found actually to increase when prices are raised.[8] The social importance of the brand, the perceived quality differences, and the fear of making a wrong choice, all affect positively the buyer's willingness to pay more. In the consumer product fields surveyed, portable stereos and tape recorders headed the list of products with reverse demand curves.

Promotional pricing. As a modified form of penetration pricing this is frequently used when the product sales fall off and the management judge-

[8] Z. Lambert, 'Product Perception: an Important Variable in Price Strategy'; *U.S. Jnl. of Marketing;* Vol. 34, October 1970, pp. 68–76.

ment is that price is the inhibiting factor. The price is set at a standard which does not fully recover all the overheads at the original turnover level. This is done in the hope that extra sales volume will be gained and that this will fully recover costs and produce profits. It is, as is clear, a pricing policy with dangers attached. It may be useful to price some items this way. These products then act as 'loss leaders' to the rest of the range, gaining entry to buyers and trailing higher price products in their wake.

Discount promotion pricing.   This technique is used where discounts play an important part in buying decisions. The technique is to set the list prices just above the market level, but provide higher discounts for buyers. In this way, a quality appeal becomes credible and buyers have the personal satisfaction of obtaining apparently high discounts. The technique has an additional advantage in that discounts need not be published in advance, but can be negotiated from buyer to buyer. Some buyers will not negotiate the full discount available to them, and the company thereby achieves a higher than average net price on those sales.

Competitive pricing.   In this situation, a price leader exists in the market, and most competitors set their prices in relation to his—either above, below, or at the same level. In markets characterised by little product differentiation and those which are highly fragmented, this tends to be the popular technique. In such markets the profit performance is usually a function of the production efficiency of the firm.

Bid pricing.   This is familiar in jobbing firms and in those supplying plant or materials. Bid pricing techniques are all competition-oriented and judged against the firm's capacity and need for the order. This is the prime example of setting prices based upon the expectation of competitors' prices, rather than having a rigid relationship with the company's own cost and demand. (*Figure 41.*)

Alternative bid levels	Company Profit	Probability estimates of winning contract	Profit factor
£9,000	£450	·9	405
£10,000	£950	·7	665
£10,500	£1,200	·4	480
£11,000	£1,450	·2	290

Figure 41 Probability technique for contact pricing. The main problem of evaluating bid prices is estimating the probabilities. This technique forces the consideration of alternative price levels and evaluates the profit which would accrue at different levels.

A probability technique may be used for setting bid prices. The probabilities are based upon subjective judgement matched with experience of the outcome of previous bids.

Product analysis pricing.   This is a British technique[9] and has been devel-

[9] L. Simons, 'Product Analysis Pricing'; Bradford University Seminar, 18–19 Jan. 1967.

oped for jobbing companies in batch production making custom-built non-standard products, and for tendering. It is particularly useful in complex production situations where pricing decisions must be delegated to middle and lower management continuously. It is a system where the pricing policy can be followed by line managers, and yet is flexible enough to take into account factors such as demand, market share requirements, and product features. The technique is built upon ascribing values to the product features —material value, added value, and product values as perceived by the buyer.

Price changes

Over the life of a product there are certain to be a series of price changes— more often than not these will be upwards. Apart from the size of the price change itself, sales can be affected markedly by two other factors, both behavioural in origin. One is the history of the company's performance in relation to price changes in general; the other relates to the actual handling of the price change.

Nimer[10], the American authority, has noted the difference between a period of 'high prices' and a period of 'rising prices'. When prices are regarded as high, customers tend to hold off buying in the expectation that they will reduce. But when prices are rising, customers tend to buy more in the expectation that if they defer the purchase they will have to pay more. Rising prices tend to pull demand from the future to the present.

Equally, falling prices can defer demand—on the grounds that buyers may wait until the prices have dropped further. Consequently a dominant company, planning to increase its prices, can announce the fact in advance and be sure that immediate demand will step up at the present prices. A small supplier has not the same option, since buyers are more easily able to switch to a different supplier.

At a time when the forecasts show that costs will continuously escalate, calling for several future price increases within the industry, the problem is whether to take one large increase or several smaller ones. It is a problem for the leaders of the market, rather than for an individual manufacturer who must probably follow his competitors. The answer will depend upon two factors. The first is the judgement of the likely point at which customers will switch to cheaper substitute products if the price rise is too steep; the second is the judgement of how far inflation will also be felt by the manufacturers of these substitute products. It may also be a long and complicated process to administer a price change, so that a series of small price changes may not be practical.

In general it is better to go for a number of smaller but significant price increases spread over time. But whatever alternative is chosen it is critical to make the move early, rather than leave the price increase to lag behind

[10] D. Nimer, 'Advanced Techniques for More Profitable Pricing'; Incomtec Seminar, London, Jan. 1966.

the inflationary costs. Companies can wait for years of ever-diminishing margins, with the price problem constantly getting worse, simply lacking courage to make the move. Industry abounds with stories of companies being forced into making large price increases in fear of their markets, and finding to their surprise that their unit sales continue with hardly a dip. At the same time there are examples of massive inflation within an industry forcing customers to switch to substitute cheaper products. In 1967, the market for catering meat products in the U.K. dropped by over 15 per cent in unit sales, as manufacturers were forced to pass on massive increases in meat prices. Within 18 months it was back at its original level. Unless there is some distinct technological change within a market, it is common to find inflation affecting most suppliers within a product field and its related substitute products to the same degree, but not, perhaps, at the same time,

Price leaders in the market are usually the first to move their prices up or down—often this is how they attain their position of leadership. On raising a price, they suffer from competitors selling against them in the short-term, although competitors are usually pleased to follow the move ultimately. To retain their leadership of the market they should not spring a nasty surprise on the competition by reducing prices quickly and without warning. If they do, they will lose the respect of their competition, which may then refuse to follow subsequent upwards price moves, and hence they will lose control and the advantage of being able to dictate the ruling price. Some markets are extremely fractious and behave wildly: such markets have poor leaders, or are fragmented.

When an individual company makes a price change it is important to minimise the hostility which will be generated within customer groups. Particularly is this so if the price change reverberates further into the distributive chain. Practices vary considerably, but the companies which allow ample notice to their customers, and give a full explanation of the reason for the change, seem to get price rises through more easily. Companies can also reduce possible enmity by providing their key customers with a moratorium on the price change for a specified time, or soften the effect with a special promotion scheme. They can bring out a cheaper, smaller, version of the product; or find some products in their range to reduce in price at the same time as raising the prices on their main items.

Companies will get their price increases through more easily if they make their changes at the same time as competition. It should not be done before, because they will be too exposed, nor later, because they will reap little short-term benefit; some customers will believe that they have moved prices twice.

When making price reductions, companies will reap greater advantage if they do so at a time when the rest of the trade is stable; and if they make a great deal of noise about the move.

The testing of price changes is a contentious subject, one on which managements expect market research to be able to provide adequate answers to the question, what will happen to sales if the price goes up or down by specified amounts? Unfortunately, it is the one subject that baffles market researchers.

There are, in fact, three problems in pre-testing price moves. The first is that we have nothing to actually 'measure'. The market demand, the competition and distribution factors, are altering continuously, in ways which are not known accurately to a company. As soon as a set of price/demand relationships is established it will probably be out of date. Secondly, price may be an independent variable to the company, but sales are dependent upon the outcome of many factors. It is not only price which affects sales. Any measure of the relationship of the two based on the history of market behaviour is certain to confuse causes and effects. Thirdly, management really wants to know what is going to happen tomorrow. Previous responses to price changes are only useful insofar as they can be expected to recur. They usually cannot be relied upon to any great degree.

The typical market research approach would be to carry out an attitude study to see what people think they would do if the price changed. Alternatively, the company might carry out a market experiment by actually changing the price in a part of the market, and measuring the result.

The first type of study is nearly useless as a predictor of buying intentions when used by itself. People have a nasty habit of saying they are about to do one thing, like voting for a politician, then changing their minds and voting for another. The second test actually assumes away the bulk of the problem. This is apart from the operational difficulties of setting up a special price in one area which will not drive buyers to the cheapest alternative source. The price change question is not about this price compared to that price; but is concerned more with the general levels of likely response to a range of different prices. Here, managements are really seeking to establish a demand curve.

Operational researchers may supply some solutions.[11] They may collect all the available data on what had happened to sales in the past at varying prices, and varying levels of competition. They should extract from these some relationship between prices and sales. Given the finding of a reliable relationship, the Operations Research man would then test his findings and validate his model by comparing the results with previous market behaviour. He would, if possible, run a market test.

There is never enough reliable evidence available. Of, if there is, it would probably take too long for the work to be done, by which time management will have made its decision and moved on. Gabor's work on pricing is closely related to the establishment of buy-response curves.[12] However, management usually end up with a series of break-even charts, and takes the plunge, willy-nilly.

[11] J. Davis, *Operational Research and Marketing*; J. Walter Thompson, booklet No. 21.
[12] A. Gabor, C. Granger, 'Foundations of Market Oriented Pricing: the Attitude of the Consumer to Prices'; University of Bradford, Pricing Strategy Seminar, 18–19 Jan. 1967.

Different Market Situations

Package Goods: Consumer

The problem for these companies is that many of their products have an inter-related demand response. Many of the items in a multi-product range company will be either substitutes or complements. A change of price on one will therefore interact on the related items. The common pricing technique is to use cost-plus, or competitive pricing. Discounts are often used by these companies for bulk order, or for overall customer turnover—but the objectives for discount practices are often unclear. Companies believe them to have a promotional effect in forcing larger orders; but the distributive trade has little freedom to alter their purchasing levels unless there is an attempt by the supplier to move the product out into the end market. Consequently the standard discounts are just taken as a matter of course. Such distributors usually negotiate for promotional discounts to be made available in addition to assist them in promotion of the product.

Many package goods companies use a form of discriminating price technique. This is where two brands of essentially the same product are produced and sold under different brand names at different price levels. Usually these brands move through different channels of trade—one going through wholesale channels perhaps; another via private label, direct to retailer groups, and so on. Companies operating in high price sectors and in distinct market segments have more freedom in price moves. Brand leaders usually are price leaders also, and have the responsibility for the equable running of the industry price levels.

Consumer Durables

Because these companies operate in distinct market categories, usually with differentiated products, they have more freedom in pricing movements. Companies in these markets frequently use a form of attitude research which attempts to indicate the degree of price/demand elasticity in their markets. For example, A.G.B. Ltd., in their Home Audit panel, continuously ask respondents whether they would be prepared to buy a colour television set at different levels of rental cost. The changes in attitude from one period to the next gives them an indication of how 'soft' the immediate market is, and this helps them to build an industry market forecast.[13] Various research studies have been published,[14] about the influence of price in these markets. Most of them have resulted in a low correlation between minor shifts in

---

[13] Audits of Great Britain Ltd., 'Colour Television Looks Rosy'; *Audit Magazine*, July 1971, pp. 2–4.
[14] D. Miln and N. Topping, 'An Application of Market Research to Price and Price Elasticity'; Market Research Society Conference Papers, 1971, pp. 79–91.

price and market demand. The influence of distributor margins is very considerable in the price which the end-user pays.[15]

Pricing techniques in these markets are often geared to a form of target pricing in an attempt to achieve an adequate return on investment. Prestige pricing techniques are used in selected market segments, and competitive pricing techniques are used where markets are fragmented. Any form of penetration price is thoroughly distrusted in this type of industry.

Plant and Equipment

Prices are developed, usually on the basis of cost plus, with an additional charge for modifications or installation, plus a servicing charge. There are so many cost and profit centres in these businesses that a standard procedure is hard to determine. In these companies cost accountants are predominant.

Most contracts are negotiated, with the various factors such as level of service and of product quality discussed together with price. The market oriented price technique is for the supplier to start with a complete product and service specification at a high price. Having established this in the buyer's mind, he then chips away at the specification until he reaches a price which is acceptable to the buyer.

The inquiry/bid system works to the narrowest margin when both buyer and seller are equally expert in deciding the specification. However, since the price must be set to cover a long delivery lead time and servicing agreement, then the element of cost forecasting, handled by the seller, makes fixed price offers hazardous. This is particularly true when there is severe competition for the contract. In times of rapid inflation, fixed price agreements for customer-built products tend to give way to escalation clauses. These work well provided that all suppliers insist on them. But the industrial buyer must judge whether the bargain he drives might not be too difficult for the supplier to deliver. If the supplier faces a substantial loss, then there will be a tendency by him to stretch the specifications, or perhaps a move to frustrate the contract altogether.

Components

These companies closely approximate the consumer durable manufacturers in their pricing strategies. Target pricing is the most popular technique. The supplier may attempt to achieve a high price level through the development of substantial service benefits. Demand elasticities are not usually very high, particularly with one-off purchases, or speciality products. Pricing techniques based upon incremental costs are common to move short-term volume and to utilise plant and labour.[16]

[15] J. Abrams, 'A New Method for Testing Pricing Decisions'; *U.S. Jnl. of Marketing*, Vol. 28, July 1964, pp. 6–9.
[16] T. Wentz, 'Realism in Pricing Analyses'; *U.S. Jnl. of Marketing*, Vol. 30, April 1966, pp. 19–26.

Materials

In supplying materials, contractual relations become more prominent. A cost plus pricing technique, based upon forecasted world prices for the materials, is frequently used. Contracts usually specify the time periods as well as the volume to be taken at the price, and fixed dates for price reviews are common. Here economic analysis and forecasting rule most of the considerations. Supply/demand curves, and elasticity ratios are constantly evolved to guide pricing decisions. Techniques for short-range and long-range forecasting commonly use econometric models.[17]

Commodity companies are quick to raise prices when competitive prices rise, but they are slow to reduce prices when costs fall.

Differentiated Products

The more differentiated the product field, the wider the span of prices offered. These markets tend to be less price-sensitive than most, particularly at the start of the product life cycle. Repeat purchases are generally more price-sensitive than first-time sampling. Any obvious risks of product failure will cause higher sales volume at higher prices, reversing the demand curve. The market may, therefore, move against the lowest priced products. It is very difficult for a manufacturer whose reputation is based upon the supply of low-price products to attempt to price up in these markets. A radical product innovation is usually required; and in quality-sensitive markets even this may be rejected for the supplier of low price varieties.

Undifferentiated Products

This is where the price wars most commonly break out. Wherever products have only narrow distinctions between them; wherever they are low-priority purchases of little importance to the buyer; wherever the products are widely known and have already been sampled by most buyers—then the prices are always set close to the minimum acceptable margin to the supplier. Companies search for product distinctions and specialised market sectors simply in order to provide themselves with some freedom in their pricing decisions.

Simulation techniques are being used to test price/volume relationships in some of these markets.[18] Price wars are a danger, since the marginal producer who finds his sales threatened knows that the market will respond to price reductions and may choose to risk everything by dropping his price. Unless he can sustain the reduction in his capital reserves, or by technological advantage, this will simply cause competitors to respond as closely as they dare. Once a price war breaks out, it is almost impossible for anyone, except the market leader, or a few leading companies acting in collusion, to stop it.

---

[17] T. Frey, 'Forecasting Prices for Industrial Commodity Markets'; *U.S. Jnl. of Marketing*; Vol. 34, April 1970, pp. 28–32.
[18] R. Stout, 'Developing Data to Estimate Price-Quantity Relationships'; *U.S. Jnl. of Marketing*, Vol. 33, April 1969, pp. 34–36.

Price wars lead to product degradation; and force markets to the point of saturation and decline more quickly. They inhibit technical innovation because the companies have no reserves for research and development. advertising programmes may suffer and promotion budgets are often spent in market forcing techniques.

Custom-built Products

These will have similar attitudes to the companies who supply plant and equipment. Here the technique of Product Analysis Pricing (*see page* 176) is most useful as a rational method of integrating the various cost and demand factors into a single pricing system which can be applied by a pricing department at middle management level.

Fragmented Markets

The leaders will lead and the minor brands will follow. A series of price levels usually operate in these markets. There is a tendency for prices to cluster together in small bands, each one in a price-sensitive sector probably relating to a market segment. Competitive pricing, promotional pricing, and discount promotion pricing techniques are common. This is due to the suppliers' heavy dependency upon the distributive trades.

Oligopolistic Markets

Economists and social commentators are much concerned about the phenomenon of 'parallel behaviour' which usually characterises these markets. When one company moves, they all seem to move. Companies in these markets often have stringent policies towards their customers in, say, the supply of credit. Such companies are seen to be large spenders on advertising; very heavy spenders on sales promotion. All this provides an uneasy suspicion in the mind of the community that they are using their undoubted power in the market to maintain an artificially high-price platform.

Oligopolists create stable markets; of which a continuing and stable price is evidence. They have well defined social structures between the businesses, each with substantial knowledge of the other. The competitors have shared values and common interests, and each respects the others' ability in at least some aspect of the industry activity.[19] They can collude, if they want to; but in doing so they know that the eyes of the world, and of the government's monopoly courts, are upon them.

There is no reason for them to have an explicit agreement on such matters; they know each other too well, they can predict the moves easily. The behaviour patterns in oligopolistic markets are consistent even though the markets, companies, and technologies are widely different. They all prefer to compete from a high-price platform, using the barriers of heavy capital

[19] D. S. Leighton, 'Competitive Pricing Strategy—A Behavioural Approach'; Bradford University Seminar, New Developments in Pricing Strategy, 18–19 Jan. 1967.

investment, heavy research and development, and heavy advertising to keep out competition. A study of the role of the price leader in such markets shows that no single company has the power to enforce monopoly prices. External competitive pressures from substitute goods, such as private label trading, and second brand trading, tend to keep price ceilings down.[20]

Concentrated Markets

Companies which have a dominant or monopoly position in their markets feel exposed when prices must be raised. Owing to their dominance, they experience the full backlash from the trade, users, public opinion and from governments, when they make price rise decisions. A degree of sensitivity to this keeps their prices down, but when costs rise and profits drop they will then use their full levering power on price levels to maintain their profitability. As has been said, 'Monopoly by itself is neither good nor bad; but it has the power to be either.'[21]

Mass Distribution

Companies operating in mass markets find their pricing decisions complex, since the effect of price changes on their distributors and, ultimately, on the end-users, must be calculated. The interaction between company selling prices, wholesale margins, retail margins, and retail prices, added to bulk and promotional discount practices is extremely complex.

Oligopsony and Monopsony

The more the company moves into a sole supply situation, the weaker becomes its price negotiating position. In a monopsonistic situation, the buyer holds the entire power. Some buyers will push the supplier down to the lowest level at which the company can operate and continue to survive. Other buyers may allow more freedom in pricing, but demand in return that certain standards of quality and performance are maintained. This happens occasionally with extremely large buyers who exercise a strong degree of control over the suppliers' specifications. With intractable buyers, in opsonistic markets, the suppliers may be forced to collude over price, in order to survive.

Example: Product Pricing

Background

Yale Security Products is the successful British division of Eaton Corporation (U.S.A.). The company's name has always been synonymous with security since the introduction of the original pin-tumbler mechanism by Linus Yale.

[20] R. Knox, 'Competitive Oligopolistic Pricing'; *U.S. Jnl. of Marketing*, Vol. 30, July 1966, pp. 47–51.
[21] H. Wilson, 'Monopolies Debate'; House of Commons, 1948.

They are in a five-year expansion programme which is aimed to satisfy the increasing needs of the market for high-quality aluminium hardware.

Problem

In September 1967, Yale studied the sales of a product which initially looked bound to succeed. The Mercury Nightlatch was a smart-looking lock that incorporated a deadlock device for improved security. Contrary to their predictions, however, the sales performance of the product showed it to be lagging significantly behind the estimated sales level. Yale's problem was how to improve the turnover and profitability of this product.

Solution

The solution involved a relaunch of the product together with a technical improvement, improved packaging and, mainly, a revision of the price level.

The company wanted the new version of the Mercury to possess significant differences so that it would stand out from the other products in the range.

Technical and Design Improvements

The company knew that a market existed for an *automatic* deadlatch, one that did not require a key to deadlock the bolt. However, although it was an important design change it would give the product the differentiating feature for which Yale was looking. It was decided therefore to incorporate this improvement in the new version.

Furthermore, Yale had sponsored a consumer study concerning the closing and locking of doors, and an idea generated from this was examined by their own design consultant. The end result was an asymmetrically shaped key. This was designed to be distinguishable from other keys and to be easy to determine whether or not it was upside-down.

Packaging and Promotion

Hardware is often found in rather drab packs, and this was the case with the original Mercury Lock. It became obvious that an improvement in the packaging of this article was required, together with further advertising, and point-of-sale display material.

The initial idea of a transparent film pack was found not to be feasible. The final choice was a cardboard pack displaying 'Yale' in orange against a green background. It had a window showing the lock that was described as 'Automatic Deadlock'. The technical and selling features, of double locking, concealed fixing, and three keys supplied, were also announced. Finally, the complete package, which supported other messages, was covered by a transparent sleeve.

Pricing

The original Mercury Lock which incorporated the deadlock principle was sold at about £1·44. However, this price was only slightly above that of an ordinary lock; about 5p. The differential was not enough to cause potential customers to reason out why there was a difference in price. The lock was, in fact, underpriced.

The new features in the product, and the promotional campaign, obviously involved substantial expenditure. To cover this, and to clearly establish a price differential, Yale decided upon a new price of £1·85. (In October 1970, a competitive lock with virtually the same function could be purchased for about £1·13.) This put the lock firmly in the upper price bracket. The price comparison with other products (Mercury's price having increased by over 40p) would, it was felt, cause people to question the reason for the new price. Consequently, they would become aware of and, it was hoped, interested in the automatic deadlock selling point.

Result

The initial sales level, for the improved Mercury lock, of six times that of the original version, has now settled to a five times level. This product can now be considered a success, and is highly satisfying to Yale.

P.M.

The Operation Variables

13. Planning for Sales

In this mammoth subject of sales organisation, which is well documented, there are three areas of planning weakness in most companies. The first is the allocation of sales resources to different types of sales and market situations. The second is the development of specific plans to increase the profitability of existing key accounts. The third is the conceptual framework in which the size of sales force and its structure are judged.

In industrial purchasing situations it is not necessarily the purchasing officer alone who the company must influence. The phenomenon of the Decision Making Unit in industry provides a particularly intractable problem for sales. This is where a clutch of three or more individuals from different functions within the business all have a say in the purchasing decision. In one company, over three departments had a say in 80 per cent of the purchasing decisions, while the purchasing officer used his own initiative in only 2·5 per cent of the decisions.[1] In another case the Board had to approve all purchasing decisions valued at over £50.

Inertia is the great weakness of British buying, and some suppliers enjoy enormous profit margins because their customers do not want to take the risk of upsetting the settled routine of things, or to investigate alternative sources of supply. A study of the steel strip industry revealed that almost three-quarters of the companies had relied on the same suppliers for ten years, even though there were over 20 companies capable of supplying the goods. That is as much to the detriment of the competing supply company salesmen as it is to the buyers.

Selling is preoccupied with the seller's need to convert his product into cash.[2] The salesman thinks in terms of deals which he negotiates; the products are useful vehicles to him in this process, but little more.

Personal selling is just a part of the 'total marketing communications' function. However, for most industrial companies it is the focal point where all succeeds, or not. The sales deal turns to some extent on the individual

[1] A. Thorncroft, 'The Forgotten Man of Selling'; *Financial Times,* 5th Aug. 1971.
[2] A. Wilson, 'Marketing—The Great Abstraction'; paper delivered to the British Electrical and Allied Manufacturers 8th Publicity Conference, Nov. 1963.

abilities of the salesman; but the primary influences relate to the adequacy of the product in fulfilling the requirements of the buyer. It is also affected by the degree to which the product or company has been pre-sold by advertising and promotion, and the timing of the offer. Salesmen need far more than their wits to live by.

There are different varieties of selling jobs which require different skills; each company operates two or more of these levels concurrently. Seven varieties of selling task have been identified:[3]

(1) Positions where the salesman's job is primarily to deliver the product, for example, milk, bread, fuel oil. His selling responsibilities are secondary to providing good service with a pleasant manner. Few salesmen of this kind originate many sales.

(2) Positions where the salesman is primarily an inside order-taker. For example, the department store assistant behind the counter finds that most of his customers have already made up their minds to buy. All he does is to serve them. He may use suggestive selling and upgrade the merchandise they buy, but beyond that he has limited opportunities.

(3) Positions where the salesman is also an order-taker but works in the field such as grocery or toiletry merchandisers. As with the delivery salesman he must have a pleasant personality and supply good service but he does little creative selling.

(4) Positions where the salesman is not expected to take an order but is used to build goodwill or to educate the actual, or potential, user. The drug company sales representative calling on doctors fills this role.

(5) Positions where the major emphasis is placed on technical knowledge, for example the engineering salesman, who is primarily a consultant to the 'client' companies.

(6) Positions which demand the creative sale of tangible products such as vacuum cleaners, refrigerators, and encyclopaedias. Here the salesman often has a double task—first he must make the prospect dissatisfied with his or her present appliance, and then begin to sell his product.

(7) Positions requiring the creative sale of intangibles such as insurance, advertising services or education. This type of sale is usually more difficult than selling tangibles because the product is less readily demonstrated and dramatised.

The allocation of resources by market situation

One great flaw in centralising the sales management system is that it leads to superficial thinking that the selling situation is roughly the same everywhere; that one basic sales strategy will be adequate, with occasional modification for local influences. The great flaw with regionalising sales management is that too much account is taken of local influences and varying levels of regional management ability have power over crucial parts of the decision making process. So whatever sales structure is used, the result is always a necessary compromise between the local and national objectives desired and the resources available.

[3] R. McMurry, 'The Mystique of Super Salesmanship'; *Harvard Business Review*, March–April 1961, p. 114.

The sales resources are always scarce when measured against the opportunities available. In setting their objectives, sales planners take the easy way out, by taking their existing resources and determining what can best be achieved with them. If there is a marginal opportunity which can be realised with additional sales resources, then they will argue the case for increasing the sales budget. However, the conceptual planning flaw remains—sales resources determine the objectives, instead of the other way around.

This attitude causes several bad side effects. First, there is a drive towards continuing to do what we are doing now, *in the way we are doing it now*, but, simply, more efficiently. Secondly, it causes sales management to think of their function as being separate from the rest of the marketing communications process, and not inter-related with it. Thirdly, the sales plan and its routine are thought to be internally consistent to sales, rather than to the marketing mix overall.

In allocating sales resources to different market situations the interaction of two most significant factors must be recognised. The first is that a few accounts may be vastly more profitable than the rest, and these are usually the large ones. Heavier concentration is therefore needed upon these. Secondly, in some areas of the country, or in some distinct markets, the company share will be strong, and in others it will be weak. The balance between pioneer calling on new prospects and service calling on existing customers, and the amount and type of promotional support must reflect these factors.

Figure 42 shows four basic market situations. The shaded dots represent the company accounts and the open dots represent those of competitors; large dots represent key accounts.

In *Market 1*, the situation shows that the company has a fair amount of business, but it is within the smaller accounts; competitors have a hold on the key account prospects. In circumstances like this, the local field sales organisation requires specialised help. A specific campaign, stretched over time, is needed on each key account. These accounts will not be opened by increasing the mailing shots, and cold calling. A full speciality selling approach may be required, developed for each account prospect in turn. This may involve the services of a full technical team, and senior management personnel in order to approach such accounts at the appropriate level. In allocating extra resources to this type of problem, the appropriate *type* of sales activity needs to be considered.

In *Market 2*, the company has a dominant share of the available business. It is a more difficult task to defend areas like this than it is to attack them. The emphasis must be laid on retaining the business within the large and profitable accounts. The level of pioneer sales activity can be set at the point at which the smaller accounts may be eroded and lost. New small accounts are needed to replace them.

Defensive selling requires fast and accurate information flowing back to the company. The cues and signals of danger in large accounts usually can

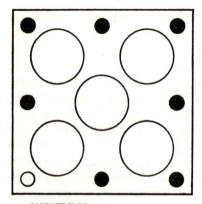

MARKET TYPE

(1) Area dominated by large number of small accounts.

Pioneer approach to selected large accounts needed, using speciality selling techniques.

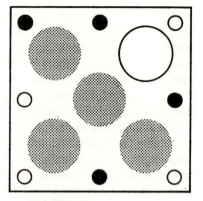

MARKET TYPE

(2) Area dominated by company share of the total market.

Defensive service calling; pioneer to replace lost small accounts; close control needed.

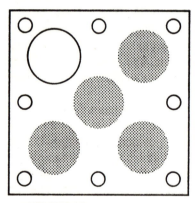

MARKET TYPE

(3) Area dominated by large company accounts.

Normal mix of pioneer and service selling.

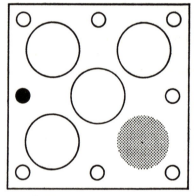

MARKET TYPE

(4) Weak area

Re-launch campaign required.

Figure 42 The mix of pioneer and service selling.

be detected by a salesman who is trained to look for them. The problem in most companies is that they have no adequate management system for listening to, or debriefing, the salesmen.

Selling is a lonely and hostile job. The salesman takes many aggravations in his stride—from his own management as much as from customers and competitors. He has a tendency to report all his problems at length, often with equal emphasis given to the large and the small matters. He needs psychological reassurance as much as physical help. He is expected to overcome most of his problems himself. When detecting signs of competitive activity in key accounts, he must have help from his immediate management automatically. If there is no method of highlighting these key account problems in his feedback system, then management cannot engage. The salesman often feels reluctant to ask for help, regarding it as a reflection on his ability, or he may not recognise the problem as being serious.

The trouble is that by the time the salesman is beginning to detect the trouble, the buyer is likely to be well on the way to making up his mind. A buyer who is reviewing his routine purchasing pattern is disturbed, and he is aware of the full range of terms capable of being offered by the usual field salesman from his normal supplier. He wants something more; perhaps a new price, a revised level of service, or some dissatisfaction put right.

Once a customer has changed his pattern of purchase, then in the short term it is almost impossible to win him back. The psychological barriers are too great, and the buyer is reluctant to admit error. He will want to give his decision a full run and he accepts flaws in the standard of service which he would normally reject from his usual supplier. But the period of his goodwill to the new supplier lasts for a relatively short time. It pays to continue to call on old accounts for a standard sequence of calls, or for a set time. Some of them return.

Defensive selling, where the accent is on fast and accurate feedback of information, is alien to the nature of salesmen and their managers. Their training and instincts lead them to be aggressive and subjective—not sensitive to cues and objective in reporting.

One company manufacturing equipment for laundries resolves this reporting problem by allowing its salesmen to issue a 'Flash Report' whenever a key account is running into trouble. The salesman can only use the system for serious problems, and such a report is delivered to all executive members of the Board, and the request for action carries the authority of the managing director, even though it may be issued by the field salesman or his manager. The technique is a little abrasive upon inter-departmental relationships, but it does save trouble in many key accounts.

In *Market 3*, the company already holds the key accounts in the area and simply needs additional business. In this case it is proper to use the usual technique of increasing the field sales resources. This is done either permanently by adding to the level of pioneer calls required, or temporarily by moving in a team of men for a campaign. The problem should lend itself to relatively easy solutions, since the attack is upon the smaller accounts where competition can be expected to be weaker.

In *Market 4*, the total company situation is weak. There are few key accounts, and little small business. Merely adding to the sales team is unlikely to unseat entrenched competitors, particularly in the key accounts. In these areas, it is best to assume that the market is virgin, that the company has no business already, and to start an attack on the market from scratch. The plans for very weak territories should be similar to launching plans. A full-scale campaign, including the involvement of head office management, the use of technical teams and speciality demonstrations, is required on the key accounts. Full advertising, promotion, and price support is required to back up the efforts of a strong field sales team which concentrate upon pioneer work to develop the area.

Size of Customer

Average monthly purchase	*Total Customers* 100%	*Total Sales* 100%	*Total Profit* 100%
Less than £20	35%	16%	2%
£21–£50	40%	38%	8%
£51–£100	20%	30%	50%
£101 and above	5%	16%	40%

Company with high delivery costs and low bulk discount figures.

Figure 43 Typical customer profit skew analysis. Company with high delivery costs and low bulk discount figures.

There is a theshold effect in allocating sales resources; up to a minimum level of effort the operation is unproductive, but at increasing levels the rates of return become greater. The last stage is reached when the rate of return for every additional unit of expense steadily diminishes.

Strategies for key accounts

Most companies divide their existing accounts into grades of profitability or size. An *A* grade account is a large one, *B, C,* and *D* are relatively smaller and receive less sales support. *Figure 44* describes how resources can be allocated to each size of account. High sales inputs in terms of numbers of calls, or level of management responsibility, are deployed against the larger accounts, in each journey cycle.

One of the ways of economising on sales service for small accounts is to apply a mix of telephone calls with personal sales visits to these accounts. One person can make up to fifty telephone calls each day, compared to less than half this number of personal sales calls—even in tightly packed areas. The industrial salesman may be lucky to make three calls per day, in widely dispersed territories.

Telephone selling need not be done by a girl in the sales office, although this is the standard practice. The salesman can visit a territory and use the flat spots in his day—usually around lunchtime and late afternoon—to telephone small accounts, and check on whether a personal visit is required. The economies flowing from such an operation when carried out on a formal

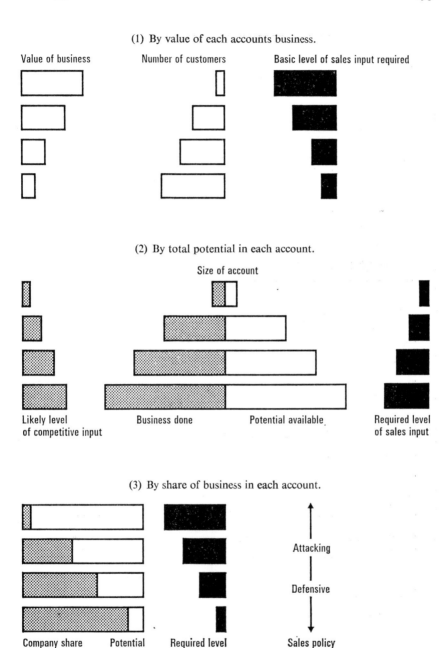

Figure 44 Allocating sales resources to existing accounts.

Targets 1971

PRODUCTS		MARKETS			
		Gin	Whisky	Vodka	Total
	Miniature	700	4,000	500	5,200
	13 oz.	6,000	15,000	500	21,500
	26 oz.	10,000	20,000	500	30,500
	Total	16,700	39,000	1,500	57,300

Action Contacts to be made :

1. Must establish contact with Chief Buyer as he handles vodka line where we have little information. Must also contact Marketing Department to try and establish brand plans. Suspect Company will put strong effort behind vodka, and ease off gin

Call frequency. Need to increase to every four weeks except in pre-Xmas period when every two weeks.

Objectives of call :

1. To identify size of vodka business and future intentions.

2. To stress our technical expertise to combat price competition

3. To increase gin business by indicating better bulk discounts on slightly larger order

4. To increase whisky business by offering stock back-up.

Support required:

1. Agreement to increase whisky stock back-up. Technical staff to vist customer to advise on running bottle line

2. Member of senior management to help contact Chief Buyer

3. Market Research department to supply any information available on vodka market

Figure 45 Customer strategy form, industrial goods example—glass containers.
(*Source:* M. T. Wilson, *Managing the Sales Force*, pp. 40–41, Gower Press, 1971)

CUSTOMER STRATEGY FORM

Salesman   R. McCarthy   **Date**   11 October 1970

Name of customer   XYZ Bottlers Company Limited

Main Street

Newtown,

Telephone Newtown 123

Current contacts   F Smith, assistant Buyer

J Jenkins, works Manager

Product/Market matrix 1970

		MARKETS			Trend	Total
		Gin	Whisky	Vodka		
PRODUCTS	Miniature	1,000 / 600	5,000 / 3,000	? / 500	Increasing because of airline business	6,000 / 4,100 +?
	13 oz.	10,000 / 5,000	20,000 / 12,000	? / 500	Static	30,000 / 17,500 +?
	26 oz.	25,000 / 5,000	50,000 / 18,000	? / 500	Decreasing because of tax and price increases	75,000 +? / 23,500
	Trend	Static	Slightly increasing	New line seems to be increasing		
	Total	36,000 / 10,600	75,000 / 33,000	? / 1,500		

Number of units in grosses

Competitive activity

Competition very strong in 26oz bottles because of price. Also trying to attack our miniature bottle sales

and planned basis have to be experienced to be believed. Many sales managers are firmly set against the use of the telephone for selling, but the business does not exist where some use for the telephone within the sales operation cannot be found. As a method of screening prospects, for locating the decision-influencers, for information gathering about competitors, it is superior, in many cases, to a field sales call.

Few companies grade and number their sales prospects as opposed to existing accounts on a planned basis, except those selling to relatively few customers in opsonistic type markets. The analysis of key account prospects is usually done on a subjective basis, through a formal report from each salesman.

Even fewer companies grade their existing key customers for the amount of potential which remains in their account. Suppliers in opsonistic markets again are the exception. Key accounts need a control system which shows an objective estimate of the potential remaining; and a plan for developing this potential.

The type of sales activity which can be used to develop each key account varies with the share of the business which the company currently holds. If the company's existing share of the total business available in a key account is large, then a defensive policy is required. The emphasis here is on keeping the price high, the discounts low, supplying added value, and a high level of service. If the share of the business is low, then an aggressive policy can be used involving price offers, promotions, competitive comparisons and so on.

Figure 45 is taken from M. Wilson's 'Managing a Sales Force' and shows an example of a customer strategy form for a glass container company.

The organisation of different levels of sales management responsibility for key accounts is also required. The managing director of most companies will have some degree of contact with the main customers of the business; but senior executives are traditionally reluctant to fill in the appropriate forms. Reporting procedures should start at the highest level of sales management responsible for specific accounts. Target sales objectives should be set for each account. The results need to be compared to the objectives, and each key account reviewed periodically. Each level of management should have its clutch of personal accounts to control. In this way, the company is certain that the 20 per cent of the customers which produce 80 per cent of the company profits are being developed individually by the appropriate levels of sales and other management.

Determining the size of the sales organisation

The determination of the correct sales force size appears to be a relatively easy problem which lends itself to tidy measurement. In fact, it is just as uncertain as any other marketing decision involving human behaviour. Kotler has drawn a decision-tree, *Figure 46*, for a particular problem where

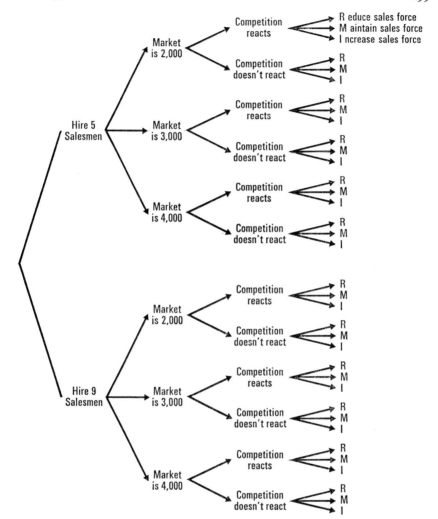

Figure 46 Decision tree for decision problem on size of sales force.
(*Source:* P. Kotler, *Marketing Management, Analysis, Planning and Control*, p. 181, Prentice-Hall, 1967)

a manufacturer is uncertain whether he should increase, retain, or reduce his sales force. The tree shows only two alternatives which have been narrowed down from many; that of hiring five salesmen, or nine salesmen.

Such a manufacturer faces a number of difficulties with this problem. Because he has imperfect market knowledge he must assess the range of potential market response which is attainable from the use of different levels of sales inputs. He must allow for the distribution 'skew' as only a small proportion of the total customer potential will account for a large volume of purchases. The sales cost of reaching each customer prospect is more or less constant. Even though this is recognised, he must allow for competitive reactions, in advertising, promotion and selling, to his tactics. Finally, he should build in some estimate of the gross margins which will result from different product mixes being sold to different customer groupings.

Two companies sell to a market with a gross margin potential of £500,000. One company goes for large volume, an 80 per cent share of the market, and uses 100 salesmen. The other company goes for a 50 per cent share of the market and uses a smaller sales force.

The sales per man in the small force will be very much higher than the sales per man in the large force. The small force will 'cream' the territory, going for the larger and profitable customers. The larger sales force will go for the same customers but must also search more widely for the marginal customers. The small force goes for penetration, while the large force must go for coverage.

The table shows the result based upon each man costing £2,000 and the man in the small sales force pulling $6\frac{1}{4}$ times the rate of the man in the large force.

Number of salesmen	100	10
Gross profit margin earned per man	£4,000	£25,000
Total gross margin sold	£400,000	£250,000
Cost of sales force	£200,000	£20,000
Overhead and profit contribution	£200,000	£230,000
Share of the market	80 per cent	50 per cent

Figure 47 How you could be more profitable with a smaller sales force.

The usual method of determining the size of the sales force required is called the salesman's workload approach. It is built upon the known level of activity which each salesman can undertake on average during a period of time. There is an implicit assumption about the productivity of the salesman's calls.

(1) The existing customers are grouped according to their size or their profitability.
(2) A required level of call frequency on each customer group during the year is judged.
(3) The number of accounts in each group is multiplied by the call frequencies desired; this provides a figure for the total calls on existing customers per year.
(4) The total number of required new accounts in order to (*a*) replace lost accounts, and (*b*) to develop territories, is judged.
(5) The conversion rates of new accounts opened to pioneer calls made is calculated, allowing for recalls. This, multiplied by the number of desired new accounts, provides the total number of required pioneer calls.
(6) The total existing calls figure is added to the total pioneer calls figure, providing a grand total of all sales force calls required during the year.
(7) The average number of calls a salesman can make in a working year is calculated, if necessary, using work study analysis.

(8) The size of the required sales force is determined by dividing the total yearly calls required by the total calls possible, per man.

The trouble with this technique is that it does not allow for customer clustering, and averages can be very misleading when used in a particular territory. It takes no account of potential except in the implicit assumption that the necessary number of new accounts can be achieved with an average level of effort, and that they will yield an average profit. The system does not deal well with the problem of structuring the sales organisation at various levels of management, in order to handle key accounts.

Territory Potential Approach. Provided that an existing sales organisation has a large number of sales areas, and sufficient historical sales data to allow for the projection of reasonable statistical estimates, then a method based upon an estimate of the various levels of productivity accruing from different amounts of sales input might be used.

Salesmen attack territories by creaming the larger accounts first. Salesmen operating in territories with high potential can be expected to produce more sales per man than those operating in areas of low potential. Nevertheless, their higher sales are less than proportionate to the increase in potential. For example, sales in a territory which has 1 per cent of the total national potential might be £100,000. Compare this to, say, a territory containing 5 per cent of the total national potential, where from the same size of sales force the sales can be expected to be higher, perhaps £200,000, but not five times higher.

Using the data from various levels of sales forces input, it may be possible to produce a sales productivity curve via statistical analysis. The method assumes the desirability of creating territories with equal sales potential. It ignores such factors as the mix of accounts in each territory, and their geographical dispersal.

Sales force structure

By territory. This is the traditional method of structuring sales forces. Each salesman handles the full range of company product in a specified area. It works well in companies with a homogeneous set of products and markets where the technical content of each is not high. Salesmen in multi-product companies quickly become order takers; as markets and products become more diversified, so the salesman needs more specialist technical support.

His responsibilities in this structure are clearly defined, however; it is easy to compare the performance of one man with another. The highest cost of all—the time spent in travelling—is reduced to the minimum. The main advantage is the comparability of salesmen, and the low cost, through minimising non-productive time.

Product structured sales forces. This is more common in companies with a diverse and highly technical content to their products; or in very large multi-product companies. One drawback is that salesmen from each product division travel over the same routes. Furthermore if the customers are the same for the diversified product ranges then confusion is caused when two salesmen from one company call independently on the same buyer.

Market structured sales forces. Sales forces can be organised to develop different types of customers, different channels of distribution, different individual customers, or different sizes of account. If the customer groups are clustered, as they often are in industry, then the system works well, because each man is familiar with his customers' type of business, and problems. However, where customers are scattered, there is a wasteful overlapping of teritorries.

All companies, whatever their structure, have different types of sales activity operating concurrently. There may be order takers in the office, salesmen in the field who can draw on technical consultancy for key accounts. Creative sales negotiations may be operated at Board of Management level, where major reciprocal trading deals are settled.

In addition, nearly all companies have a mixed structure of some kind in their sales force, while laying their greatest emphasis on one of the systems described. In the consumer goods company selling to mass markets, there will be an area sales force, plus a small head office negotiating team to handle key accounts. They may be joined by a specialised team to handle cash and carry wholesale business, and perhaps even a development team of young salesmen who are pushed from area to area to handle pioneer work.

Market Situations

Package Goods: Consumer

In these markets, salesmen tend to be less influential than other factors such as the power of advertising. Field salesmen are often of the order-taking variety. The concentration of buying power means that the creative selling task is in the hands of the top speciality salesmen. There is often an emphasis on what is called 'selling-out' rather than 'selling-in'. This means assisting the distributor to sell; sometimes by 'selling-through', that is, actually finding customers for the distributor, and passing the orders back through him. The sales force costs are often high in relation to the value of the goods sold and there is great emphasis on efficient journey planning, and sales cost-effectiveness.

Consumer Durables

There is stronger emphasis on personal selling: particularly on techniques of 'selling-through' distributors. Territories in general are more diverse. The expensive nature of the product puts a premium on creative selling techniques, and a degree of consultancy work is involved, particularly through supplying merchandising help in-store. Sales costs are usually a lower proportion of the total product cost, and stress is laid on finding salesmen with high personal skills.

Plant and Equipment

Salesmen in these fields are consultants and supply a two-way information flow. They are responsible for the education of their customers in the latest technical developments and for reporting back opportunities and developments in the market place to their companies. Seventy-eight per cent of company maintenance engineers claim that visits from salesmen are amongst their two most important sources of information on products.[4] Product knowledge is the key to success in these industries. It has been named as the factor which makes for the most outstanding difference between the best salesmen and the ordinary man in these companies.[5] Much of the selling task is carried on at high company management level. Sales costs are low as a proportion of the business done, and product or market-structured sales forces are common.

Components

These are the companies facing the greatest difficulties with the structuring of their sales forces. Their products are usually complex, the product use is diverse, and the technical content may be high. An element of consultancy work is required. The balance of pioneer selling and existing account service is very difficult to adjust. Because of the problem of buying clusters, with various pockets of industry located in different geographical centres, it is often difficult to provide territories of equal size and potential. This makes comparability between individual salesmen's performance difficult.

Service levels provide difficulty—both after-sales service and maintenance. Often these essential services are run at a net loss, making profitability calculations from different sectors of the market difficult.

Large sales forces selling to industry may lend themselves to mathematical model building devices to assist in structuring and size decisions.[6]

Materials Supply

Salesmen for these companies deal with the highest volume of orders per man of any kind of sales force. One-sixth of all salesmen in the repeat industrial product area are personally responsible for more than £200,000 in sales volume each year and some can exceed £1 million.

It is very difficult to evaluate the contribution of these individual salesmen for a number of reasons. First, the opening of a new account may be the

[4] Industrial Market Research Ltd., *How British Industry Buys* (Table 8); Institute of Marketing, 1967.
[5] 'Salesmen Under the Microscope'; *Institute of Marketing*, 1968, p. 18.
[6] A. Easton, 'A Forward Step in Performance Evaluation'; *U.S. Jnl. of Marketing*, Vol. 30, July 1966, pp. 26–32.

result of activity by several individuals in the selling and technical teams. Secondly, most of the repeat orders come in without the salesman influencing them. Thirdly, the geographical clustering of customers makes the allocation of equal-size territories difficult. Fourthly, the influence of reciprocal trading practice, which is stronger in this field than in any other, closes off much of the free market.

Differentiated Products

Where products and market segments are widely diverse, then a mixture of different sales structures will be used.

Undifferentiated Products

The requirement in these companies is for a higher level of creative sales ability than for any other. It is usual to find selling practices being operated at all levels of management, and by all departments in the business focusing on sales. Many of these companies are highly sales-oriented.

Custom-built Products

Here the emphasis is on locating prospects. Selling must be operated constantly, because few orders are repeated automatically. The order-getting process is usually influenced by several people making up a team, with the salesman in the role of being a contact executive. Sales forces are usually structured by customer type or size.

Fragmented Markets

In these markets, field sales activity is usually frenetic, because of the need to force products through distribution. Sales costs are often high.

Oligopolistic Markets

Supplier's sales forces are highly efficient, often dominating the supplier/buyer relationship. The very active end of these markets often witness rivalry between distributors who compete fiercely for the business of the end-users—as in the market for tyres, for example.

Concentrated Markets

When companies are in a dominant position in their markets, their sales forces concentrate on service for existing customers. Such companies are often status conscious. There can be a lack of aggression in these markets and this is reflected by the sales forces which are often difficult to motivate. Sales salaries may be high, although the total costs of selling as a proportion of the business done may be low. Salesmen in these companies prefer to act as consultants. More sales aggression is experienced when markets are growing and can be exploited.

Mass Distribution

Companies in mass distribution markets often structure part of their sales forces according to (*a*) the power of the buyers who place large orders, and (*b*) through different channels of trade. Mass distribution makes for large sales forces and often a relatively low level of sales ability in individual salesmen. The accent is usually on helping distributors to sell the product to end-users through merchandising and promotion techniques. Trade forcing practices, such as special offers and personal incentives, are frequent.

Oligopsony

Companies operating in oligopsonistic markets find that great power flows to their salesmen, who are often the main arbiters of company policy. The sales force cost is low and the salesmen are few in number, but each has a great share of total responsibility. The individual customers are all-important, and each is developed as far as possible. In product fields with a high technical content, the salesman may be the leader of a team which serves the customer at various levels in the organisation.

The salesman in this company is highly respected for his ability to successfully hold a few accounts. In some companies there may be a fear that the man will leave and take his personal goodwill with him. This risk, ever-present, will be hedged by senior management contact at appropriately higher levels of customer management.

Monopsony

In the monopsonistic company, the chief executive and his close colleagues will form the sales team. The customer and his demands are all-powerful for the future of the business.

Example: Reorganising Sales

Background

Crosfields Farm Foods (South-Western) Ltd. is a feedstuffs company, part of a larger group, which serves the south-west of England.

Before 1968, 75 per cent of sales were scattered through 15 retail companies which had been acquired over the years. There was no direct control over these companies, and each had a fair amount of autonomy in its decision making.

The problem

The company was drifting. Its situation was very difficult as the farm feed market became particularly competitive and intensely difficult to operate profitably.

The sales force was committed to traditional ways of doing business. Sales representatives tended to hang on to their existing contacts, instead of finding new business.

The methods adopted

Consultants were appointed under a government grant scheme which subsidised half the cost. The consultants diagnosed a lack of marketing expertise. An experienced sales manager, Mr. Peter Green, was appointed.

The rural retail outlets began to be integrated. The scattered sales force was reduced gradually by about 30 per cent. This was achieved almost entirely by natural wastage and voluntary retirement.

Sales representatives, who formerly worked haphazardly under Branch managers, were put under five area managers, who each reported to the sales manager. Management by objectives was introduced to the sales force, and organised discussion and reporting procedures ensured a constant two-way flow of information.

Each of the five areas was provided with a different objective, a separate spread of business, and a separate policy to meet local circumstances.

Previously sales representatives dealt with problems of distribution and administration within their territories, under their Branch managers. This was changed so that each man concentrated solely on his selling task, with distribution being reorganised under central command.

Area managers now spend at least three hours in the field every month with each man. Training is carried out on a systematic basis, but locally. Under a training manager, comprehensive programmes are drawn up to fit the sales and product knowledge needs both of the individual and team. Induction courses are provided from outside, through commercial services for basic sales training.

Back-up services were improved. A specialist technical services department was set up to improve the quality of advice given to customers, and to improve the technical knowledge of the salesmen.

Results

The sales cost of marketing each ton of feed was reduced by 20 per cent in two years. In the same time, the turnover for each sales representative was increased by one-third. In the same period, the average earnings of each salesman were increased by 25 per cent under a new structure. The company's return on capital employed has nearly doubled, with sharply increased trading profits.

The methods used by the company are now in the process of being applied to other areas of the parent group's business.

J.W.

14. Physical Distribution

'In the corner of a typical manufacturing plant, a manager says, "There's nothing in there that would interest you." On the door it says Despatch Department—you go through that door and you are in original chaos. Yet, the despatch department is where the labour costs are. The despatch department, as often as not, is unmanaged. It is considered as donkey work, and the head of production puts a donkey in charge of it. The head of production is a technical man, and he is interested in engineering aspects, and not in the area of physical distribution. The marketing manager is not interested in the despatch department nor in the plant warehouse either, and so these are in no man's land. The department is under the plant roof, but you have a very hard time trying to find the costs, because they are in "miscellaneous manufacturing overhead". Unless you start the management of physical distribution in the finishing room, you cannot manage physical distribution at all. At best you can improve things a little.'[1]

When Peter Drucker told this to a conference on physical distribution management, he was advocating the use of an integrated systems approach to the subject. He and other writers have argued the case consistently, and techniques of system development have been perfected. However, management generally has remained deaf. The case has been proven over and over again; story after story has appeared in business publications, showing how specific companies saved enormous sums through examining their total distribution system instead of parts of it. Rival managements are not convinced.[2]

As long ago as 1912, the need for physical supply co-ordination was detected. 'The essential element in any business activity is the application of motion to material.'[3]

Physical distribution is a cost area, and purely a cost area. All one can do by physically moving stuff is to harm it—one can spoil it, break it, scratch

[1] P. Drucker, 'The Frontier of Modern Management'; talk to Annual Spring Conference, National Council of Physical Distribution Management, April 6, 1965.
[2] D. Foster, 'Distribution: The Achilles Heel'; *Marketing*, March 1971, pp. 40–43.
[3] A. W. Shaw, *Some Problems in Market Distribution*; U.S.A. 1912.

it, soil it, stale it, and discolour it. As a cost centre of business it is seldom looked at as an entity. The cost of transport of finished products, which is what managements normally examine, might be up to 10 per cent of what the customer pays. (*Figure 48.*) Yet the total cost of moving stuff all the way along the business process, including through the channels of distribution, might be higher than 50 per cent of the price the final customer pays.

Drucker tells the story of an oil refinery in Japan, where 85 per cent of the sales of petrol are concentrated in two urban areas, including Tokyo. With a refinery in each area, the company's supplies travel no more than

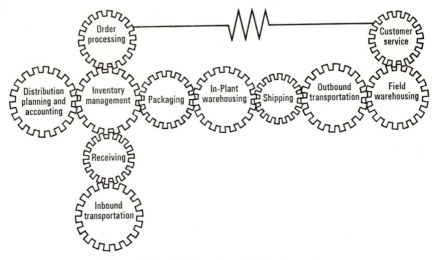

Figure 48 Activity 'cogs' in a distribution system.

(*Source:* W. M. Stewart, 'Physical Distribution: Key to Improved Volume and Profits'; *Journal of Marketing*, January 1965, p. 66)

20 miles to the users. But the company sells its petrol to one national wholesaler; which in turn sells it to a regional wholesaler; which in turn sells it to a local wholesaler, who finally sells it to a retailer. As a selling process it may make sense. But unfortunately the petrol is actually handled accordingly. It is pumped into a lorry at the refinery, and taken a short distance to the tanks of the national wholesaler. It moves into these tanks, and out of them again into another vehicle which takes it to the tanks of the regional company. They store it, then pump it out and carry it to the local wholesaler, who stores it, and finally moves it out to the retailer. It is loaded and unloaded eight times, when two would do. It could obviously be moved straight to the retailer, no matter where the papers go, or how the mark-ups are distributed. If the management had felt like going out with the lorries and following it through, they would have found out. But managements are traditionally reluctant to do this. Every time the material is moved it wastes and deteriorates.

The physical distribution problem is going to get worse. First, the economic pressure causes some buyers to place small orders frequently, so that they can reduce their stocks, while others place large orders to force up the discount terms. This distorts delivery schedules. The competitive pressure means a concentration of manufacturing stocks above minimum economic levels, so that out-of-stocks do not occur. New product development trends have resulted in a welter of varieties, shapes, colours and sizes, and consequently slower movement of each item. The growing power of the large buyers has pressured manufacturers to supply direct deliveries, moving the burden of transport to the supplier, and away from the distributor. The degree of service is being constantly increased so as to provide an edge in marketing advantage by reducing delivery lead times.[4]

There are three basic types of physical distribution structure: the first is where the company has a single plant and delivers to a single market area. Usually the location of the plant is near to the market; depots are sited next to the manufacturing unit, and the cost is relatively low.

The second type is the most common, where a single plant exists, but delivery must be made to several markets which are geographically dispersed. The choices open to the manufacturer are to transport direct to customers in each market, transport to a depot in the key markets, and/or to use a distribution agent in less important markets.

The type of physical distribution method used might also vary from market to market. Company-owned lorries might deliver to large and nearby markets, with commercial services used for distant and small markets.

The optimum distribution method is a function of several inter-related factors. These are the number of drops, their geographical clustering, the acceptable delivery frequencies and pattern, the size of the drops, and the capacity of the transport. (*Figure 49.*)

Calculating the most cost-efficient method of distribution is more complex in companies which service multiple markets from multiple plants. The two problems here relate to (*a*) minimising the transport and stock costs in the factory to warehouse situation given the present facilities, and (*b*) the longer-term problem of deciding whether the present number of warehouse and distribution centres is minimising the total distribution costs.

The problem of managing physical distribution is that it is the centre of a mass of conflicting demands. The demands of production are to clear their stocks as soon as they are made, to eliminate inventory costs and to reduce the necessary storage space. The demands of sales are for depots to be located as close as possible to markets. Sales also require stocks to be sufficiently high to meet all reasonable customer demands, on all product items, with the fastest possible delivery time. The demand from financial controllers is to minimise the stock levels everywhere, and to minimise other elements

---

[4] W. M. Stewart, 'Physical Distribution, Key to Improved Volume and Profits'; *U.S. Jnl. of Marketing*, Vol. 29, Jan. 1965, pp. 56–70.

of capital which might be tied up in vehicles or warehouses. They would wish to throw the burden of distribution so far as possible on to customers.

The crucial factor, which few companies consider, is to establish the level of service which is acceptable to the customers in relation to competitors' levels of service, and to provide the least-cost physical distribution method to meet this level.

Standards are required for the various components making up customer service. There will be a tolerable level of out-of-stock occurrences which

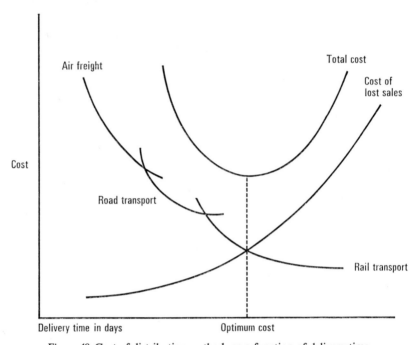

Figure 49 Cost of distribution methods as a function of delivery time.

(*Source:* P. Kotler, *Marketing Management, Analysis, Planning and Control*, p. 427, Prentice-Hall, 1967)

all customers will allow—and some will allow greater margin than others. Customer service as a function of physical distribution is far more complex and subtle in its effects on buyers than traditional cost and profit models suggest. If this factor seems critical, then it can be established with the use of attitude research or simulation studies.[5]

The responsiveness of customers to various levels of delivery discount needs to be established. In most markets customers are less responsive than is popularly supposed.

The degree to which forecasting errors, special promotion schemes or

[5] R. Willett, P. Stephenson, 'Determinants of Buyer Response to Physical Distribution Service'; *U.S. Jnl. of Marketing Research*, Vol. VI, Aug. 1969, pp. 279–283.

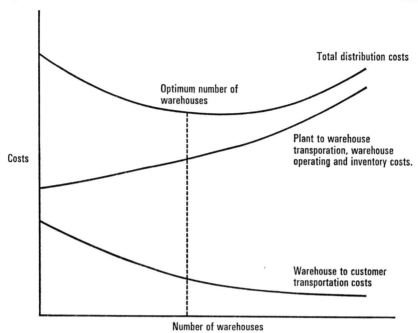

Figure 50 Distribution costs versus number of warehouses.

(*Source:* W. M. Stewart, 'Physical Distribution: Key to Improved Volume and Profits'; *Journal of Marketing*, January 1965, p. 68)

rush deliveries affect input and output relationships needs to be established and built into the basic system.

Reducing distribution costs

There are two points of attack on physical distribution costs. The first is upon the individual cost elements which make up the distribution chain. The second is on the manner in which these costs alter, when changes in the system occur.

For example, the total costs will change when the number of warehouses are changed, or when the level of customer service is altered. (*Figure 50.*)

A cost analysis is required from every aspect of the chain. Starting with the inbound transportation of materials to the plant, their receipt and handling, the analysis will include the management of finished stock, packaging, in-plant warehouse, bulk transportation, field warehousing, delivery transportation, customer service, parts service, order processing and traffic control. In most companies these costs belong to separate budgets within different divisions. However, the effect of a change in total distribution procedure cannot be measured until the total cost is known of all the factors. This is the traditional area for unearthing skeletons in the system, where, for example, a man is employed on one side of a table to check goods out,

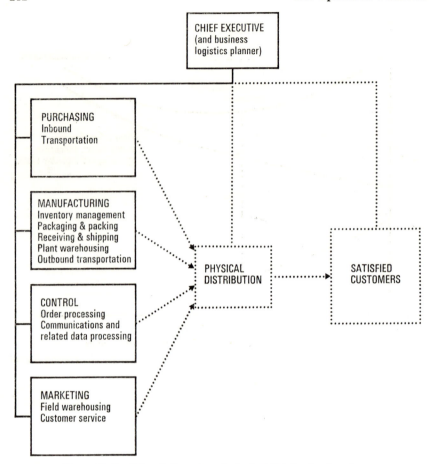

Figure 51 Traditional allocation of physical distribution functions.
(*Source:* W. M. Stewart, 'Physical Distribution: Key to Improved Volume and Profits'; *Journal of Marketing*, January 1965, p. 68)

and a man belonging to another department sits at the next door table to check goods in. It's worked that way, perhaps, because they have always done it like this. (*Figure 51.*)

The opportunities for saving costs lie in six areas.[6]

(1) The simplification of the total system. The elimination of one warehouse; or the final product fabrication plant placed nearer to the main market— would be examples of system simplification.

(2) Reduction in stocks. By consolidating stocks at fewer centres, less balancing of stocks is needed; or stocks can be lowered through more frequent deliveries. The cost saving resulting from reduced stocks might more than offset the on-cost of transport.

[6] R. Maffei, 'Modern Methods for Local Delivery Route Design'; *U.S. Jnl. of Marketing*, Vol. 29, April 1965, pp. 13–18.

(3) Improvements in packaging. Smaller, more dense, more uniform package sizes permit greater efficiency in handling. Sizes of cartons which are common to several products will reduce packaging cost.

(4) More efficient methods and procedures. This refers to the selection and use of the most efficient handling procedures, warehouse location, space utilisation, warehousing and transport methods, as well as the use of equipment.

(5) Use of technological innovations. There have been a significant number of technical improvements made in equipment for materials handling, stock, and in control through the use of computers.

(6) Channels of distribution. One reason for high cost may be found in the channels of trade being used. Some trade margins are notoriously higher than those of other channels which might do the same task equally as well.

A 'total cost' approach was developed in America[7] in 1965, and has made considerable impact upon the management approach to this problem. This takes the impact of distribution on each cost of the business, emphasising those costs which are significantly affected by distribution policies and practices. Sets of alternative policies in distribution are drawn up and measured for their impact on these costs. Finally, the decision which maximises overall company profits is selected.

The approach is shown in *Figure 52*. This problem related to the number of warehouses the company should have. The graphs show that for each factor of costs, a certain number of warehouses would yield the optimum return. Each factor has its own built-in logic, and so each curve is shaped differently. The sum of all the curves shows one optimum point, which is the optimum number of warehouses the company should have in order to maximise its returns. The graphs show that even if some of the distribution costs are cut to their lowest practical level, the total costs may actually increase.

The use of operations research

To study the entire physical distribution process and to evolve an integrated system is so complex that some form of operations research is inevitable. Operations research can be used when the problem is sufficiently complex to present a number of alternative factors to be balanced against each other, and when chance factors are influencing the problem. It is also desirable when the scale of operations is so large that the potential return from such a study is high, and will justify the research cost.

There are four main steps to be applied:

(1) A statement of the problem. This sounds easy, but in fact it may present the researcher with his hardest problem. The problem as specified by the production manager will be totally different from that presented by sales; and again will be different from that presented by the transport manager,

[7] R. LeKashman, J. F. Stolle, 'The Total Cost Approach to Distribution'; *Business Horizons*, Vol. 8, Winter 1965, pp. 33–46.

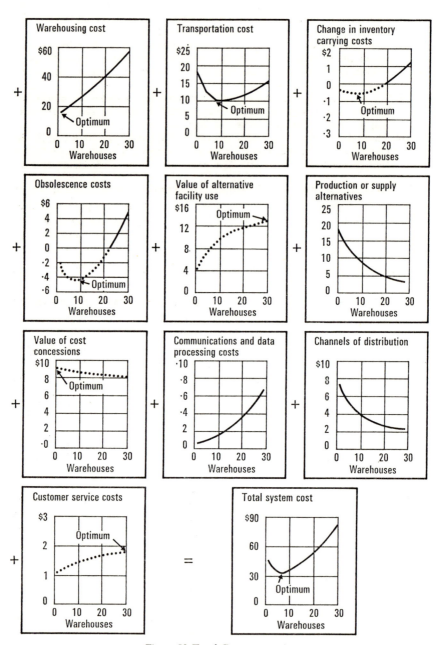

Figure 52 Total Cost approach.

(*Source:* R. Le Kashman, J. F. Stolle, 'The Total Cost Approach to Distribution'; *Business Horizons*, Vol. 8, Winter 1965, pp. 33–46)

or the financial chief. The objectives for the research study will be similarly conflicting from each management source.

(2) The construction of a model for the problem. This is the essence of the operations research approach. It can range from the establishment of a relationship of the work involved in some physically measurable property, to an extraordinarily complex model of the entire market system.

(3) At some point, various techniques such as linear programming, queueing theory, or simulation testing, will be applied to the model to obtain a solution.

(4) Interpretation. This involves securing the active support of the people involved. It is difficult, since it involves their support also for the final implementation stage.

Market Situations

Package Goods: Consumer

With perishable products distribution costs can be very high indeed; stock movement is very rapid and depots are located near to markets. The effect of date-stamping perishable products puts a tremendous added strain on distribution. It is not unusual for physical distribution costs alone, within the total process, to be as high as 20 per cent of the company selling price. With long life products the problem is eased. Such companies often are concerned about the total costs of distribution including channels of trade. This leads to the considerations of eliminating wholesalers.

Consumer Durables

These companies have greater freedom in setting their levels of customer service than companies in packaged goods, but they are constrained by competitors' service levels. Spare parts processing may be very complex, and order control can be difficult. Having high value products causes these companies to be anxious about carrying undue stocks.

Plant and Equipment

Distribution through company-owned services is unusual, and carriers are contracted in most cases. Physical distribution is not generally a high proportion of the total costs, but stock holding costs can be high. Parts service and replacement is a problem, particularly for outdated equipment.

Components

Order processing, supply of spare parts, and the mix of plant locations and markets, makes distribution complex and often costly for these companies. Rush deliveries form a major part of the nuisance factor. Stock costs can be high.

Materials

Materials usually are supplied according to known patterns of demand and delivery requirement. The materials handling cost may be high and may be capital-intensive, with special vehicles designed for the task, and special lifting or pumping equipment required. Distribution costs are very high. Although they might not form a large proportion of the total product cost, they lend themselves to system design and to operations research. The most startling cases of cost reductions while maintaining service levels generally have occurred in materials supply companies.

Example: Reducing the Costs of Physical Distribution

Background

A simple case history of a successful use of operations research techniques was presented at a seminar held at the Management Study Centre in early 1970. The case is adapted here from *Business Administration*, July 1970, and was presented by J. R. Webster, of Business Operations Research Ltd.

The problem

Delta Limited—to give the company a fictitious name—manufactures a range of expendable consumer goods at three factories sited in a roughly triangular configuration in the Midlands. In considering what kind of distribution pattern would provide best service at minimum cost, its managers applied a formula often used: warehouse costs + transport = distribution costs.

As a result of calculations based on this formula, they decided to build a single main warehouse to supply four stock carrying depots. Between them, these would service some 80,000 wholesale and retail outlets.

Before implementing this decision, Delta called in consultants to evaluate the plan. The consultants' OR team re-examined the problem from scratch, collected much additional data, and finally applied standard mathematical techniques to elicit firm facts on comparative costs on a vast number of alternatives.

The consultants formulated several problems. What type of depots—stock carrying or 'shunt' (parcel clearing houses) should Delta operate? Where should the main warehouses and depots be located and what size should these be? What geographical areas should be served by each satellite, and how many vans would each need? Should Delta do all its own deliveries or contract some of them out?

The method

First task was to analyse costs affecting warehouse location. For the main warehouse these were freight costs from the factories and transport costs to customers in the warehouse vicinity. For shunt depots, costs were depot and van operation and increased main warehouse costs; for stock carrying depots, costs were depot operation, trunking between main warehouse and depots, van operation and stock holding.

Van costs, on a fixed pence-per-mile basis, were applied to calculate annual fixed costs when the main warehouse and satellite depots were located at varying distances from the factories and from one another; and for depots of either type and of different sizes. Results, combined with depot operating costs, added up to show that even if throughput of parcels was considerably higher than the present estimate, the cost of shunt depots would remain significantly smaller.

The next task was to select four depot sites that would minimise the annual van and depot operating and carrier costs. The average number of parcels carried per call and total parcel capacity of a five-ton van were established. Van performance was reduced to a mathematical formula. Result of the calculations was embodied in a graph that showed how many parcels each van could deliver in an eight-hour working day when a depot was situated at distances measured in five-mile steps up to 80 miles from the drop points.

The following data were used to discover the optimum location for each shunt depot: average daily number of parcels delivered to each locality in the delivery area (via analysis of historical information); a list of about 40 towns potentially suitable for depots; road distance from the main warehouse to each depot; road distance from each depot to each feasible drop point.

Computer programmes calculated a set of feasible van routes from each potential depot site. Constraints ensured that as far as possible each route most efficiently utilised eight-hour van days. Then the cost of each van route was calculated on the basis of van costs, variable shunt depot costs, and costs incurred in sorting parcels delivered in Delta vans to shunt depots. Every combination of non-overlapping routes from the depots was then costed out to find the cheapest.

Results

The table shows the extent to which the consultants' proposals reduced annual running costs, and compares capital costs of the original and the new scheme. The new proposal also allowed 95·4 per cent of goods to be delivered by Delta vans, as compared with the 90·2 per cent achieved by the original scheme.

Annual Operating Costs £'000	Original proposal	New proposal	*Estimated Capital Costs £'000*	Original proposal	New proposal
Van costs	166	264	Vans	121	125
Depot costs	151	28	Trunkers	50	0
Carrier costs	65	37	Depots	348	103
Trunkers ex main warehouse	29	0	Main warehouses	1316	1357
Factory to warehouse costs	233	208			
Extra main warehouse costs		38			
Total	644	575	*Total*	1835	1585
Saving	£69,000 p.a.		*Saving*	£250,000	

15. Marketing Communications

Communication requires three elements—a 'source', the 'message' and the 'destination'.[1] The 'source' encodes the message in such a way as to make it easy for the destination to understand the message. The message itself is made up of signs, which the destination decodes. In the persuasive communications process there is a 'feedback'. The destination tries to interpret the message more fully; so he encodes another message, often in the form of a question, which the source then decodes.

Marketing communication is really a series of two-way communication flows between a rich variety of sources and destinations, which act in parallel. The process is also sequential, so that a series of parallel communications move the prospective purchasers in steps through the learning cycle. These potential purchasers will move from a state of ignorance to a point where the prospect optimises his knowledge with his degree of personal need for the product.

Communication is not just a simple type of interaction, but comprises a number of critical parts. The process is dynamic, and the parts are interdependent.

In marketing communications there are three additional problems. First, the required destinations of the message are spread to a multitude of places and people, so that a 'communications organisation' is required to help. The organisation can take the form of a sales force, publishing house, television station and so on. Such organisations are characterised by a high degree of message output, and a low degree of feedback. Second, several vehicles of communications must be used concurrently, some of which are primary vehicles, such as advertising and personal selling, and some of which are secondary, such as letter writing, or packaging designs.[2] Thirdly, at different stages of the purchasers' adoption of the product, varying degrees of cost-effectiveness will apply to the different forms of media. For example,

[1] W. Schramm, *How Communication Works, the Process and Effects of Mass Communication*; Urbana, University of Illinois Press, 1955, pp. 3–26.
[2] R. Colley, *Defining Advertising Goals*; New York, Association of National Advertisers Inc. 1961, pp. 49–60.

advertising is usually the most cost-effective method of creating wide-scale awareness quickly. However, personal selling or other word of mouth communication are usually more cost-effective at the time of the buyer's decision.

Buyer behaviour models

To understand and control the marketing communications process it is necessary to relate the problem to the more common theories of buyer behaviour.

There are four standard theories, of which two are more generally acceptable to practising marketing men.[3] It should be noted that any particular individual may not fit permanently into one of these models. However, they do depict how a buyer may react under certain circumstances for a period of time.

The traditional theory of buyer behaviour is called the *Marshallian Economic model*—the origin of which goes back as far as Adam Smith in the eighteenth century.

The theory is based upon man behaving in an entirely rational manner, carefully calculating the effect of the consequences of his purchases, and maximising his utilities. He will carefully assess such factors as price and value, and make an optimum choice. Economic factors alone cannot explain all the variations in sales, and the theory in general is discredited by marketing men. There are those who hold that it has greater relevance to industrial purchasing situations.

The Pavlovian learning model views buyer behaviour as an associative process. It has four central concepts. Drive, which is the individual's internal stimulus that impels him to action. Cues, which are the environmental stimuli. Response, which is the buyer's reaction to cues. Reinforcement, which is the tendency towards rewarding experiences so that responses will be repeated. Advertising and copy strategy is often developed on the lines of Pavlovian theory, but it is not a complete theory of behaviour.

The Freudian model is based on psychoanalytic motivations. Man attempts to gratify his needs, frustration leads him to perfect subtle means of satisfaction, and guilt or shame causes him to repress some of his more basic urges from his consciousness. In applying this theory, there have been many bizarre hypotheses about what may be in the buyer's mind when he makes certain purchases. Motivation research based on this model can, and often does, lead to useful insights for creative men, but it also leads to some highly fallacious answers.

The Veblenian Social-psychological model. This sees man as primarily a social animal. His wants and behaviour are largely moulded by his present

[3] P. Kotler, 'Behavioural Models for Analysing Buyers'; *U.S. Jnl. of Marketing*, Vol. 29, Oct. 1965, pp. 37–45.

group membership, and the group to which he aspires. The best known example is in Veblen's theory of the leisure class. His hypothesis is that much of economic consumption is motivated by prestige-seeking, rather than by intrinsic needs. This model has been used for much marketing segmentation strategy. The effect of his social class on his attitudes, the influence of 'reference groups', that is, those to whom he aspires, must be taken into account. The 'face-to-face groups' which have the most immediate influence on his tastes and opinions also contribute to the construction of the Veblenian theory of buyer behaviour.

Marketing men agree that the effect of small groups with whom the buyer comes into contact have a most powerful effect upon his attitudes. Family, close friends, neighbours, those with whom he works, all wield great influence. There is a fascinating array of evidence on the subject in all the studies of communications and sociology.

The Hobbesian organisation model. This is the only theory to be developed relative to industrial purchasing decisions. The differences between the industrial buyer and the buyer as an individual are that he is paid to make purchases for others, and that he works within an organisation. The theory holds that the industrial buyer steers a careful course between satisfying his own personal needs and those of the organisation. The buyer has private aims and ambitions and yet he tries to do a satisfactory job for the company. The importance of the model is that buyers can be swayed by both personal and organisational arguments. The best 'mix' of the two is not a fixed ratio, it will vary from buyer to buyer, product to product and with the type of organisation. Where there is substantial similarity between the products offered, then the buyer has less rational basis for his choice, so that he can be swayed more easily by personal or emotional motives. But where there are great differences in the product offerings, the buyer pays more attention to rational factors.

Other chapters in this book deal with the primary expense functions of marketing communications, that is, sales, advertising and sales promotion. These operations have been run for many years before any realistic theories of purchasing behaviour were developed. They were being used long before we came to understand all that we do about the persuasive communications process.

It is possible, however, that in the search for increasing marketing productivity, we may have lost sight of the need for creative solutions to basic marketing communications problems. Creativity has to do with the development, proposal and implementation of *new* and better solutions. Productivity has to do with the efficient application of *current* solutions. We may have been repeating past experience for too long.

Leman[4] proposes that marketing communications affect both 'sales'

[4] G. Leman, *Sales, Saleability, and the Saleability Gap*; British Bureau of Television Advertising, 1968.

and 'saleability'. For example, he distinguishes between advertising and sales promotion in consumer product fields by saying that advertising affects long-term saleability rather than sales, through its slow and progressively incremental effects. Sales promotion, on the other hand, exploits saleability to get a short-term advantage. Promotion therefore has non-incremental effects on saleability. In fact, he goes on to suggest that a very high level of promotion may have a negative affect on saleability. This may be due to its influence in weakening consumer attitudes towards the quality of the product itself. Some advertising may have a short-term result, particularly in direct-response product fields.

It seems that the idea of separating the saleability of a product as a distinct entity may provide important guidelines for product policy in the marketing communications area. At least it provides a rational basis for the general corporate desire to maintain product image. Such desires have been weakening in many markets in the face of intensifying competitive pressure.

A Harvard Business School study,[5] shows that company reputation is a powerful factor in the industrial purchasing process—although its importance varies with the technical competence of the buyer. The study showed that the better the company's reputation, the better are its chances of getting a favourable first hearing for its salesmen, and of getting early adoption of the product. Although salesmen from well-known companies have an edge over other salesmen, the study showed that customers expect more from the high reputation company, and they judge its performance differently. The amount of personal risk to which the buyer is exposed proves to be a vital factor in his decision and the company with the high reputation always has the edge.

The study also showed that a sound sales presentation from a less well-known company can be just as effective as a poor presentation from the better known one. Indeed, the researchers found that buyers were often willing to give 'help' unconsciously to the less well-known company salesmen, by lowering their expectations.

Message source credibility. The study was originally run in order to explain the phenomenon of what is known as the 'source' effect in communications. The persuasive power of a message is governed by at least three factors.

(1) The degree to which the source of the message is recognised as being materially dependent upon the outcome of the message. A salesman scores low credibility against the 'expert' within the family.
(2) The degree to which the message itself, its timing and appeal can be adjusted according to the response of the receiver (in seeking further information or registering disbelief). Here the salesman scores higher than advertising.
(3) The degree to which the source of the message is acknowledged as credible. A well-known company will score higher than an unknown company.

[5] T. Levitt, 'Communications and Industrial Selling'; *U.S. Jnl. of Marketing*, Vol. 31, April 1967, pp. 15–21.

1. Message delivered face to face by third party independent of source where information can be exchanged (such as professional consultant).

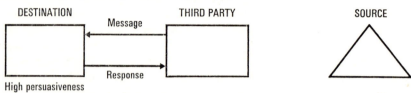

High persuasiveness

2. Message delivered face to face by someone identified with the source and where information can be exchanged (such as salesman).

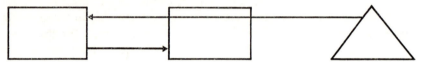

3. Message delivered face to face by an 'independent' third party where information exchange is limited (such as a public lecture by an expert).

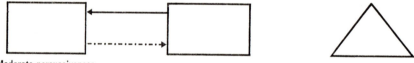

Moderate persuasiveness

4. Message delivered face to face by a third party identified with the source and where information cannot be exchanged (such as a market trader).

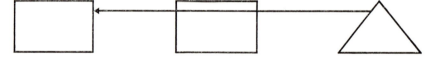

5. Message published in sound or printed form by a third party independent of source (such as editorial mention).

6. Message published in sound or printed form with the source identified (such as an advertisement).

Low persuasiveness

Figure 53 The source effect in communications (in descending order of persuasiveness).

Word-of-mouth communication

Undoubtedly the most neglected part of marketing communications theory lies in one of its most influential areas: word-of-mouth communications. Yet informal conversation is probably the oldest mechanism by which opinions on products are developed, expressed and spread. In the last 20 years social scientists have developed a substantial body of data on the role of word-of-mouth in the process of new product diffusion.

Few textbooks deal with the subject and there is hardly any material published for practising marketing executives. Indeed, we seem not to have proceeded far from 24 years ago when a textbook by Sandage concluded that there was no way of measuring accurately the forcefulness of word-of-mouth.[6] That may still be true, but word-of-mouth exists for our products whether for good or ill, and whether we can measure it or not. Its influence in certain purchasing situations is terrifyingly clear, particularly with 'fad' products sold to younger age groups. But slimming foods, personal products, drugs and do-it-yourself markets are all highly sensitive to word-of-mouth. Wilkinson's razor blades practically were launched on it.

There have been some attempts to influence word-of-mouth communications commercially. Traditionally taxi drivers have been used to spread stories; and 'mystery shopper' promotion techniques are sometimes used to reward shop assistants who recommend specified brands. Many products have been advertised using the theme, 'here is good news—pass it on'. Some advertisers have adjusted their campaigns to the word-of-mouth comments which their products receive. For example, the cinema industry adjusts its distribution policy according to the likely word-of-mouth response. If the picture is a bad one, they aim for rapid distribution building up to saturation quickly, with cinemas showing the film simultaneously. However, if the film is a good one, the distribution slows to a creeping pace, allowing favourable word-of-mouth to build up.[7]

In a U.S. study of the purchasing behaviour of buyers of small electrical appliances[8] it was discovered that word-of-mouth was more frequently mentioned than any other external source. Another study of industrial buyers showed that word-of-mouth tended to be more important at the later stages of the adoption process. This study noted the effect of within-firm communications between colleagues, and intra-firm communication between 'experts' in the industry.[9]

Most of these studies have shown the importance of the so-called 'opinion leader'. There is little doubt that some people tend to be more influential

[6] C. Sandage, *Advertising: Theory and Practice*; 3rd edn., Chicago, Richard D. Irwin, p. 271.
[7] L. Handel, *Hollywood Looks at its Audience*; University of Illinois Press, 1960.
[8] J. Udell, 'Pre-Purchase Behaviour of Buyers of Small Electrical Appliances'; *U.S. Jnl. of Marketing*, Vol. 30, Oct. 1966, pp. 50–52.
[9] J. Martilla, 'Word of Mouth Communication in the Industrial Adoption Process'; *U.S. Jnl. of Marketing Research*, Vol. VIII, May 1971, pp. 173–178.

than others and it has been assumed for some time that opinion leaders have a set of behaviour patterns which mark them out from the 'mixers' and the 'followers'. One of these characteristics is reputed to be a higher exposure to media of various kinds. This gave rise to the 'two-step hypothesis', in that the messages flow first from television and print to opinion leaders, and then onwards to less active sections of the population.

However, a British study set up to test this hypothesis,[10] rejected this conclusion. Opinion leaders do exist, of course, and the evidence is that they may be the people who reinforce new ideas, known to the whole group, by being the first to translate them into practice. The opinion leader may perhaps be identified by his willingness to innovate and to take risks.[11]

Marketing executives do not like using the word-of-mouth process because of the problem of possible distortion. This may have been true under conditions of stress, such as rumour-mongering in wartime. However, studies of the process when undertaken in normal settings have shown that word-of-mouth is relatively reliable and undistorted.[12] There has been virtually no research carried out into the problem of word-of-mouth acting as a retarding force within the market. It is entirely possible for opinion leaders to discourage change or, indeed, to unseat a previously favourable opinion. Particularly is this true of the early stages of the adoption process, when a favourable opinion might be held only weakly. Manufacturers degrading the quality of their product have often found that buyers have passed the word along, and sales have dropped drastically.[13]

In summary, there are three reasons why word-of-mouth is an important medium of persuasive communications, one which operates whether the company wants it to or not. First, it is thought by the receiver to give reliable and trustworthy information, through the source of the message being perceived to be independent of the outcome of the message. Secondly, in contrast to advertising and sales promotion, such personal contacts offer social support. Thirdly, the message is often backed up by social pressure to conform, perhaps even under supervision.

The opportunities for manufacturers to actively exploit word-of-mouth appear to lie in four main areas. The first is through the development of interesting and imaginative products; or through presenting them in interesting and imaginative ways, designed to cause people to talk. Secondly, through the creation of novel sales and advertising appeals, with similar objectives. Thirdly, through the mounting of unusual and interesting activi-

[10] M. West, 'Opinion Leaders, a Study in Communication'; Papers of the Market Research Society Conference, Brighton, 1969, pp. 145–188.
[11] J. Engel, R. Keggereis, R. Blackwell, 'Word of Mouth Communication by the Innovator;' *U.S. Jnl. of Marketing*, Vol. 33, July 1969, pp. 15–19.
[12] J. Arndt, *Word of Mouth Advertising*; Advertising Research Foundation, New York, 1967.
[13] S. Cunningham, 'Some Comments on the Relationship Between Rumour and Informal Communications'; Unpub. paper, Harvard Business School, 1963.

ties which are relevant to the marketing strategy but nevertheless designed to stimulate conversation within customer groups. Many sales promotions activities meet this requirement. Fourthly, through the mounting of press and public relations schemes so that company information is disseminated in such a way as to divorce the source of the message from its content.

At the least, the company should be aware of the threat of adverse word-of-mouth criticism. While it may be true that to ignore criticism is probably the best way of defeating it, nevertheless, this is an option which the company should have available along with other alternatives. At base, the company should be aware of the simplest principles of corporate communications. This means having control over all the visual and verbal communications media in which it deals.

Uncontrolled marketing communications

To see the extent of the communications problem which companies face it is necessary to examine their procedures. *Figure 54* shows a series of dia-

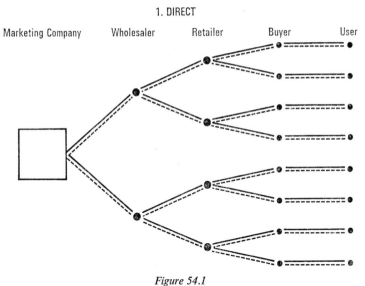

Figure 54.1
Figure 54 The complexities of the marketing communicating process.

grammatic models of the company communications process. This assumes that a company deals with a wholesaler, who deals with retailers, who sell to buyers who may be different from product users.

As can be seen from the models, the total communications system is hopelessly complex. At *Figure 54.1*, the simple sequential process which takes the message from marketing company to wholesaler to retailer to buyer to user, is shown—and each process is two-way, with feedback communi-

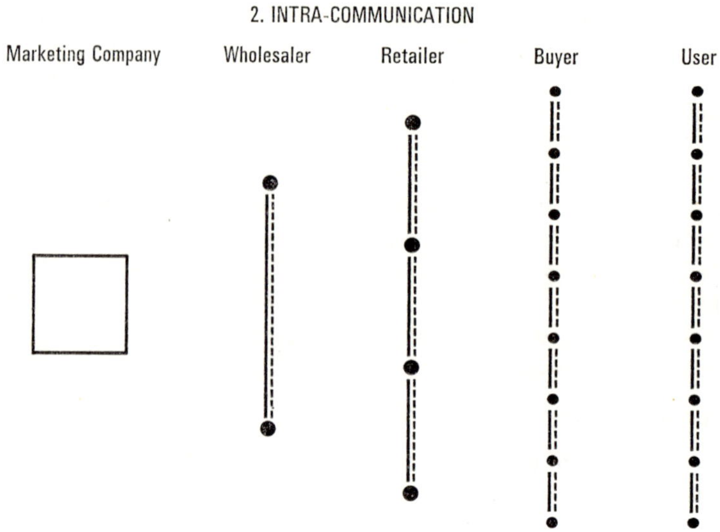

2. INTRA-COMMUNICATION

Marketing Company   Wholesaler   Retailer   Buyer   User

Figure 54.2

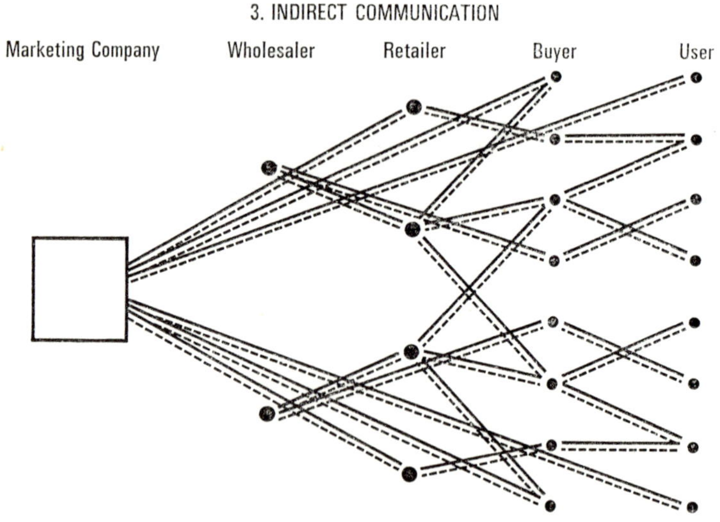

3. INDIRECT COMMUNICATION

Marketing Company   Wholesaler   Retailer   Buyer   User

Figure 54.3

Figure 54 The complexities of the marketing communicating process.

cations returning along the same paths. At *Figure 54.2*, the intra-personal influences are shown—more delicate in their nature and out of the direct influence of the marketing company. *Figure 54.3* shows that the marketing company makes some attempt to influence the further ends of the chain through advertising, packaging and merchandising. *Figure 54.4*, shows that there

4. WORD OF MOUTH INFLUENCES

Marketing Company   Wholesaler   Retailer   Buyer   User

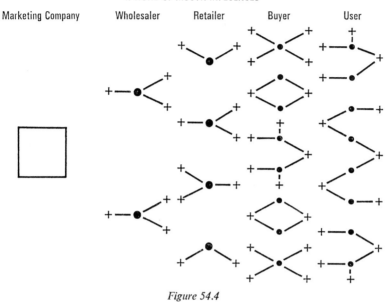

Figure 54.4

5. VEHICLES OF COMMUNICATION

Marketing Company   Wholesaler   Retailer   Buyer   User

Advertising; Packaging;
Merchandising;
Literature; Letters;
Telephone; Sales;
Editorial;

Company signs;
Vehicle livery;
Documentation
(invoicing etc.);
Word of mouth

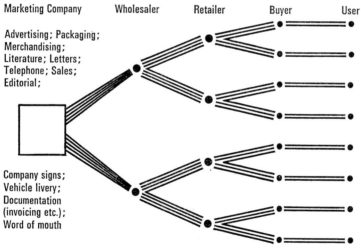

Figure 54.5

Figure 54 The complexities of the marketing communicating process.

6. MULTITUDE OF COMMUNICATION POINTS

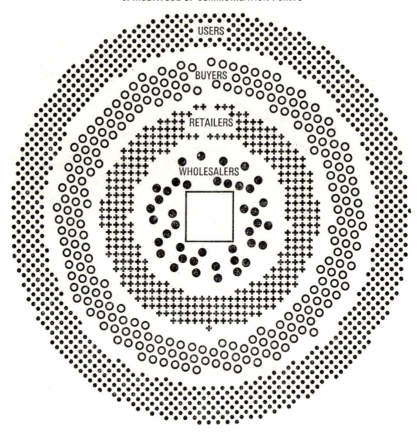

Figure 54.6

Figure 54 The complexities of the marketing communicating process.

is a multitude of influences acting on each buyer—from competitors, from exposure to independent sources, by word-of-mouth. The manufacturer attempts to influence these sources usually as a side effect of his advertising and promotion programme, and through public relations techniques. *Figure 54.5* shows the total range of communications vehicles which are used by the marketing company. Not only do they include advertising and sales promotion, but also the entire range of secondary media, such as letters, telephones, company documentation, vehicles and so on. These vehicles thin out as the company reaches further down the buying channels. For the sake of clarity only one wholesaler has been shown on these models; he has two retailer customers only, each having two customers. Finally, *Figure 54.6* shows that the total number of decision, buying and communications points runs into thousands, even for small companies.

If a similar model were to be drawn for industrial companies it would show the same problem, only slightly worse. At least in the consumer markets these are discrete relationships easily traced, identified and influenced. Within industry, the great difficulty lies in tracing the 'decision making unit', the decision influencers at each step of the adoption process. Having identified them, the problem is to reach them. At the same time, the deciders must be identified and reached, followed by the buyers. In most cases the influencers are not the same as the buyers. The relationships involved are hopelessly delicate, interdependent and complex.

Figure 55 shows the strength of the problem facing the marketing man

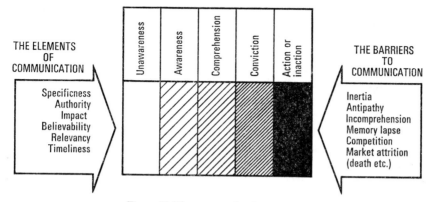

Figure 55 The communication process.

(*Source:* L. W. Rodger, *Marketing in a Competitive Economy*, p. 184, Associated Business Programmes Ltd.)

who must introduce factors such as specificness, authority, impact, and credibility into a series of messages. These must be relevant and timely, and must be passed on through each of the complex channels previously described.

There has been little formal research into this total problem. One study has been published relating to a planned strategy for what was called Visual Communications.[14] This was defined as 'the visible, distinctive, and consistent projection of related company, division and product identity into its markets'. Under this technique, each medium is visibly designed to support the other. The closest approach to it is a corporate identity programme.

An audit is carried out on all the visual communications materials, internal to the company and external to its markets. This pin-points areas of visual weakness and areas of strength. It looks for relationships between the media, such as packaging which may not relate visually to the advertising. Weak brand identity, poor brand reputations, varying styles of company logotypes,

[14] G. Stahl, 'The Marketing Strategy of Planned Visual Communications'; *U.S. Jnl. of Marketing*, Vol. 28, Jan. 1964, pp. 7–11.

printed literature which is inconsistent, are typical examples of problems. From this audit, a series of specific objectives are drawn up relating to the company's messages, the way they are presented and the inter-relationship of the various vehicles of communications. Frequently such an audit turns up great communications weaknesses. For example, in financial accounts— reminder letters about overdue accounts may be badly written. Consider transport—the vehicle washing programme or repainting schedule may be too lax. In field sales, a hand-written letter may be sent by salesmen to customers on any spare piece of paper. Notice boards and company signs may also prove to be weak.

Public relations as a factor. Just as there has been no proper exploitation of word-of-mouth communications in marketing, although everyone knows of its existence, there has been no serious theoretical case made out for the role of public and press relations within marketing. Perhaps this is because it faces the same measurement handicaps as word-of-mouth. It is difficult to define, its objectives are difficult to quantify, and its effect is inextricably mixed up with the returns from other communications forces such as advertising and personal selling.

It is quite clear where its purpose usually lies. It has its primary aim set on improving company 'saleability' as defined by Leman. Where it is used for the long-term build up of company or brand reputation, for example through company sponsored books, educational programmes, films, and corporate identity programmes, the returns are earned far into the future. The returns from this kind of activity are untraceable. They flow back through the company obtaining easier sales interviews, buyers being more willing to 'adopt' new ideas because the source is credible, through more favourable word-of-mouth communication, and so on.

But public relations has been used also for its power to reach select groups and to provide a shorter-term direct effect on sales, just as advertising can be used in the same way.

It has been pointed out by a marketing authority,[15] that public relations is in many ways a sharper weapon than advertising. It ought to be used to influence the small groups who are in a position to influence sales, or who belong to a group which is influential in moulding opinion within the market.

A study has been published[16] showing how public relations techniques have been used specifically to create opinion leaders. It was used to help launch a series of pop records. Social leaders amongst students such as sports captains, secretaries of student bodies, were contacted and invited to join a select panel to help evaluate pop records. They were told that they were specially selected, that they would be paid a token fee for participating,

[15] L. Heath, 'What Marketing Expects of Public Relations'; Inst. of Public Relations, Winter Conference, 1967.
[16] J. Mancuso, 'Why Not Create Opinion Leaders for New Product Introductions?'; *U.S. Jnl. of Marketing*, Vol. 33, July 1969, pp. 20–25.

and that they would be free to leave the panel at any time. They were asked to answer a few simple questions each month. The total cost of the experiment was £2,000. Several of the company records hit the top ten charts in the test cities without contacting any record stations for plugs. and without advertising. At the time, over 200 new competitive records per week of this kind were entering the market.

We are concerned here with examining public relations only in its connection to the marketing process. Community relations programmes can be developed to assist personnel problems; financial public relations schemes to influence the sources of capital; parliamentary liaison to influence legislation. These are all part of the overall function of public relations. To consider its role within the marketing communications process, the press relations aspect of the subject must be examined, since that is where the greatest emphasis is laid by most marketing companies.

Press relations schemes are the most common form of public relations activity, particularly within industry. They have an advantage against advertising, that the source of the information is perceived to be an independently-minded editor. He apparently has no interest in the outcome of the stories other than in their intrinsic interest for his audience, and in the fact of their accuracy. Against this, must be set the fact that the message cannot be controlled by the marketing company either as to the publication in which it appears, its length, its presentation, or its timing.

A study by a trade association of different forms of media seen by buyers in the chemical industry,[17] showed the great importance of technical journals to the companies in that field, compared to other media, such as direct mail, and exhibitions. They asked respondents to rate comparatively the usefulness of the media they used. In this evaluation, editorial items in technical journals came out as most useful followed by advertisements in the same journals. Manufacturers' leaflets and catalogues appeared fairly low.

Percent of Respondents listing First:

	percentage
Editorial items	30
Technical Journal Advertisements	23
Manufacturers' representatives	22
Leaflets	13
Exhibitions	7
Catalogues	4
Others	1

Source: ISBA study of Advertising in the Chemical Industry.

[17] E. Shankleman, 'The Tools of Industrial Selling and their Deployment,' paper to the National Industrial Marketing Conference, University of Sussex, 22 Sept. 1967 (from a study by Incorporated Society of British Advertisers into advertising effectiveness in the chemical industry).

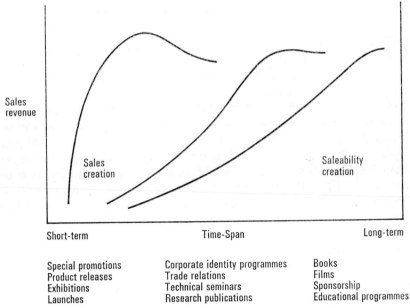

Sales revenue

Sales creation

Saleability creation

Short-term   Time-Span   Long-term

Special promotions	Corporate identity programmes	Books
Product releases	Trade relations	Films
Exhibitions	Technical seminars	Sponsorship
Launches	Research publications	Educational programmes

Figure 56 Time-span of marketing responses to public relations.

Figure 56 shows the likely time span of return against various types of public relations activity. Where the emphasis is laid on obtaining immediate sales, it is used to provide a short-term energising boost to the total marketing activity. Examples include a company launch, or the release of product news. The decay effect of this activity will be rapid unless there is a continuous use of varying kinds of activity. Constant promotion provides the company with a cumulative market reputation for 'activity' or 'size'.

Other types of activity such as sponsored sports, or films, can hardly affect sales in the short-term. They are designed to improve the general reputation and saleability of the company's name. Sometimes, short-term sales opportunities are built around these events, but in this case they act merely as a facilitating device for exposing immediate prospective buyers to company products.

Because of the peculiarity of the costing system for public relations, there is a totally different configuration from the promotional payoff curve, compared to that of, say, advertising.

Figure 57 shows a comparison of expected results from standard press relations work compared with results from advertising. The payoff from advertising expenditures occurs after a certain minimum expense level has been reached, called the 'lower' threshold. It then steadily increases with incremental returns up to the point when the rate of increasing returns begins to diminish. Press relations work has a much lower threshold of minimum expense, but diminishing returns set in more quickly. This is because press

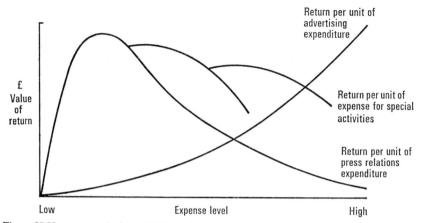

Figure 57 How press relations within marketing may be highly cost effective against advertising at low levels of expense: but it decays quickly.

In most markets, advertising begins to increase its rate of return once the lower threshold of expense has been met. Beyond this level, there are incremental returns until the market reaches advertising saturation level. The levels vary from market to market.

Advertising space must be purchased at commercial rates; the labour cost of planning, preparing and controlling add up to around 15 per cent—the cost of the agent.

Press relations is entirely labour cost, with much lower levels of absolute expense being incurred. The labour cost varies with the type and amount of activity generated. The editorial space is 'won' on the strength of the material and its interests for the readers.

Given the appropriate subject the returns from press relations at low levels of expense are likely to be significantly more cost effective than advertising at this level. But, unless special factors prevail, the rate of return decays rapidly. This is partly due to *story interest fatigue*; and partly because *editorial saturation* sets in quickly—editors are notably reluctant to constantly use news of individual companies.

The *decay rate* can be held off if special factors prevail, such as sponsorship activities; charity support; and promotional stunts. But such activities usually increase the material expense cost of public relations; they are usually expensive in themselves, with often doubtful returns from key media. They may also suffer from the problem that they are not related to specific sales points of the product.

relations is not a 'purchasing' activity except for relatively small items such as printed material. Success is a function simply of time, ability, and newsworthiness and the expense is mostly in labour costs. Advertising, on the other hand, is primarily a purchasing activity. The time costs account for only 15 per cent or so of the expense, (the agent's margin, plus company staff), the rest is purchased space or time. Advertising, as with public relations, is also sensitive to ability in exactly the same area—creativity, and programming.

The nature of the creative aspects of the two subjects is different. Advertising creativity is concerned with the presentation of audio-visual sales messages. Public relations creativity concerns events, creating circumstances where sales messages can be released. These are expected to generate interest or activity through an influential third party, such as an editor.

The two functions, advertising and public relations, are not comparable in their overall influence on marketing operations. Advertising will usually be the greater because more can be spent on it before diminishing returns set in, providing it with greater power in the communications mix. But up to a certain point of expenditure, the returns from public relations activity may be higher, £ for £, than they will be from advertising.

There is a sharp limit to the amount of interest which can be generated and sustained amongst the relatively small band of key publications which will take material continuously. The active participation and help of intermediate audiences such as editors is voluntary and is vital to the success of

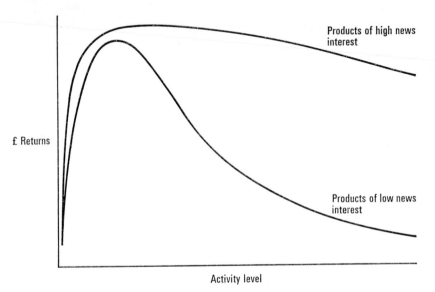

Figure 58 Interest fatigue.

the exercise. Advertising has no participation problem until it reaches the final audience. In media terms, the advertiser obtains whatever he chooses to pay for, and it is just the attention of the ultimate buyer which is required. In press relations work, the active assistance of an intermediate third party is required for the dissemination of messages. This must be won largely on the strength of the story idea and its relevance to the publication. At the same time page traffic studies show a higher interest rating for editorial compared to advertising by a factor of 3.

Public relations work is sensitive to another factor which may account for its relative failure in some markets. It depends upon the intrinsic public interest in the product, the company or the subject. This is a factor which we can call 'interest fatigue'. (*Figure 58*.)

To take an extreme example, there is hardly any need for anyone to advertise the Miss World Contest. Public relations can carry the entire task, in

Britain and abroad, simply because the mass media love printing pictures of pretty girls in bikinis. The only realistic limit to the amount of publicity which can be obtained is set by the funds available for the public relations labour cost and for limited entertaining expense.

On the other hand, a company manufacturing ball bearings or shoe laces will have the utmost difficulty in getting national publicity. Relatively 'weak' stories only will be available relating to the company and its history, plans for new markets, overseas sales orders. The public relations man must make shift as best he can with this kind of material. Or artificial stunts must be devised.

Some multi-product companies with a technical background spend great sums on public relations work, and earn a continuously high return from it. When this is examined in detail, the business can usually be seen to divide itself into several discrete product/market areas. Each one requires a special service for itself. Companies in this situation suffer less from 'interest fatigue'.

There is a further public relations problem which also affects advertising planning. This relates to the limited power of some media to reach target audience groups. For example, it may be desirable to reach the student market with news of a new slide rule product. But the power of the recognised media to reach this group is very limited indeed—perhaps by using a combination of several publications a total of 30 per cent of the target audience can be reached. Through press relations the chance of obtaining the voluntary co-operation of all of these publications with a relatively uninteresting subject is extremely poor. On the other hand, it is much easier to reach accountants or engineers with the same product. The press available have greater penetration power for these groups. The newsworthiness of the product, while still not high, is better for accountants and engineering press than it is for student publications.

Added to this is one further difficulty. The interest in a company, or in its products as expressed by the appropriate media, may or may not be the same as the sales-oriented news offered by marketing management. Usually not. The result is often a compromise, with a story developed primarily because of its appeal for certain classes of media. It is then worked upon to build in some selling point for the company. *Figure 59* shows the difficulty. Strong sales messages, offered repetitively, are not suitable for the somewhat delicate mechanism of public relations.

To summarise the role of public relations within marketing; it seems that its greatest benefit lies in its ability to influence relatively small groups. Its long-term reputation-building function clearly is designed to improve company and brand 'saleability'. Its short-term sales support operations are awkward to construct and to control but they may be effective at low cost. One of its great advantages lies in the persuasive power of its message; but the message cannot be controlled easily in its form or in the timing of its presentation. Public relations, being activity- or event-oriented, works well

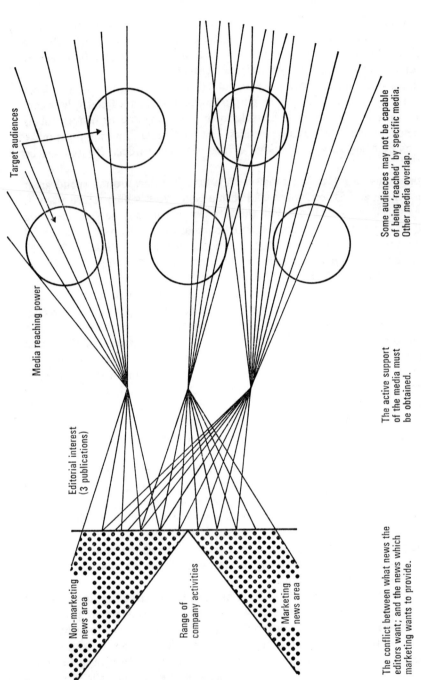

Target audiences

Media reaching power

Editorial interest
(3 publications)

Non-marketing
news area

Range of
company activities

Marketing
news area

The conflict between what news the
editors want; and the news which
marketing wants to provide.

The active support
of the media must
be obtained.

Some audiences may not be capable
of being 'reached' by specific media.
Other media overlap.

Figure 59 The press relations conflict.

at low levels of total expenditure. It suffers, however, from rapidly diminishing returns at higher levels. The response to public relations activity is subject to the amount of energy applied, the degree of creative imagination used, and the level of audience interest in the company and its activities. As with advertising, its ability to reach target sectors of the audience is constrained by the power of the media available for the task.

Example: Marketing Communications

Background

A bakery's profits were heavily influenced by sausage rolls. These accounted for only 8 per cent of the tonnage but just under 20 per cent of the total profit. Sales fell by 25 per cent over 18 months. A market survey showed that this was due to people turning more to lighter, tastier snacks, such as crisps, which were heavily promoted. Also more bread bakeries were making savoury snacks and winning sausage roll custom into their own shops.

The market is very fragmented, with many competing suppliers, some of them strong in local areas. There is little branding in the market, a very high proportion of sausage rolls being sold unwrapped through the bakery trade or to catering outlets. There is virtually no advertising within the market and the primary objective is to force distribution to stock. The product is of low priority, as a purchase, with numerous substitute products.

Problem

To arrest the decline in sausage roll sales; and to find new markets for the product.

Method

A new variety of sausage roll was produced, including more meat and with large cross cuts in the top pastry to show the meat filling clearly.

A press relations scheme was developed, using the novelty of the idea of making the sausage roll seem 'sophisticated'. The results of such a scheme are difficult to predict so plans were laid to exploit any publicity break. A story was placed with the Charles Greville column of the *Daily Mail* which talked lightly about the management problems associated with sausage rolls. They headlined the story, 'The stylish sausage roll'.

On the day the story appeared, copies of the *Daily Mail* were handed to every main customer, with samples of the new product. Small reprints of the story were placed into every wrapped sausage roll pack for two weeks. Twenty-five thousand copies of the *Daily Mail* article were posted to top buyers, and trade press advertising was booked using the newspaper story as the copy.

Further publicity was obtained; the managing director was interviewed on television for four minutes in a magazine programme; the story went on to Southern Television and on the B.B.C. news in the Midlands; it appeared in all the trade press and in two more national papers. Display material was produced to help customers to sell the sausage rolls.

No opportunity was lost in bringing the idea of sausage rolls to the attention of groups of people who could be expected to influence sales. The generation of word-of-mouth communications was actively encouraged; the entire company, its particular its sales force, were soon talking about sausage rolls, and the story caused a brief flurry of interest in the trade.

Special sample boxes of the new sausage rolls were made up and these were delivered to large potential customers who might be expected to place orders under their own brand name. These were fresh on arrival and the rolls were still warm from the oven when the buyers tasted them. The boxes were tied with pink ribbons as an added 'stylish' touch.

Results

Existing trade customers used the display material and featured the new style sausage rolls; sales began to climb again as some customers switched over from other snack products. New customers were added who had not previously bought sausage rolls. One large private label customer alone began to buy over six tons a week to sell in his shops. Within four months sales had gone back to the two-year ago level; within another four months they were 25 per cent higher again. A night shift was engaged, and a new high speed production machine was designed. An additional gross margin of over £40,000 p.a. was traced to the press relations exercise. Most of this came from new private-label customers becoming interested in what had been a low-priority product.

The press story in the *Daily Mail* itself hardly produced any extra sales— but it created the opportunity for exploitation and sales pressure which was otherwise lacking.

J.W.

16. Advertising Planning

Advertising is one of several forces contributing to the overall task of marketing communications. One single communications force hardly ever moves a sales prospect through the entire cycle of the process, leading him from a state of unawareness, through awareness of the product, comprehension about its benefits, conviction about his 'need' for it, and final action to buy it.

Only a part of one industry alone even comes close to using advertising in this way as the sole communications element. Mail order advertising in the press is the closest; even here the product is often 'sampled' first, and press advertising is only part of the much bigger mail order business which is conducted primarily through catalogues and sales agents.

On the other hand, personal selling can, and often does, carry out the bulk of the marketing communications function for many companies.

All the vehicles of the marketing communications process are mixed at several stages in order to move the prospect, inch by inch, towards the company's aim of obtaining a satisfied customer.

In its own right, advertising is not a strong persuasive force. The argument is not about how far advertising 'works', it is about how far it is cost-effective when compared to other parts of the marketing communications mix. It is more cost-efficient in some stages of the persuasive communications process than in others. For example, it can create product awareness more rapidly and cheaply than personal selling, but it is less effective at the final clinching of the sale.

There may be an argument that the very impersonality of advertising can lead to more effective demonstration of product benefits. Receivers of advertising can adopt a detached attitude to it, in a way that they find difficult to do with personal salesmen. Because of this they are forced to make for themselves the connections between the appeals of the advertised product and their own circumstances. Most large-scale advertisers would still prefer to use a personal sales force to call upon their multi-million customer groups, rather than to use advertising. As Medcalf has pointed out[1] the soap advertiser would need a sales force 160,000 strong, the size of the British

[1] G. Medcalf, *Marketing and the Brand Manager*; Pergamon Press, 1967, p. 135.

Royal Navy, in order to call upon housewives once during each weekly purchasing cycle. They would certainly sell more soap but at what cost?

In this chapter we define advertising as consisting of space, time and preparatory costs in *commissionable* media. Many companies, particularly those serving industrial markets, will also include in their budgets for advertising such matter as sales literature, direct mail, exhibitions and merchandising material.

The measurement of advertising return is perhaps the most talked-about and least understood area of marketing by company managements. Each year, the typical Board of Management reviews its expense budgets, looks at the sum spent on advertising and murmurs about the need to measure the benefits one day. Many highly complex models have been built by operations research teams within the large advertisers. Their object is to identify the precise benefits which can be obtained from different levels of advertising expense. Certainly they have enabled management to understand more clearly the process of advertising in the industry they serve, and to locate some key factors. However the question of how to establish a rate of return on the investment has baffled everyone.[2]

Perhaps an advertising man, James Wallace, may be allowed to make an uncomfortable contribution to the advertising measurement problem.[3]

> First, make a list of all the working functions of the business, such as production, research and development, maintenance, accounting, sales etc., But do *not* include advertising.
> To each one of the listed functions, allocate the exact amount of sales or profit which can properly be credited to that activity, and add up the allocations.
> Deduct the sum of these allocations from the known total of sales or profits of the business.
> What remains is the contribution of advertising.

One distinguished economist has made out a case for companies to treat advertising as a capital expense, instead of being included in the operating revenue budgets.[4] Advertising could be regarded as any other type of investment. It is concerned with spending today to achieve results in the future.

Advertising planning

The following decision areas surround advertising:

(1) Which part of the marketing communications objective is advertising suited to perform, and what level of expenditure is appropriate?
(2) What mix of advertising media should be used; with what weight and frequency?

[2] D. Wilding, 'Advertising—The Catalyst'; Market Research Society Conference Papers, April 1969.
[3] J. Wallace, 'A Perfect Measurement of Advertising's Contribution to Marketing'; *U.S. Jnl. of Marketing*, Vol. 30, July 1966, pp. 16.
[4] J. Dean, 'Does Advertising Belong in the Capital Budget?'; *U.S. Jnl. of Marketing*, Vol 30 Oct. 1966, pp. 15–21.

(3) How should the plan be phased during the year, taking into account product group needs for support, market response and seasonality, and the interaction with other parts of the marketing communications process such as sales promotion?

(4) What message and presentation forms should be used, with what variety and what weight of repetition?

(5) What are the best means of knowing what the advertising is accomplishing?

This latter point is one of the most complex problems, because at least eight factors can be identified as presenting measurement difficulties.[5]

Non-linear effects. High expenditures on promotion do not necessarily mean proportionately higher sales. Advertising 'overkill' has already been identified as one of marketing's most expensive mistakes.[6] This occurs particularly in oligopolistic consumer markets where the total sum of all the expenditures has little incremental effect on the overall size of the market. Very high rates of oligopolistic competitive advertising are used merely to support brand positions. The competing companies realise that they could all drop their expenditures proportionately and still maintain their brand shares, but no one is willing to do it unilaterally. The problem, like those of modern wars, is how to de-escalate the action without peace terms being agreed.

Threshold effects. Promotion may have no effect unless a minimum amount, called the lower threshold level, takes place. Low levels of expense in a high cost area such as advertising mean that too little communications power is being bought. The audience is hardly receiving the message, and what little is being received lacks sufficient impact. Advertising expenses seem to go critical at some level, as with a nuclear reactor. For small budgets the answer is to select a smaller task, concentrated in one sector of the audience, or at one time of year, so that although the total expenditure might be small, it is nevertheless fairly dominant in whatever is the chosen area.

Carry-over effects. Advertising does not achieve its effect immediately, but is spread over time. The memory of advertising in one period can be expected to carry-over to the next. The degree of carry over is affected by two factors at least. The first is the level of competitive advertising running in the market; the second is the length of the product purchasing cycle. If the buyer's repeat purchasing decision only comes up for renewal every few months rather than every few days, then his decisions can be 'disturbed' by competitive advertising correspondingly less frequently.

Decay effect. Nevertheless the potential repeat purchaser's memory of advertising decays over time. Strong goodwill built up at one time can be expected to weaken in the face of competitive communications pressures from all sources.

[5] P. Kotler, *Marketing Management Analysis Planning and Action;* Prentice-Hall, 1967, p. 172.

[6] D. Kelly, 'Overkill, is it Marketing's Most Expensive Mistake?' *Marketing*, June 1967, pp. 347–350.

Marketing-mix interaction effects. The results from advertising will be affected by the remainder of the marketing mix and of the other parts of the communications programme.

Environmental interaction effects. Factors external to the company, such as market response levels, economic activity, buyer's attitudes, will affect the response to advertising.

Competitive effects. The effect of advertising will be subjected to pressure from competitors' current advertising programmes. The pressure is built from what they say, the way they say it, and the power they put behind saying it.

Quality Effects. The quality of the advertising itself, its timing, its presentation, its media mix and so on, will clearly and significantly affect the sales response.

Setting the budget

All systems for arriving at advertising budgets are inadequate where the effect of advertising is not traceable but must be guessed at. Most standard methods suffer from conceptual flaws of logic. Because the 'right' answer to the problem of how much advertising to use does not exist, the least inadequate alternative, therefore, must be identified. This will be the outcome of three requirements—the least advertising waste, the least company risk (of spending too much, or not achieving the aim), and the most likely market result. The budget must be set in the light of what can be afforded, and the job to be done. The common methods are:[7]

Percentage of previous year's turnover. Where demand is known to be limited and production capacity is stable, this may be the method to use. It makes no provision for growth or for capitalising upon opportunities; and does not allow for the inflation of advertising costs. It assumes inertia. The favourite argument used by its advocates is that it is, at least, 'affordable' in the sense that expenditure will not exceed earnings. This only holds good while earnings remain constant. The system may cause them to drop, if competitors push up their advertising rate.

Percentage of future sales. At least this system has the advantage of being based upon a forecast of future sales. It does tend to encourage advertising stability in an industry. However, it may lead to over-spending in markets which are growing, and underspending in markets which are under competitive pressure. What percentage level should be used? The basic level of communications power still must be determined, and this method treats advertising as being a constant factor throughout the product life cycle.

[7] 'How to Budget for Industrial Advertising'; I.P.A., Jan. 1968. 'Setting Advertising Appropriations'; Marketing Society Study Group No. 4, 1967.

Yet new products require a higher proportion of advertising; and to increase market share requires a heavier than proportionate increase in advertising. The entire method, which is the most common one in industry, is founded upon the cliché—'if we have no information, then we will make a decision and stick with it'. It uses circular reasoning in that sales cause advertising—whereas advertising should cause sales.

Percentage of profits, or profit excess. This is a common method used by small, growing companies where advertising is not the primary communications factor. It is also used by some large advertisers who set aside a proportion of this year's profits to build up an advertising reserve for the future. Here there is even less relationship between the advertising programme and the marketing aims. This time, profits appear to cause advertising. In addition, it provides for a hopelessly unstable advertising plan, which will swing from year to year.

There is, however, one major advantage for the system. In companies which are budgeted to meet a required profit objective there is a natural reluctance to earn much more. There are three reasons for this. First it may disturb a carefully laid financing plan if the profit figure is seen to fluctuate wildly. Secondly, the shareholders in their excitement at the high profits, may require a similar return in future years. Third, the inland revenue will take a large proportion of the excess profits in company tax. This provides for the attraction of the system—when profits are in excess of the objective, any extra funds invested in market development resources such as advertising carry the implication of a 40 per cent subsidy from the tax men.

The major disadvantage beyond all, is that such a budget is liable to be slashed at the end of the financial year, if profits are down. A history of such activity within a company causes advertising managers and agencies to seek ways of spending the money early in the financial year, with an inevitable loss of performance.

Matching competition. This system helps to stabilise advertising wars, but it suffers from all the flaws of logic which apply to the other systems. In this case the reasoning runs that competition causes advertising. In practice the expenditures usually bear some relationship to the relative market shares. However, the two great problems are that competitive levels of advertising spending are notoriously difficult to calculate—particularly when competition changes its media mix radically. Secondly, it takes a considerable time for a company to respond to different levels in competitive spending. An increase in the competitive rate of spending may not be noticed for, say, three months; then it must be quantified, then the company's campaign must be similarly increased. A time lag of at least six months occurs, if not longer.

Following competitors' patterns of media spending is also dangerous, since by the nature of the system, the competitor makes all the running, and is seen to be leading the relationship.

Having stated the flaws in the system, it is only fair to say that, however elegant the rationale of the argument used by the large advertisers in oligopolistic markets to justify their high expenditure levels, in essence this is the system they are using. Advertising 'overkill' is one result of it.

Objective and task method. The system which the experts admire most, but which they find so difficult to apply, is the setting of the budget based upon an objective and task method. Here, advertising objectives are set as specifically as possible, followed by the necessary programme to reach them, plus its cost estimate.

At least the method has the merit of causing management to think through their specific advertising objectives, and to set up plans and expenditures to reach them. Over time, more experience is gained of what the programmes achieve and at what cost, so that the uncertainties begin to be reduced.

There are two enormous problems with the system, however. First, is the nature of the objectives themselves. Since advertising cannot be related directly to sales response by most companies, then another measure must be used. This could be the brand awareness level, or user penetration. But there is no knowing whether the specific advertising objective has a significant correlation with sales—although the assumption is there; and there is no knowing if it is worth reaching the objective in terms of cost. For example, the best known brand of whisky in Britain is Johnnie Walker, which has a phenomenal awareness level of unaided recall—somewhere in the 80 per cent range. Yet the brand has less than 20 per cent of the market, and by no means is the largest selling brand in this country. The detailed studies of the relationship between advertising exposure and purchasing behaviour have noted short-term relationships[8] but the conclusions are very tenuous.

The second great problem lies with the estimation of how much power, and of what kind, is needed to reach the objective.

Will an average of, say, four Opportunities To See a campaign for 60 per cent of the target audience be sufficient to attain the objective? What is the attention-getting power of the campaign, as opposed to its persuasive power? Can we be certain that the media mix we have selected will reach the spread of the audience in both the required coverage and with the required frequency? Do we require a similar objective for the total of the country, or must the campaign be weighted, area to area, or market to market? All these calculations will affect the ability of the campaign to achieve the desired objective in advertising terms, always supposing that we have sufficient information to (*a*) determine the objective, and (*b*) to measure the results, and assuming also that the advertising objective will itself have the desired effect upon sales.

[8] C. D. P. McDonald, 'Relationships Between Advertising Exposure and Purchasing Behaviour'; Market Research Society Conference papers, April 1969.

Truly advertising expenditure issues are complex. Some work has been done in the area of Bayesian theory. The Reverend Thomas Bayes was a Presbyterian minister and mathematician who lived in England in the early eighteenth century. A probability theorem developed by Bayes forms a central part of the theory. The technique is to ask management for an intuitive guess at the possible levels of sales increase which could be due to the influence of advertising. The distribution of these guesses shows the chances of attaining various levels of increase. After a series of statistical evaluations, usually involving more probability estimates, a model is constructed. This shows the key choice areas and the level of risks involved plus the expected payoff from each choice. Bayesian theory is quite useful in its simplest form to resolve complex decisions in a state of ignorance, through forcing the appropriate managers to consider the distribution of probabilities of various events happening.

Creative planning

There is no universally acceptable planning system for the development of creative advertising ideas. Each group of advertising creative executives works in a different way. The wide use of attitude research is often criticised by advertising men. They claim that it leads to the generation of concepts which recognise attitudes as they stand at present, whereas the creative task is to disturb accepted attitudes. Others claim that the use of highly imaginative and unusual approaches in advertising tends to focus the attention upon the advertising itself rather than on the product. They point out that there is no evidence that such schemes, attractive as they often are, have a more significant result upon the sales response.

There is a considerable movement away from advertising pre-testing, particularly of television commercials. Specialists in this field have moved into the area of market segmentation analysis. They provide evidence of 'spatial' areas in product fields, which no one else is exploiting, and which might respond to an advertising appeal directed in the chosen area.[9] They show, often in three dimensional form, the range of perceptions which the market holds now, of the various brands and their images.

One leading authority, Bernstein, has counselled marketing executives to be prepared to revise their entire brand strategy if they discover a method of presenting the product or the message which is distinct, and which gives them an edge in appeal over competition.[10] In advertising-responsive markets, there can be little question that a brilliant method of presenting the sales appeal may provide as much boost in brand share as a new product idea itself.

[9] Audits of Great Britain Ltd., 'Advertising Research and Creative Men—No Longer Segmented'; *Audit Magazine*, Oct. 1971.
[10] D. Bernstein, 'A Thought for St. Patrick's Day'; address to Marketing Society, 17 March, 1971.

Media selection

In terms of media selection, the extent to which companies should use press, television, magazines, posters and other media depends upon several factors.[11] First is the character of the medium, say its geographical spread or its ability to reach special groups of buyers. Second is the atmosphere in which the medium is received in relation to buying interest and ability to purchase. These factors are matched against the structure of the target audience and its media habits. The range and power of the combination of media to reach the chosen audience with the desired coverage, frequency, and at least-cost formulation are then determined. Interacting upon the media choice are creative questions which may determine some media combinations. An example would include the basic decision to use audio visual movement on television, or to rely on the printed word. Flowing from considerations of cost and creative requirement are questions of size and position, length of commercial, and time of transmission.

Media selection for consumer markets through the use of linear programming models on computers has developed very rapidly in the past ten years. Once the basic constraints of a campaign have been built in, then appropriate schedules can be developed from a very wide range of alternatives. Such constraints include the size of the budget, the minimum and maximum usages of specific media, and the required exposure rates for various categories of buyers. Under the traditional methods of media planning, only a limited range of alternative campaigns could be handled within the compass of one man's experience and knowledge.

Media planning is based upon a required number of 'bankers' to build up a certain level of audience. Specialised media are added to give the desired weight to specific parts. The tendency before the computer era was towards an over-use of certain basic media, a polarisation of competitive campaigns into similar media channels, and the inevitable bad 'skew' of exposures. The duplication of audiences between different media results inevitably in a circumstance where one section of the audience is heavily over-exposed to a campaign, while another sector of the desired audience has too light a campaign. The average of audience exposures might appear to be correct, but the distribution of exposures may be hopelessly 'skewed'. This still remains the outstanding media planning problem.

The timing of advertising campaigns. Kotler's model shows the alternative timing patterns which are available to the planner. (*Figure 60.*) There is considerable evidence that large advertisers are moving steadily towards the patterns of intermittent and alternating bursts in their schedules (box 12), rather than use continuous level spending, noticeable years ago (box 5). This is unless there are marked reasons, usually self-evident, that some other

[10] J. Hobson, *The Selection of Advertising Media*; Business Publications Ltd., 1956.

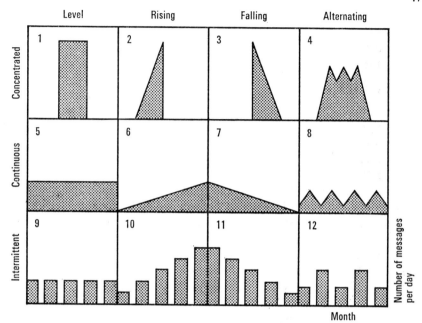

Figure 60 Advertising time patterns.

(*Source:* P. Kotler, *Marketing Management, Analysis, Planning and Control*, p. 485, Prentice, Hall, 1967)

form of advertising timing pattern applies. Rising or falling expenditures to meet high seasonal peaks in demand, or for new product introductions, may then apply.

Advertising media are becoming so costly that to continuously dominate the total of all the competitive messages being delivered would require an expenditure beyond the resources of any single brand. One 30-second commercial transmitted across all the national television networks in peak time, every night, would cost over £1 million per year. This buys the advertiser only ·002 per cent of the total audience's average viewing time each evening. The rival demands for audience attention come from programmes as well as from competitive advertising.[12] The communication cost comparison in press media is undoubtedly much the same when advertisement reading and noting averages are taken into account, rather than the much wider 'opportunities to see' measure, which tends to inflate audience figures. Large advertisers, following the principle of domination in communications theory, find that they can only afford to dominate for relatively short periods of time. Consequently, they tend to intersperse their advertising periods with sales promotion periods. During one time they will 'lead' with theme advertising, to the extent that they hope to exert more advertising pressure than

[12] Audits of Great Britain Ltd., 'Do you Plan to Burst your Advertising Schedules?; *Audit Magazine*, April 1971, pp. 7–8.

their direct competitors at this time. In the next period, the advertising is cut down to the level of supporting sales promotion schemes. These are designed to capture the interest and attention of the distributive trade and of customers at the point of sale.

Advertising research

When the total of advertising expenditure in Britain amounts to £600 million or more, as it does, with the large-scale mass advertisers accounting for half of the expenditure, the total cost is about equivalent to building one new aircraft carrier. Yet there is probably more research to support the manufacture of an aircraft carrier than there is to measure advertising effectiveness. One-tenth of 1 per cent of the total mass advertising expenditure amounts to £300,000. If half of this amount is actually spent on researching effectiveness, it would be a wildly optimistic guess. If it improved the effectiveness of marketing goods through retail shops by only one-thousandth part, then as a result sales would rise by £10 million—or marketing and distribution costs would reduce by up to £3 million. These hypothetical figures would be regarded as conservative by most economists; they are useful only insofar as they indicate the tremendous scope for savings in advertising and for finding out how to make it more effective.

Expenditure on advertising research in most companies is truly an investment of capital, which can be expected to pay off over five years or more of total advertising expenditures. One of the factors it would undoubtedly show is that advertising campaigns are changed much too frequently.

There are six areas related to advertising in which research can help:[13]

(1) Who to direct the advertising at? Consumer advertisers are well aware of the problem of identifying their audience. Most industrial advertisers, however, have a long way to go before they are aware of all those people who can influence the buying decisions—and whom they cannot reach through personal selling. And they have only limited data relating to their media habits.

(2) What to say in the advertisement. Why do people buy? Why do they not buy? Why do they stop buying? The research techniques for measuring these aspects of the problem are well proven—depth interviews and attitude studies. Unfortunately, most advertisers are too busy making decisions based upon the reasons they imagine are causing people to buy.

(3) When to say it. The time of peak enquiries does not always correspond with the time of peak sales—in most industrial buying situations there is a long lag in between.

(4) How to say it. This is a tricky area of advertising pre-testing where the techniques could be developed, but few are willing to pay for them. Highly structured interviewing techniques, problem-oriented and small samples, all too often show that contrasting advertising approaches are not significantly different, although common sense says otherwise. Such tests usually fail to show why one campaign is better than another. Advertising

[13] H. Gordon, 'Yes, Virginia, Research Helps Make Better Advertisements'; *U.S. Jnl. of Marketing*, Vol. 31, Jan. 1967, pp. 64–66.

research, which shows simply accept/reject results, is clearly inadequate. What is needed is more diagnostic research—and research techniques which are not geared to specific theories of advertising.[14] However, they cost more, and they assist managements' comprehension of the communications process, rather than compare advertising schemes.
(5) How well did the advertising do? Message registration, advertising recall, customer action, inquiry response. In most cases it is difficult to connect advertising directly with sales response and it may be uneconomic to try.

Industrial advertising

The role of advertising compared to that of personal selling in industry is of generally less importance. Yet paradoxically some industrial marketing companies in specialised product fields manage to rely on it entirely with little support from field sales. Just as the consumer package goods company cannot do without field salesmen in some part of its overall marketing communications programme, so the average industrial marketing organisation has a critical need for advertising. It is to solve the problem posed by *Figure 61*. Most people who take part in buying decisions refuse to see sales engineers. At general management level, only two directors in ten will see salesmen; they cannot be reached except by word-of-mouth, direct mail, advertisements and exhibitions. The process of getting to them should be viewed as sequential. When they *do* see salesmen it is because they have been influenced to do so by their colleagues through word-of-mouth or by advertising. And sales engineers provide them with their most important source of information on products. But somehow they must be persuaded to see them first.

Evaluating industrial advertising's contribution. In one reported case,[15] that of a general machinery manufacturer, the contribution of advertising was estimated for each step of the sales process. These steps were listed as: making the contact, arousing interest, creating a preference, making specific proposals, closing the deal, and keeping the customer sold. Each step was assigned a weight reflecting its importance. Creating a preference and keeping the customer sold were considered the most important steps and assigned weights of 25 each. Arousing interest and making proposals were next in importance, with weights of 15 each.

Advertising contributed towards the fulfilment of each step. It was regarded as more important for some steps than for others. For example, 30 per cent of the 'making contact' step was attributed to the role of advertising, a third of the 'aroused interest' was attributed to advertising, but only 10 per cent of the 'preference creation' and 10 per cent of 'keeping the customer sold' was attributed to advertising. If the weight of each step in the sales process is

[14] A. Cohen, *At the Receiving End: Five Case Studies of Advertising Research*; J. Walter Thompson Company Ltd., booklet No. 22, 1967.
[15] C. Freeman, 'How to Evaluate Advertising's Contribution'; *Harvard Business Review*, July–Aug. 1962, p. 137.

In industry personnel with these functions → consider, in the percentages shown, these factors to be amongst the two most important when obtaining information on products*	Board (general management)	Operating management	Production engineering	Design and development engineering	Maintenance engineering	Research	Buying	Finance	Sales	Others
Catalogues	39	36	45	64	34	64	52	32	44	76
Direct mail	12	9	14	6	31	21	23	14	5	27
Sales engineers' visits	66	61	60	67	78	64	64	60	73	40
Advertisements in trade press	14	32	28	22	21	15	12	23	24	24
Exhibitions	15	17	11	11	47	15	9	19	14	12
Demonstrations by manufacturers	50	41	35	26	37	21	37	38	45	22
Other	6	4		6			5	5	35	

Figure 61.1 Methods of receiving information on products—all industry.

Example: In industry generally board members who play more than an occasional role in purchasing, in 66 per cent of cases consider sales engineers' visits to be amongst the two most important methods of obtaining information on products.

In industry personnel with these functions → see or do not see sales engineers, in these percentages, as given below*	Board (general management)	Operating management	Production engineering	Design and development engineering	Maintenance engineering	Research	Buying	Finance	Sales	Others in company	Others outside company
Percentage of all personnel who see sales engineers	18	52	36	45	38	26	74	13	15	13	3
Percentage of personnel who take part in purchasing who DO NOT see sales engineers	78	44	42	23	41	50	13	71	78	60	83
Percentage of personnel seeing sales engineers and NOT playing more than an occasional role in purchasing (i.e. wasted visits)	7	8	9	6	45	25	11	73	46	48	58

Figure 61.2 Effectiveness of Sales Engineer's Visits.

*In industry generally 26 per cent of research personnel see sales engineers. However 50 per cent of research personnel who play more than an occasional role in purchasing do not see sales engineers. Further 25 per cent of research personnel who see sales engineers do not play more than an occasional role in purchasing. Notice that 78% of general managements who do take part in purchasing decisions claim never to see sales engineers.

(*Source: How British Industry Buys*, pp. 88–89; Sponsored by Industrial Market Research Ltd./ Institute of Marketing, 1967)

multiplied by the portion attributed to advertising, the total influence of advertising can be derived as indicated in the table below, which is taken from the study.

	Importance in Sales Process ×	*Importance of Advertising Contribution* =	*Share of Advertising Contribution*
Making contact	10%	30%	3%
Arousing interest	15%	33·3%	5%
Creating a preference	25%	10%	2·5%
Making a proposal	15%	0	0
Closing the sale	10%	0	0
Keeping the customer sold	25%	10%	2·5%
	100%		13%

One way for an individual company to estimate the weights to apply to various aspects of advertising is to construct an ends and means matrix for the company, as shown in *Figure 62*.[16]

Ends / Means	Create awareness	Stimulate interest and favourable attitudes	Need gate	Generate enquiries	Take and execute orders	Maintain customer relations
Press advertising						
Direct Mail						
Personal calls						
Exhibitions						
Public relations						
Technical literature						
Others						

Figure 62 Selling: ends and means matrix.

Researching Industrial Advertising. One single market study can be carried out, often at relatively low cost, to assist the construction of industrial advertising schedules.

A sample of potential buying companies can be contacted, using industrial research techniques, involving small samples, interviewed at length. The

[16] E. Shankleman, 'The Tools of Industrial Selling and their Deployment'; Paper to the National Industrial Marketing Conference, University of Sussex, 22nd Sept. 1967.

questionnaire examines first the nature of the current buying practice within the customer group. It identifies the steps of the decision process, and indicates who influences each step—from screening suppliers, to selecting a range of alternative quotations, their evaluation, testing and final choice.

The questionnaire then identifies the key factors in the product area which influences each person's decision. It asks each decision influencer how he receives information relating to products of this kind, followed by a company and brand awareness check. Finally, questions relating to the aided and unaided recall of trade and business magazines are asked. In this way, a reasonably complete dossier on the company communications process is built up, and can be expected to remain unchanged in most markets for a number of years.

Market Situation Factors

Package Goods: Consumer

Clearly, here one finds the mass advertising programmes. When purchasing cycles are short, then advertising must be run frequently. In these companies the primary job of the marketing manager lies in the area of allocating the advertising expenditure, directing, controlling and measuring it.

Consumer Durables

Advertising is most likely to be seasonal. Often it is promotion related, and frequently operated with a careful watch for its effect on the distributive trade. Heavy emphasis is laid on point of sale support. The advertising is directed at creating product awareness and not clinching the sale.

Components

Advertising is usually product related, concentrating on the 'lead' products in the range. Creative approaches concentrate more on the functional aspects of products. Such companies are heavy users of direct mail. Much of the problem for these companies is to locate potential customers, and advertising is used frequently to obtain direct response in the form of sales enquiries or requests for literature. Many companies, serving industrial markets which are scattered, rely on advertising with a telephone follow-up for their entire selling operation to small customer prospects. Particularly is this true of differentiated products sold in small quantities.

Plant and Equipment

Most of the advertising for these companies is part of a corporate communications task, even though company products may be featured. The primary problem is to influence people whom the sales engineers never meet, particularly those at Board of Management level, and to create company awareness.

These are the heavy advertisers in the business and financial press which can be used to create an atmosphere of confidence and high reputation for the organisation.

Materials

Material suppliers are heavy users of corporate communications programmes, to influence many different audiences apart from the buying decision influencers. Many of them rely on their consumer product advertising campaigns to carry-over into the industrial buying sectors. Because the companies are large they run campaigns to influence the sources of finance; the shareholders, and other outside groups who are influential to their goodwill.

Differentiated Products

Companies concentrate on establishing their differences, and reinforcing their appeal to distinct market segments.

Undifferentiated Products

The creative appeal is more likely to be related to peripheral factors such as company service, or to less rational motives on the part of buyers.

Market Structures

Campaigns in fragmented markets are usually product and company oriented. They appeal directly against competition, with strong emphasis laid upon effect of advertising directed at the distributive trade. Oligopolists use advertising as a strategic weapon to close off their markets from competition. They can sell over the heads of the distributive trade by using their advertising power with the end-users. In concentrated markets, advertising becomes more general in its effect, and is used to support the overall market and company reputation.

Distributive Characteristics

As one moves from mass distribution to opsonistic and monopsonistic markets, the emphasis on advertising runs from very high indeed down to almost nil. Even those companies selling to opsonistic markets, however, like the reassurance of a public reputation within the trade, and frequently run advertising campaigns to this end. Much of the distributor co-operative advertising work is done in these markets, where buyers are provided with funds to conduct campaigns which will help to move the suppliers' products.

Example: Advertising Testing

Background

One large advertising agency, The J. Walter Thompson Company, operates what it calls a 'creative workshop' through its research subsidiary company.

In 1968, it published a booklet showing the results of advertising tests for a variety of clients. This is adapted from the published results of pre-testing Pin-Up home-perm advertising.

The method

The starting point of every creative workshop is a briefing form which sets out the creative strategy. This is defined in terms of the impressions which should be implanted in the minds of the consumer. People within the 'target group' of the audience are contacted, shown the advertising and interviewed to discover how their ideas, beliefs and feelings with respect to the product relate to those defined in the strategy. The questions are 'open-ended', a free response is encouraged and interviewers probe intensely at critical points of the interview. About twenty interviews are usually sufficient.

The problem

Pin-Up home-perm is a product with certain unique advantages. The advertisement tested was designed to communicate the ideas that Pin-Up's exclusive foam neutraliser makes it easier and less messy to use than other home-perms, and gives better control of the final result. The advertisement tried to convey the impression of a modern product, used by young, fashionable, sophisticated women rather than by teenagers. The intriguing headline—'You can do anything with Pin-Up'—and the model in the advertisement had a significant contribution to make to the mood conveyed. Accordingly, it was important to ensure that the headline stopped short of innuendo, and that the model was not too sophisticated to be acceptable, both in herself and as a symbol of the product.

The test

The target group for the Creative Workshop consisted of 20 home-perm users under the age of 45 in the lower middle and working classes.

The foam neutraliser made a great impression on the women interviewed, and the advantages—no drips and no mess—were immediately seized on:

'It says there's no mess, just foam, and that is a good thing, I suppose—you don't want it running down your neck.'
(Lower middle class/22)

'The only home-perm with a foaming neutraliser.'
(Lower middle class/33)

'It's got this foam neutraliser in it so you don't get the mess and drips like you do with a lot of other perms.'
(Working class/42)

'It's a new type of foam neutraliser one. It doesn't drip and you get all the hair covered with it. I suppose the foam seeps through the rollers and covers it evenly, and of course it produces a first-class result. You get a professional look to your hair, not a home-perm look.'
(Lower middle class/31)

The headline succeeded in stimulating interest in the advertisement:

'It chains your attention to Pin-Up . . . you notice it.'
(Working·class/39)

'It draws your attention to it—to the advertisement—you see that first and it makes you wonder what it's about.'
(Working class/42)

But there was no suggestion that a double-entendre was read into the head-line, and in general it was thought to mean simply that Pin-up was an adaptable product, suitable for all hair types and styles:

'It doesn't matter what style and cut, you get the best with Pin-Up . . . I think it sums it up in a few words.'
(Lower middle class/33)

'That you can perm your hair in any style you wish to . . . well, I think, as I said, it covers everything.'
(Working class/40)

The one aspect of the advertisement to excite controversy was the hair style. A few women commented that the style was soft, light and natural:

'It didn't look so set as most perms. It looked more natural, it didn't look as if it was just permed.'
(Working class/43)

But the majority of the women interviewed made unfavourable comments. One or two felt the style was too sophisticated to be appropriate for a home-perm product:

'The sort of people who are going to have that sort of hair style are going to have it done at a shop.'
(Working class /19)

Rather more criticised the style, not as being too elaborate, but as looking ruffled and untidy:

'Her hair is all scraggy, and personally I don't believe in it if that's what it does, and I'd go mad if my hair was like that . . . it was all over the place, it looked as if she'd been out in the wind.'
(Lower middle class/18)

'I think, myself, it looks most untidy. It looks as if she's just got out of bed and hasn't done it yet.'
(Lower middle class/31)

'The hair style looks as if it's gone frizzy.'
(Working class/31)

'She looks as though she's been out in the wind a lot—she looks a bit ruffled.'
(Working class/36)

'All her hair was going all bits everywhere.'
(Lower middle class/16)

It was clear that the hair style depicted in the advertisement was beyond the experience of many of the home-perm users and, paradoxically, too sophisticated to be an effective symbol of sophistication.

Result

The test showed that the advertisement had a great deal to commend it. But the model's hair style was likely to lead to misunderstanding. Accordingly, it was decided to take a photograph of the model with her hair styled less extravagantly, and the advertisement was run in revised form.

J.W.

17. Planning Sales Promotion

Sales promotion can be described as the hysterical arm of marketing operations. In the next ten years an element of rationality will steadily be introduced into sales promotion planning in consumer product companies as a result of forecasting models being developed based upon consumer panel figures.

Evidence needs to be gained about the delicate relationship between brand-switching and variances in advertising and sales promotion activity. Once this is done, then sales promotion in consumer markets will take its place with advertising and selling as a respectable activity, making a real and measureable contribution to marketing efficiency.

Until the time when appropriate models will be built and validated, then the emotion will prevail. The great difficulties involved in measuring the effect of sales promotion lie in problems connected with its synergistic effect on other activities. Other difficulties include its transient nature, being usually short-term; the proliferation of different types of scheme; and the rich multitude of specific problems it is called upon to resolve.

The great worry which besets brand marketing strategists lies in evaluating the long-term effect of successive sales promotion schemes. Their effect on both the attitude of the market towards the brand, and the cumulative effect of all the competitive promotions on the purchasing habits of the buyers, needs to be studied (*Figure 63*).

Allocating funds between advertising and sales promotion

The general methods used to set advertising budgets have already been discussed in the chapter on Advertising. The difficult problem arises in deciding the allocations between the two main streams of activity, advertising and promotion.

Competitive split method. The most common method is to decide the overall promotion allocation by one of the arbitrary systems previously described, and to subtract from it the essential support expenses. Display material, salesman's aids, literature, price lists, and trade mailings are the kind of expenses which must be incurred to keep the operation going. From infor-

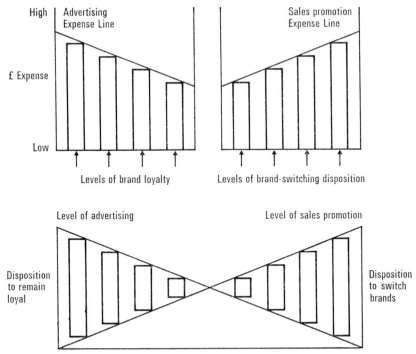

High | Advertising Expense Line

£ Expense

Low

Levels of brand loyalty

Sales promotion Expense Line

Levels of brand-switching disposition

Level of advertising

Level of sales promotion

Disposition to remain loyal

Disposition to switch brands

Figure 63 How more sales promotion may harm your market. As the ratio of sales promotion to advertising increases there is a tendency for the market to concentrate on purchasing for artificial reasons. The culminative effect is to force the market into brand-switching habits. The market becomes fragmented with special offers; there is then a focus upon shop loyalty rather than brand loyalty and a consequent fight for distribution. This leads to further sales promotion activity and an ultimate weakening of the brand identity.

mation obtained through retail audits, or through consumer panels, a calculation is made showing the ratio by which competitors are splitting their allocations. Rules of thumb might show one market as having a 2:1 split in favour of advertising; another fractured market might show a 2:1 split in favour of promotion. Knowing the competitive allocations, a decision is taken to follow the split. Alternative tactics include the use of a higher advertising proportion, or higher sales promotion proportion, depending upon which theory of the persuasive communications process is currently in vogue with marketing management. The advantage of the method is that it tends to stabilise the total spending in the market through keeping the basic flaws in the system constant over all competitors, through time.

Discretionary allocation method. A slightly more realistic approach is taken by those companies which recognise the interaction between objectives and costs. These companies decide their overall promotion budget requirements as before. They determine the minimum funds they require for theme advertising to just hold their market position. They do the same for sales promotion, calculating the absolute basic cost to hold their share. The difference between this basic budget and the total funds they are prepared to spend, to achieve whatever position in the market they require, is now a 'discretionary' factor. This must be allocated between advertising and sales promotion. At this point the companies list their primary problems, and their sub-problems, in order to decide what types of activity are required to resolve them. This is matched against the discretionary funds available and an allocation is decided. The method suits growing markets because of the size of the discretionary funds available. It also tends to boost the level of advertising spending against sales promotion because the basic and essential advertising costs are so much higher than those for sales promotion.

Synergistic method.   When more data becomes available about the interactive effects of various promotion activities, then companies will begin to use the model-building synergistic method. Synergy has been described by Ansoff as the $2+2=5$ principle. Through interaction, the whole is greater than the sum of the parts. This method requires that all the key problems and sub-problems are listed, and developed into objectives. The problems will be related to (*a*) the market and its development, (*b*) the product and its position, (*c*) the distributive trade, both selling-in and selling-out, (*d*) the company organisation such as sales force, or physical distribution.

A search then is made of all the likely combinations of activity in order to resolve the problems with the best use of the synergistic effect. The solutions are quantified as to their cost and their effect. The least cost formulation for optimising the objectives is calculated, which in turn sets the budgets and the allocations. The activity is finally programmed.

The method has the benefit of flowing from the problems identified by the company; and the basic constraints, such as minimum desired levels of advertising expenditure, can be built into the calculations. It is more flexible than the other methods, but it will be almost impossible to trace whether the judgements as to the optimum 'mix' of promotional expenditures are correct.

The theory of promotional payoff.   *Figure 64* shows the 's' curve theory of promotional payoff as developed by Industrial Market Research Ltd.

If the company is promoting in a given market, the relationship between the extra buyers attracted and the promotion expenditure will be in the shape of a normal Sigma curve. The exact shape of the curve will alter marginally as the target group buyers in the market change; as the costs of promotion inflate; and finally owing to the carry-over effect of previous promotions. The effect of promotion in one period will be to an extent affected by the response in the previous period, although the decay effect of sales promotion schemes is usually sharp. Also the fixed costs of advertising and selling can be expected to inflate so that the initial position of the C1 plot will alter.

it on to his customer. In most cases he is asking for a disguised increase in his margin—usually in the form of a cost subsidy of some kind. The same study showed that over half of all grocery buyers wanted to abandon all forms of incentive offer, except price cuts. (*Figure 66.*)

	Per cent of buyers in favour of price cuts only
All stores	53
By store type:	
Multiples	62
Co-operatives	67
Voluntary chains	21

Figure 66 Proportion of buyers wanting only price cuts, and not other incentives.

(*Source:* Retail Business 129, November 1968, *Dealer Incentives* (Marketing Advisory Services Ltd.), p. 27)

The giant retail multiples are using their negotiating power to force manufacturers to join in their co-operative advertising campaigns. Many do so willingly, knowing that display and stock levels are guaranteed. Others have refused to participate because of their dislike of losing control over their advertising appropriations. These are schemes where the media selection is done by the store, and in the store's own interests, rather than those of the manufacturer.

Objectives for promotions

Many lists have been made of all the possible reasons for running a sales promotion scheme; but most of them relate side advantages of different types of scheme as 'objectives'.

A Marketing Society study report was explicit on the subject, condensing all the reasons into the following categories:[4]

(1) Increasing consumer sales.
Either the same people can buy more, in which case the appropriate promotion scheme might be a giveaway or special price offer; or more people can buy the product in the first place, which might call for sampling, or a money-off voucher scheme.
(2) Holding sales level against competition.
This might be in terms of consumer sales or of brand share, and self-liquidators or competitions might be considered.
(3) Increasing distribution in depth.
By increasing stockholdings in existing outlets, or through the use of trade offers, this objective might be reached.
(4) Increasing distribution in width.
This may be done by using promotions designed to open new accounts, perhaps through an opening order offer, or through a banded pack consumer offer.

[4] 'Measuring Trade and Consumer Promotions'; Marketing Society Study Group Report No. 5, 1968.

W.O.M.P.—K

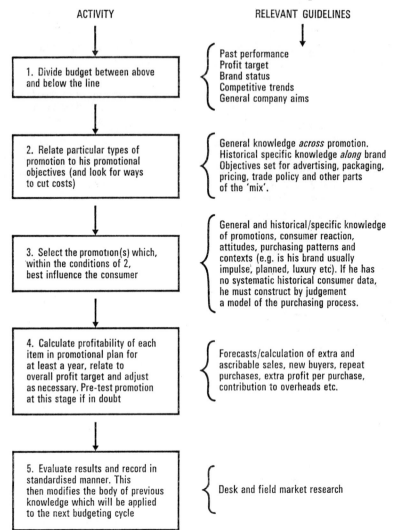

Figure 67 The planning procedure for sales promotion.

(*Source:* M. C. J. Barnes, C. D. P. McDonald, R. T. J. Tuck, Thompson Award Silver Medal Paper, 1969, 'Evaluating Below the Line Expenditure'.)

To these must be added the objective of motivating the sales forces towards a multitude of objectives, usually through the use of competitions, incentives, or bonus rewards. (*Figure 67.*)

The most common types of consumer promotion

This section is adapted from a study prepared by Miss Ann Morgan for the advertising agents, Ogilvy, Benson and Mather Ltd.[5]

[5] A. Morgan (Miss), *A Guide to Consumer Promotions*; Ogilvy, Benson and Mather Ltd., London 1970.

Competitions. These tend to appeal to younger housewives of the upper middle class groups. Competitions do not suffer from the disadvantages of many other types of promotion scheme, in that the costs are not open-ended—they can be determined in advance, and there is no need to pack specially prepared versions of the product.

On the other hand, competitions need a high level of direct advertising support, and the costs are rising rapidly as manufacturers search for more original and sometimes exotic prizes.

It is essential to have good distribution in the chosen area, and it is necessary to secure the shopkeeper's goodwill in order to display the entry forms.

The crucial decisions relate to the structure of the prizes—whether to have a pyramid structure with one big prize, some good seconds and thirds, or whether to offer a larger number of less valuable prizes. Experts differ as to which is the best, but experience shows that entries do increase if most contestants have a good chance of winning something however small.

Competitions can achieve their marketing objectives even though the number of entries is relatively small, particularly if the aim is to promote display, or to provide a vehicle for product publicity.

Free premiums. This is where the consumer receives a free gift at the moment of purchase. Such gifts are usually classified as with-pack, in-pack and on-pack premiums. Each type has subtle differences in its appeal.

The search for the ideal premium is related to several factors. These include the association of the premium to the product and its use, the links with the advertising creative strategy, the cost and value of the gift, and its originality.

(1) The with-pack premium has an immediate appeal because it is given away separately to the pack, and does not suffer from the problem of the manufacturer having to pack the premium with the product. This type of premium is useful for stimulating consumer trial. There is good display potential, and if a collectable item is offered, it can be used to stimulate repeat purchasing.

However, the scheme does need planning a long way in advance, and it may be necessary to give the dealer a handling charge for his assistance. There needs to be constant supervision and monitoring of displays, and this makes the with-pack premium less suitable for small outlets. The promotion should be advertised and there should be overprinting on the pack itself, and on the premium, so as to prevent misappropriation.

(2) The in-pack premium. The gifts can be fairly inexpensive and this type of offer usually ensures good product display in-store. On the other hand it may be difficult to pack on high speed production lines, and there will be considerable limitations on the shape and size of the premium. Advertising is essential for the success of this type of premium.

(3) The on-pack premium. Advertising support is not absolutely essential with the on-pack premium, and there is greater flexibility in the shape and size of premium which can be used, although severe constraints will

operate on display space in-store. The display value of these offers is very high. The on-pack premium can stimulate repeat purchasing through offering a voucher against the next purchase; and a collectable item may be used to stimulate repeat purchasing. Storage and carriage are more difficult, but packaging is often easy, provided the production line does not operate at very high speed.

With all premiums it is essential that the item offered is known to the consumer and is one which he or she wants. If it is an item which the retailer normally stocks, then an allowance must be made to him for his loss of profit on normal sales. It is crucial to synchronise the timing of stocks in the trade with the break of advertising support.

Most premiums need pre-testing so that the estimates of consumer off-takes are as accurate as possible. If premiums stocks run short, then the company may be held to be misleading the consumer.

Free mail-in premiums. These are the free gifts for which consumers apply by sending in packet tops, bottle tops, and such like. The gift may be an item, or money, or a voucher against the next purchase. With this type of premium it is possible to offer a more expensive gift since not everyone will apply for it, and there is considerably more scope in the range of items which can be offered. It is not so dependent upon the retailers' co-operation, and does not interfere with packing lines. It is particularly useful for products which move through a very wide variety of outlets.

The trouble is that the financial commitment is open-ended, and the costs increase directly with the success of the offer. The great danger is when companies considerably underestimate the offtake, having to pay more for rush extra deliveries, even if these are available. The problem of overestimating the demand is equally difficult, since remaindering stocks through special clearing houses can also be expensive. The incentive to the consumer is less immediate, and the post and packing costs can be high.

Such premiums need advertising support, and flexible supplies of the item. If money vouchers are used, then the apparent cost of the offer rises. In other words, offering an item *worth* 20p may only cost the company 12p plus postage and packing. But offering a voucher for 20p costs exactly that, plus postage.

These premiums are the ones most often run regionally, or with heavy pre-testing to evaluate them.

Free premiums with continuous coupons. This is where tokens are packed with the product, collected by the consumer and mailed to the company to obtain free gifts. The scheme is used to ensure brand loyalty and to cause repeat purchasing, and is particularly helpful in undifferentiated product fields.

There is some difficulty experienced in sustaining the excitement, and the biggest handicap is that the scheme is virtually impossible to end without dropping the product. Very expensive catalogues are required, and the scheme needs a strong administrative organisation to handle it.

Personality promotions. In these schemes, housewives are rewarded with money or a gift, if they have the product in the home, or are using an item at a specific time, and can prove this when someone calls on her.

These schemes were at one time very fashionable and highly successful, but the novelty has now worn off somewhat. The person calling is usually given some special name, and advertising support to announce his or her presence in the area is essential. The scheme is very useful for boosting the entire marketing operation in one area; salesmen can link in to open new accounts, existing stockists will order more, both the frequency of consumption and trial sampling rates go up. The schemes always create a great deal of excitement, and can be used for product publicity purposes in the area concerned.

However, the schemes are expensive to run. They require very extensive preparation, and to some extent the costs are open-ended. The advertising needs to be supplemented by a door-to-door leaflet, distribution, plus display build-up in the shops.

There is a danger that the schemes may not now be legal, although this has not been tested in the courts at the time of writing.

Money-off and banded packs. This is a price cut marked on the pack, or the banding of two or more units together to make a composite pack. The benefit to the consumer is immediate and obvious, and such schemes can be used to reach a wide variety of marketing objectives. These range from increasing rates of consumption to countering competitors' moves and forcing distribution. A popular product can be used to carry the sale of a less popular product, to encourage trial sampling. The promotions are usually expensive, since the price cut must be fairly deep[6] and the retailer will expect his normal margin. If price cuts are run too often, then consumers may be resentful at having to pay the normal price. Such offers, when operated widely by all competitors in a market, cause brand switching and weaken repeat purchasing patterns and brand loyalty.

Money-off vouchers. This is a coupon redeemable in stores against the purchase of the products. The coupons can be distributed in a variety of ways, say through newspapers, door-to-door delivery, or by putting the voucher on another product. The vouchers can also be of several kinds, offering different money values, or an offer against the purchase of a variety of different products. The advantages of the scheme are that it can help force distribution, and avoids the need for special printed packs. It is particularly useful to support new product launches.

It is difficult to assess the redemption rate, however, and the costs are

[6] 'Money-off Promotions'; *Nielsen Researcher*, July–Aug. 1964, pp. 3–7.

open-ended. There may be a problem of misredemption. Companies have been known to find that they are subsidising the sales of competitors' products.

The essentials of such schemes are that good distribution of the coupon must be obtained, together with good distribution of the product. The price cut must be deep enough to move consumers from their normal purchase habits, and to go to the bother of taking their coupons with them when they shop. Trade co-operation is essential, and the total cost of the promotion can be very high.

Sampling. This is the traditional technique for launching new products and for widening trial users. The consumer is given some of the product free, or allowed to use it during a given period. The samples can be distributed in a number of ways—a demonstrator in-store; given with another product; distributed door-to-door, advertised for consumers to write in. Mass sampling is by far the quickest way to obtain widespread consumer trial, and it creates excitement.

The disadvantages are that it is extremely expensive, not only in distribution costs, but also in the preparation of the samples. The products need to have a demonstrable advantage which the consumer can perceive. It needs good sample distribution control to prevent them going astray, and it needs the co-operation of the trade. The conversion to product usage will be assisted if the opening sample also carries a money-off voucher for the first purchase.

Self-liquidating premiums. This is a premium offered to the consumer in return for proof of purchase plus money. The manufacturer aims to recover the cost of the entire scheme from the money paid by the consumer. The advantage to the consumer is that the offered price is a reduction on the normal retail cost of buying the item.

In the short run, self-liquidators can increase purchasing and consumer trial; self-liquidators also provide a good excuse for elaborate displays in-store and they add excitement to the products. One advantage is that the operation can usually be mounted quickly to resolve a short-term problem, such as countering a competitor's move.

The items need to be not only wanted by the consumer but original and newsworthy. As shops carry wider and wider ranges of goods, it is increasingly difficult to find premiums which they are not currently selling—otherwise the manufacturer must compensate them for loss of profit. Liquidators need advertising support, and it is difficult to achieve long-term sales impact with them. The estimation of demand is difficult, and flexibility of supplies is needed. The saving in cost to the consumer must be seen to be significant, and this means using premiums on which there is a high trade margin Problems of administration, packing and postage must also be watched.

Individual outlet promotions. This refers to promotions which are organised by the retailer in his individual shops. The usual types are related items promotions, where two products from different manufacturers, which are normally related in purchasing, are promoted at the same time. This can be achieved using a banded offer; a deep price cut; or an in-store demonstration.

The advantage is that these promotions are highly flexible, although they are usually designed to solve the retailer's problems rather than those of the manufacturer. Manufacturers have much less control over this type of promotion, but retailer co-operation is assured. If the manufacturers supplies merchandising or demonstrating staff, then the costs can be very high when measured against the additional gross profit resulting, although in absolute terms the costs are relatively small. This type of promotion penetrates deeper into each outlet, but lacks coverage.

Multiple group promotions. These are the schemes which are designed by manufacturers to be run exclusively in a group of outlets. Retail groups like this form of promotion, and the absolute cost of the promotions can be fairly low. Provided that the multiple has good control over its outlets, then retailer co-operation is assured. If the promotions are advertised, there is a danger of irritating other multiple groups which normally stock the products. The promotions lack coverage, which is restricted naturally to the areas where the group has outlets. These promotions can be very valuable to manufacturers whose distribution is limited to a few multiple groups—those with a near-opsonistic distribution network.

Trading stamps. The trading stamp schemes either have the bonus stamps given to customers by the multiples themselves who normally deal in stamps; or they are packed with the product in the pack. To manufacturers they have some of the advantages of the free continuous promotion schemes, using coupons, and retailer co-operation is assured. Sometimes an advertising subsidy is required by the retailer to promote the scheme. The disadvantages are that trading stamps are opposed by a number of very large retailer groups who will not accept the stamps enclosed with the package. Schemes of this kind do not win the customers' loyalty to the brand because they have a variety of sources from which to collect stamps. Furthermore, the schemes are not under the control of the manufacturer.

Trade promotions

Bonus offers are the most popular and frequent type of promotion aimed at the distributive trade. There are various methods by which the offer can be made to the trade. For example (*a*) a cash discount as a percentage of turnover, (*b*) cash per case, (*c*) against a certain quantity order over a specified period, or (*d*) related to another product in order to force its distribution—these are the most common.

A deferred discount is often given to retailer groups who purchase an agreed volume over, say, a year, and this can be an effective way of holding retail support. Such discounts tend to be self-perpetuating, however, and are very difficult to drop—they are also quite difficult to avoid giving even when the total order does not quite hit the target in the time specified, unless the manufacturer is in a dominating market position.

Extra goods. These are popular, particularly to force the distribution of new products. In this way, free goods are made available against specified order levels. This is the traditional method of stock-loading the trade. The company offers, say, one free case in six; it is particularly useful for countering competitors' planned activity before it starts. The danger in filling up the distributive pipeline with too much stock which cannot be moved quickly by the trade is self-evident and is very harmful to future trade relationships where it occurs.

Coupons. Where consumer schemes are operating, trade support is frequently sought by the offer of coupons packed in the outer case.

Gifts. It is not easy to draw the line between giving gifts and bribes. Many multiple group head offices refuse to allow any kind of gift to their shop managers. But gifts are often given for opening orders; and they are often given to the shopkeeper who co-operates in a self-liquidating premium scheme. He can usually keep the item which has been used in his display, once the scheme is over.

Other trade schemes. Mystery shoppers are popular as a cheap method of forcing display. Somebody simply walks into the shop and if the item is on display, or if the assistants recommend the product, then they are immediately given a cash prize or gift. Similar schemes have been run as consumer promotions, but they need very heavy advertising support, and are not popular.

Trade competitions are popular with manufacturers attempting to secure goodwill and to provide their field sales with additional selling features. Often the retailer who supplies the customer who wins a consumer competition will also qualify for a prize.

The trade usually participate in self-liquidating offers on similar terms to those offered to consumers.

Promotions within the Sales Force

There are four accepted ways of motivating salesmen. The first is by varying commission rates. The second is by offering a special bonus against the achievement of specific targets. The third is by a sales contest; and the fourth is by an incentive scheme involving gifts.

Commission rates. The commission must be a high enough proportion of the salesman's take-home pay, before it will motivate him—if one-third of his earnings or more is variable according to his performance, then his response will be high.

The problem with commission rates is that they tend to be regarded as part of normal salary, and salesmen become irritated if there is a change in their circumstances such as a territory alteration, or product withdrawal. Commissions do not always reflect performance; sometimes they are the chance result of a particularly good territory. Target setting is a difficult problem; individually the targets are always either too high, causing a disgruntled salesman, or too low, causing an unnecessary loss to the company. Nevertheless, the standard commission system is the most widely used, wherever there is a traceable effect between the salesman's efforts and the results.

Special bonus. To work properly, the bonus must be fairly substantial in relation to the man's total take-home pay. The problems of target setting and unjust results apply as in commission schemes. However, the bonus has the advantage of being set usually for a very special task—such as a sell-in, for new accounts opened, or for a special territory campaign when the men are away from home. It is usually run for a limited time period.

Bonus schemes are often inflexible. They lack excitement, and thus may not provide the expected incentive to the sales force.

Sales contests. Contests are popular with sales managers because they introduce an element of competition between the individuals in the force, and because they generate excitement. Contests can work well, and are liked by sales forces, provided that four conditions are met.[7] The first is that the contest must motivate virtually every participant. The second is that the contestant should achieve specified and pre-selected targets. The third is that they should sustain enthusiasm throughout the period. Finally the contest should be capable of paying for itself out of the gross profit earned on increased sales.

The problem with contests is that the top men win too frequently. Even if their targets are adjusted sharply upwards after a win, they become expert at finding ways of 'saving' themselves, and their customers' orders, for the next contest they want to win. The second problem is that most of the sales force give up trying after they have had a poor start, and see the leaders forging ahead.

Prize structures, timing and variable target setting during the contest period can resolve some of these problems. In effect, the main contest then becomes a series of very short-term contests, in which the entire team stops and starts afresh, with new targets.

Points schemes. The great thing about points schemes, whether they add up to cash prizes, gifts, travel, or other awards, is their flexibility. They are

[7] K. Gazzard, 'A Step-by-step Guide to Sales Incentive Programmes'; *Incentive Marketing Magazine*, Oct.–Nov. Dec. 1965.

W.O.M.P.—K*

not usually offered competitively between the men, although this feature can be built in from time to time. They are usually offered simply for the performance of the man against his target—and he and his sales manager agree the target.

Points schemes are as useful for the newcomer to the sales team as they are for the high flyer. They have the additional advantage of enabling the salesman to work according to his own choice of ambition—particularly this is true of gift schemes. If gifts are offered from a catalogue, one man may decide to save up many of his points for a boat, or some other expensive item. Another may just set out to equip his home with small appliances as he wins sufficient points for them. The value of the gifts is higher than the cost of them to the company, and this is an added attraction in the scheme. Gift prizes provide recognition and are a permanent reminder to the winner and his friends. Such points schemes nearly always require an outside service company to prepare the catalogue, and handle the administration.

Evaluating sales promotion

Most of the methods of pre-testing sales promotion schemes follow those for testing advertising. Qualitative research using group discussions, or semi-structured interviews can test the general acceptability of an idea. Quantitative research has become popular in the past three years. It is designed to provide information about which of several alternative promotions is most likely to be effective in reaching specified goals, as well as an estimate of likely demand for premiums.

Much pre-testing work can be handled on the sequential basis recommended by Sampson and Hooper.[8] A number of ideas can be 'screened' through, say, jury panels. The selected alternatives can then be tested for their impact, and the likely market response, in specially designed market experiments, or through attitude evaluation. The essential thing about pre-testing promotion is to produce the results quickly, and relatively cheaply.

Post-testing promotion is often concerned with measuring the gate after the horse has stumbled through. The evaluation can be made relative to the results of other promotions in such areas as brand awareness, trial sampling, brand-switching or in the number of competition entries. Alternatively, the promotion can be measured for its results relative to the objectives set for it—such as in sales results, or in distribution levels, or in profit payoff.

Industrial promotion

The more exotic forms of sales promotion used by consumer goods companies have never been popular with industrial marketing companies, apart from leaflets, direct mail and exhibitions, on which industrial spending is heavy. The industrial buying process appears to be more 'rational' and less

[8] P. Sampson and B. Hooper, 'Evaluating Below the Line Expenditure'; Thompson Silver Medal Winning Paper, 1969, pp. 95–121.

responsive to sales appeals which are disconnected with the product's performance. Again, the nature of the industrial buying decision is that many people are involved in the final choice. Most of them are unknown to the manufacturer—and these people are difficult to motivate by standard promotions. Indeed, most industrial companies guard their technical reputations so carefully, that they will not be associated with anything which smacks of gimmickry.

Yet they do it all the same. The annual company golf match, to which leading buyers are invited, is a common feature of industrial companies. The chairman may take a party to Glyndebourne twice a year; the company may own a pleasant villa in the south of France and open it for visitors—in this way, customers are rewarded for their loyalty. Prospective customers may be invited to visit the supplier's premises and be entertained appropriately. Customers' operating management may be invited to special seminars run by the suppliers, often featuring international experts as speakers.

In their subtle way, industrial companies are indulging in sales promotion activity, sometimes with great effect. However, it is more usually carried out without a basic plan, without a set of precise objectives, and with little measurement of the effect. These criticisms may appear harsh, but industrial marketing companies usually reject any method of forcing markets which is not related to providing additional discounts.

Without a plan these sales promotion activities will often have a badly skewed distribution in their effect. For example, it is often the same buyers from the same companies, those who are known to be friends of members of senior management, who are invited to the annual company 'affair'. Without a plan for distributing the benefices where they will have most effect for future company business, they will be placed repetitively, and will concentrate on rewarding existing customers, rather than motivating new customer prospects.

Industrial companies also make use of other forms of sales promotion techniques, similar to those in the consumer markets. Giveaways are used, often in the form of some item of technical assistance. The annual Christmas present or company diary is common. Again, their distribution is usually only roughly planned, with no measurement of their effect.

Product sampling, and free trials, are popular in some companies particularly where this has become a tradition in the industry. Cash offers and disguised discounts are another feature in common with consumer goods companies. Customer contests have been known where the nature of the contest can be tied in to the sales features of the product.

The three big questions for the industrial marketing company entering the sales promotion field for the first time are as follows. Firstly, can reasonable objectives be set in business terms for this exercise, and can the results be measured? Secondly, is this promotion one which can be stopped in the future if company circumstances alter? The problem with the annual golf match, or the yearly bottle of Scotch, is similar to the problem of roller skating. Once the things have started it is a difficult job to stop them, without upsetting someone. Thirdly, if the promotion is successful, will the direct competition respond in similar manner? It is very easy to devise a successful promotion in industry, only to find that within a short time it has become common practice for all competitors to operate similarly.

Market Situations

Package Goods: Consumer

The basic chapter has been written with this type of company in mind, since it is in these markets that the most prolific users of sales promotion forcing techniques are to be found.

Consumer Durables

Most of the price cutting in these markets is operated at store level, occasionally with manufacturers providing help in the form of advertising subsidies. Promotional schemes (such as competitions) are mostly designed to draw attention to the product rather than to force sales. These products are 'considered' purchases and peripheral benefits are not likely to influence sales, but they can influence the way the product is merchandised and displayed. Most promotion schemes are linked directly to shop multiple groups through tailor-made promotions. A degree of promotion is operated at the retail level[9]—very often in the form of generous trade-in allowances for old equipment.

Industrial Marketing Companies

These all take a softer line on sales promotion, and direct their activities at existing customer groups. Occasionally corporate image building promotions are undertaken through the sponsorship of sporting events, or the provision of educational grants.

Concentrated Markets

Companies in these markets usually prefer to remain fairly aloof from sales promotion activity. Often, however, they encourage a degree of promotion activity within the distributive trade.

Oligopolistic Markets

Companies in these markets usually direct the bulk of their promotion activities towards the final user of the products, while providing the trade with incentives to ensure adequate stocks and display. The overall objective of their promotion schemes is to provide a boost for the brand share within the total market.

[9] Audits of Great Britain Ltd., 'All Change for Household Appliance Markets'; *Audit Magazine*, April 1971, pp. 2–4.

Fragmented Markets

Companies in these markets usually concentrate their attention on promotions which will help to force products into and through the trade. Promotions to the end-users are run provided that they serve as an adequate vehicle for obtaining distribution.

Mass Distribution

Again, the emphasis will be on the distributive trades, concentrating on selling-through for wholesalers and selling-out for retailers. The emphasis is on the entire series of push-pull relationships which must be motivated at each stage.

Oligopsonistic Distribution

Here any promotion will be softer and designed specifically to either secure the goodwill of the relatively few buyers, or to physically assist them in their business. Customers' promotions usually receive support from suppliers' budgets, even though the degree of control over the promotion which the supplier can expect to have is minimal.

Example: Testing Sales Promotion

Background

Field testing sales promotion schemes assumes away most of the problem, because the tests relate to only a few alternatives which have already been selected from a range of *n* possible options which exist at the start.

The problem

Even allowing for the fact that most of the theoretical alternatives have been screened out, the marketing man may be faced finally with a few very simple and obvious alternatives. Having fixed his objectives in terms of new users, or increased existing brand usage, he is left with a guess as to what will be the outcome of several variables. The levels of promotion cost will affect sales results greatly; but with most promotions their cost is also affected by the sales result they achieve. And the type of promotion used will also affect cost and demand simultaneously.

Store testing

Contimart Ltd. have devised a promotion testing service in-store for package goods advertisers.

A brand manager in a company making shoe polish wanted to run a price-cut promotion. He felt his choice lay between three alternatives. He could offer 1p off one tin; or 2p off one tin; or offer one tin free for each one purchased.

A representative sample of 20 supermarkets and self-service stores in the north-east of England was split into control and experimental groups. The interviewers visit the shops to check that merchandising material was laid out as specified, and that no undue out-of-stocks occurred. The experimental

The Operation Variables

and control groups were matched by check-outs and by turnover. The field staff eliminated other stray variables which would affect the results in a local test, but which would not occur in a national operation. Co-variance analysis was used in the calculation of results, taking in sales figures previous to the promotion.

In the specific shoe polish case, a series of tests showed that the 1p offer doubled the sales during the promotion; 2p multiplied sales nearly three times; and the 'one tin free' offer multiplied sales nearly seven times. Subsequent sales levels and final shares of the market were also predicted for each scheme.

The problem with running such tests in one's own stockists, is that there will be inevitably non-representation of the sample of shops, and company bias in one form or another will certainly skew the results. Using a normal store audit service does not provide the necessary level of field control to eliminate all the stray variables and to ensure that merchandising specifications are met. So the test shops must be set up under the appropriate disciplines.

The results of three different sets of promotions are shown. For all three products the greatest sales increase was significant at the level of 95 per cent confidence.

	Test period sales as percentage of sales in pre-test period	
Brand A: *Toothpaste*		
No promotion	▬▬▬	131
Offer of tights	▬▬▬▬	189
Reduced price	▬▬▬▬▬▬▬	337
Brand B: *Shoe polish*		
No promotion	▬	82
1p off one tin	▬▬▬	161
2p off two tins	▬▬▬▬	235
one tin free	▬▬▬▬▬▬▬▬	540
Brand C: *milk powder*		
No promotion	▬▬	130
2½p coupon enclosed	▬▬▬▬	212
Reduced price	▬▬▬▬	216
½ pint free	▬▬▬▬▬	271

Source: Audits of Great Britain Ltd: 'The True Test of Sales Promotion'; *Audit*, April 1971.

18. Conclusion

Does marketing make people do things they would not otherwise do? Or is it simpler than that—does marketing merely reflect changes in society? Confusion on the question often reigns, but the truth is easy. It does both.

The sum of what we do does help to formulate people's attitudes and scale of values. We are helping to build a materialistic society. We cannot avoid it. Yet, at the same time marketing must respond to people's changing wants and circumstances. But things may be changing too fast, even for us.

We now rest upon an explosive force. Something is happening today which has never before happened in the history of mankind. A technical explosion is taking place which is beyond the control of anyone. The pace of progress is accelerating beyond belief. In the time it takes you to read this final chapter, men will have published twenty new and significant scientific papers. Is marketing adaptive enough to stand the pace? Are there enough people in our business with a comprehension of what it is that we are doing—individually and collectively? Is not marketing a social science rather than a business mechanism to be perfected?

See how the rate of change has speeded up. Take measurement for instance. In the fifteenth century, if you could gauge distance to an accuracy of one part in one thousand you were doing well. Now, today, you can measure correctly to one part in one hundred million.

In the twelfth century you could mark the passage of time correctly to about one quarter hour per day. Now you can do so accurately to one second in three thousand years. By doing more than a million calculations per second, a computer will have completed the equivalent of 60 man years of work in the time it has taken you to read this paragraph. The total body of human knowledge is currently doubling every ten years. A man who has obtained his Ph.D in physics may be out-of-date five years after he has qualified. It has been said that a marketing manager is unlikely to be able to comprehend all the working language of his subordinates in fifteen years' time. They will be specialists with a jargon all their own.

The marketing function feeds off information. Knowledge and measurement are the nourishment of marketing. Can marketing men absorb the necessary information for the efficiency of their jobs?

The question becomes academic and ridiculous when one considers the size of the problem. An average person reading twelve hours a day for fifty years can read up to 18,000 technical books in his lifetime. There are about 30 million books in current publication in the world today. There is a flood of facts and paper which is totally impossible to control. Marketing men must be selective in their absorption of information. But the process of selection may blind them to what is going on next door.

Since 1850 the English population grew more than five times but jobs grew more than eight and a half times and goods and services 34 times. In this period of improving machines and methods, jobs multiplied faster than the population and goods and services faster than jobs. Yet in 1800 our economy was 80 per cent agricultural and 20 per cent dependent on the power of human and animal muscle. Today's British farmer produces enough food for himself and 12 others. Yet the biggest cross that the British economy has to bear is the fact that we invented the Industrial Revolution. We are now saddled with docks and mines that should be stripped out and started again; a road and rail transport network that is chaotic; and a set of systems and attitudes of mind which are years out-of-date.

It is very hard to get people to accept that they have been doing things the wrong way round. It means that history, tradition and experience take second place to genuine conceptual ability. The ability to see old things in a new way. Our standard attitudes inhibit change. Yet it is vital that we have an open attitude to change, because it will happen whether we are prepared for it or not. And the only way we can deal with it is to recognise the forces which cause change and to plan accordingly. Otherwise we swing about at the mercy of every random influence.

Look at some of the changes which will be with us in the next thirty years.

In ten years' time we will all be witnessing a wide-scale revolution in energy supply. The cost of gas drawn from the North Sea and piped into our homes and factories will turn the consumer durable industry topsy-turvy. Many manufacturing giants will turn to gas for their heating requirements. What will this do to the markets for electricity, oil and solid fuel? Change them out of recognition.

Hard on the heels of this gas revolution will come atomic energy. Contrary to all forecasts, the cost of atomic energy has been slashed dramatically. Today's cost of producing atomic energy for industrial use is only 7 per cent of what it was in 1960. This fuel source will be available in the foreseeable future almost everywhere on an inter-continental scale. The distinction between the haves and the under-developed have-nots will begin to diminish rapidly.

Nearly every major consumer goods field we can think of is in for some kind of revolution in the next 25 years. The food industry itself will be subjected to the introduction of the domestic microwave oven. The microwave oven, already being used in parts of the catering industry, provides instant cooking in a matter of seconds for prepared foods. The resolution will develop first in the catering trade, but already an American company has developed a microwave oven for the home. This piece of equipment consumes only 1,300 watts, which is little more than an electric toaster. It can bake a cake in four minutes, and cook a 4 lb roast in twenty minutes.

Such a development will change the whole structure of the food manufacturing business. Centralised power will be vested in the hands of a few manufacturing giants with marketing facilities and resources to provide complete meals in packs. The anarchy and chaos which disfigure the food distribution practice of this country today will be things of the past. Even today only 25 per cent of all the food we eat is in branded packaged form. Small manufacturers and processors will exist, surely. But they will be selling to the marketing giants, not to the retail trade.

The consumer, however reluctantly at first, will ultimately accept microwave ovens because they will liberate the housewife entirely from her major domestic chore, that of preparing and cooking food. With time and money available for people to pursue individual and family interests, this in turn is likely to cause a second revolution among the entertainment and leisure industries.

What about other major revolutions in which we shall be engulfed by the year 2000?

First, communications. There will be a tumultuous revolution in information supply and assessment. There will be vast increases in computing and telecommunication networks and widespread use of electronic storage and retrieval of information. Possibilities arising from this will be television, telephones and worldwide weather warning services using satellites. Television links will be used between firms instead of business channels and data stores will exist in the home. Libraries, paperwork and typists could be near abolished and newspapers as we know them could be changed out of recognition.

There will be worldwide spontaneous reporting of news. Second, there will be the revolutionary consequences of biology. We will have a deeper understanding of living systems, including the human brain. We may be able to manipulate the genetic structure. The possibilities arising are an alteration of cell heredity; the transplantation of organs and wide use of artificial limbs and organs—the modification of the developing brain—the conquest of viruses, heart disease and cancer are possibilities. There will be a better understanding of human behaviour as a result and a danger of 'mind control' techniques.

We may begin to exploit the oceans. This could produce new protein sources and obtain minerals from seawater and the seabed. We may be able to control weather and climate by warming or cooling seawater.

We have touched already upon new forms of energy but we have not mentioned the use of fuel cells as small power units for energy storage. We may have fuel cell generators in the home. Almost certainly there will be fuel cell batteries for cars, and oil companies may be the dodos of the industrial world. One good thing—at least the transport will be quieter than it is at present. Electric cars on rails: why not?

There will be a continuing race between food and population and the world population may have increased up to 70 per cent by A.D. 2000. There may also be a 50 per cent increase in the expectation of the life of children in poorer countries.

There will be a growth of knowledge with a great advancement of education. We may look forward to the day when 90 per cent of the world's children will be at school, compared with only 50 per cent today.

The flood of fact and information is a fundamental problem of our age by itself. It will become worse. The role of the individual will be weakened to the point of non-existence. Or so it will seem.

Although each of us is beset by far more information than we can hope to absorb, nevertheless we do have an advantage over the 700 million adult illiterates in the world today. We can read and we do know we have a problem.

Whether we think that the changing pace of progress is a good thing or not, there is one unassailable fact. We can't stop it. We can try as far as possible to keep up with our own end of it. At best we can each take one little sector and try to advance our knowledge in that area we have chosen in such a way that all society can benefit.

The marketing process is contributing greatly to all of this. It is not initiating the developments, as many think. It is responding to an activity which it is powerless to control. Nevertheless, all this scientific progress is being channelled through the marketing function. We are responsible for its exploitation.

None of us can foresee where all this will end. Let us hope it will end well for humanity. Whether it does or not may largely depend upon whether those of us connected with advancing development in the world understand what we are doing.

This is why we need to regard marketing as a social science. This is why we need to have a comprehension of the fundamental principles of marketing behaviour. So far, we merely scratch the surface of knowledge.

As marketing men we must help to channel these scientific developments to the benefit of an unsuspecting society. The penalty for failure may be vested upon our grand-children. The reward for success may be earned by the under-developed in the world.

Bibliography

GENERAL MANAGEMENT

Peter F. Drucker, *The Practice of Management*. (William Heinemann Ltd., London, 1954.)

Peter F. Drucker, *Managing for Results*. (William Heinemann Ltd., London, 1964.)

H. Igor Ansoff, *Corporate Strategy*. (McGraw-Hill, U.S.A., 1965.)

E. Peter Ward, *The Dynamics of Planning*. (Pergamon Press Ltd., Oxford, 1970.)

J. K. Galbraith, *The New Industrial State*. (Hamish Hamilton, London, 1967.)

Richard Bailey, *Managing the British Economy*. (Hutchinson, London, 1968.)

Peter C. Sanderson, *Computers for Management*. (Pan Books Ltd., London, 1969.)

Anthony Jay, *Management & Machiavelli*. (Hodder & Stoughton Ltd., London, 1967.)

Robert Townsend, *Up The Organisation*. (Michael Joseph Ltd., London, 1970.)

SOCIAL PSYCHOLOGY

D. Krech, R. S. Crutchfield, E. L. Ballachey, University of California, Berkeley, *The Individual in Society*. (McGraw-Hill, Maidenhead, 1962.)

Josephine Klein, *Working with Groups*. (Hutchinson & Co., London, 1961.)

John Cohen, *Behaviour in Uncertainty*. (Geo. Allen & Unwin Ltd., London, 1964.)

John Cohen, *A New Introduction to Psychology*. (Geo. Allen & Unwin Ltd., 1966.)

Vance Packard, *The Status Seekers*. (Longmans Green & Co. Ltd., London, 1960.)

MARKETING MANAGEMENT—GENERAL

Aubrey Wilson (Editor), *The Marketing of Industrial Products*. (Hutchinson & Co. Ltd., London, 1965.)

Robert Bartels, *Marketing Theory and Metatheory*. (American Marketing Association, 1970.)

Leslie W. Rodger, *Marketing in a Competitive Economy*. (Cassell/Associated Business Programmes, 1971.)

Victor P. Buell, *Marketing Management in Action*. (McGraw-Hill Inc., 1966.)

Thomas L. Berg, *Mismarketing*. (Thos. Nelson & Sons Ltd., London, 1970.)

Colin McIver, *Marketing*. (Business Publications Ltd., London, 1959.)

Hector Lazo, Ph.D., and Arnold Corbin, Ph.D., *Management in Marketing*. (McGraw-Hill Book Co. Inc., 1961.)

C. G. A. Godley and D. S. Cracknell, *Marketing for Expansion and Europe*. (Longman Group Ltd., London, 1971.)

MARKETING ANALYSIS AND CONTROL

Philip Kotler, *Marketing Management: Analysis, Planning, and Control*. (Prentice-Hall, Inc., Englewood Cliffs, N.J., U.S.A., 1967.)

Steuart Henderson Britt and Harper W. Boyd, Jr., *Marketing Management & Administrative Action.* (McGraw-Hill Inc., U.S.A., 1963.)

A. S. Johnson, B.A., A.C.W.A., *Marketing and Financial Control.* (Pergamon Press Ltd., Oxford, 1967.)

Thomas L. Berg and Abe Shuchman (Editors), *Product Strategy and Management.* (Holt, Rinehart and Winston, Inc., U.S.A., 1963.)

Gordon Medcalf, *Marketing and the Brand Manager.* (Pergamon Press Ltd., Oxford, 1967.)

John Stapleton, *How to Prepare a Marketing Plan.* (Gower Press Ltd., London, 1971.)

John Winkler, *Marketing for the Developing Company.* (Hutchinson & Co. Ltd., London, 1969.)

C. Graeme Roe, *Profitable Marketing for the Smaller Company.* (Directors Bookshelf, London, 1969.)

Paul Ellis (Editor), *Hardy Heating Co. Ltd.* (British Broadcasting Corporation, London, 1968.)

Terry Coram, *Cases in Marketing and Marketing Research.* (Crosby Lockwood & Son Ltd., London, 1969.)

Henry Deschampsneufs, *Marketing Overseas.* (Pergamon Press Ltd., Oxford, 1967.)

MARKETING INFORMATION

Aubrey Wilson, *The Assessment of Industrial Markets.* (Hutchinson & Co. Ltd., London, 1968.)

Gordon Wills, *Sources of U.K. Marketing Information.* (Thos. Nelson & Sons Ltd., London, 1969.)

Morris James Slonim, *Guide to Sampling.* (Simon and Schuster, Inc., U.S.A., 1960.)

D. Elliston Allen, *British Tastes.* (Hutchinson & Co. Ltd., London, 1968.)

M. J. Moroney, *Facts from Figures.* (Penguin Books Ltd., England, 1951.)

Wm. A. Bagley, *Facts and How to Find Them.* (Sir Isaac Pitman & Sons Ltd., London, 1962, 1964.)

Albert Battersby, *Sales Forecasting.* (Cassell & Co. Ltd., London, 1968.)

MARKETING PRODUCTS AND PRICING

R. N. Skinner, *Launching New Products in Competitive Markets.* (Cassell/ Associated Business Programmes, London, 1972.)

Peter M. Kraushar, *New Products & Diversification.* (Business Books Ltd., London, 1969.)

E. J. Davis, *Experimental Marketing.* (Thos. Nelson & Sons Ltd., London, 1970.)

Elizabeth Marting (Editor), *Creative Pricing.* (American Management Association Inc., 1968.)

Albert J. Bergfeld, James S. Earley and William R. Knobloch, *Pricing for Profit and Growth.* (Prentice-Hall, Inc., Englewood Cliffs, N.J., U.S.A., 1962.)

Bernard Taylor and Gordon Wills, *Pricing Strategy.* (Staples Press Ltd., London, 1969.)

MARKETING—THE OPERATIONAL VARIABLES

Nicholas A. H. Stacey and Aubrey Wilson, *The Changing Pattern of Distribution.* (Business Publications Ltd., London, 1958.)

M. T. Wilson, *Managing a Sales Force.* (Gower Press Ltd., London, 1970.)

David Rowe and Ivan Alexander, *Selling Industrial Products.* (Hutchinson & Co. Ltd., London, 1968.)

Henry Deschampsneufs, *Selling Overseas*. (Business Publications Ltd., London, 1960.)

E. B. Weiss, *The Vanishing Salesman*. (McGraw-Hill Book Company Inc., 1962.)

Dr. A. Tack, *The Sales Manager's Role*. (World's Work Ltd., London, 1968.)

Heinz M. Goldman, *How to Win Customers*. (Staples Press Ltd., London, 1958.)

Norman A. Hart, *Industrial Publicity*. (Cassell/Associated Business Programmes Ltd., London, 1971.)

Martyn P. Davis, *Handbook for Media Representatives*. (Business Publications Ltd., London, 1967.)

J. W. Hobson, *The Selection of Advertising Media*. (Business Publications Ltd., London, 1956.)

Ralph Harris and Arthur Seldon, *Advertising In Action*. (Hutchinson & Co. Ltd., London, 1962.)

Ralph Harris and Arthur Seldon, *Advertising In A Free Society*. (Institute of Economic Affairs, London, 1959.)

D. S. Cowan and R. W. Jones, *Advertising In The 21st Century*. (Hutchinson & Co. Ltd., London, 1968.)

Martin Mayer, *Madison Avenue U.S.A.* (The Bodley Head, London, 1958.)

William A Belson, *The Impact of Television*. (Crosby Lockwood & Son Ltd., London, 1967.)

E. Hereward Phillips, *Fund Raising Techniques and Case Histories*. (Business Books Ltd., London, 1969.)

Alan Toop, *Choosing The Right Sales Promotion*. (Crosby Lockwood & Son Ltd., London, 1966.)

E. B. Weiss, *Merchandising for Tomorrow*. (McGraw-Hill Book Company Inc., 1961.)

Index

Page references in italic represent a figure

Baxters, 45
Bayes, Rev. Thomas, 245
Bayesian theory, 245
B.B.C., 237
beef, 43
behaviour, patterns of, 6
behaviour, people's, 3
Bernstein, D., 245
Bird's Eye Foods Ltd., 126, 127
Board of Management, 5, 94, 167, 193,
    202, 240, 252
brand identity, weak, 229
brand loyalty, 117
brand management structure, 56
brand reputations, poor, 229
brand-switch, 116
break-even analysis, 157
break-even point, 144
Broads Builders' Merchants Ltd., 150
Brooke Bond, 112
budget centres, 66
    codes, 66
budgeting:
    base, 31
    draft, 79
    hierarchy of systems, 61
    tight, 75
        advantages of, *77*
business analysis, 157
    stage, 155
Business Research Organisation Ltd., 216
buyer('s), 3
    attitude of, 260
    behaviour, 219
        models, 219
    grocery, preferences, *260*
    need, 136
buying influences, 93
buying/selling categories, *13*

'Cannibalising' sales, 44
capital goods, demand for, 173
capital intensive companies, 17
cash flow graph, 69
check list, the, 156
chemical industry, 231
Coca Cola, 43
Collins, B., 159
communication(s):
    company process, 225
    complexities of marketing process, *225,*
        226, 227, 228
    marketing, 237, 239
        process, 239
    models, 225-9
    mix, 234
    process, *229*
    public relations, 230

factor, 230
source effect in, *222*
total system, 225
uncontrolled marketing, 225-37
visual, 229
word-of-mouth, 223, 230, 237
    exploiting, 224
competition, 11, 47, 122
competitive reactions, 200
competitive structures, 126
competitor's product list, 156
components, 2, 8, 108, 125, 149, 167, 181,
    203, 215, 252
computer systems, 15
concentrated markets(ing), *9*, 10, 27,
    44-8, 97, 108, 122, 150, 168, 184,
    204, 272
consumer durables, 148, 167, 180, 202,
    215, 252, 272
consumer markets, 116, 256
consumer products, *7*
Consumer Research Officer, 99
Contimart Ltd., 273
controls, 37
copy strategy, 219
copying machines, 152
corporate planning and development
    division, 84
cost centre, 66
cost-plus, 173
costs:
    annual, running and capital, 217
    opportunities for saving, 212
    reducing, 75-7
Crosfields Farm Foods Ltd., 205
Crosse and Blackwell, 45
custom-built products, 12
customer clustering, 201
customer satisfaction, 12
customer strategy form, *196-7*

Daily Mail, 237
Davis, E. J., 124
decision analysis systems, 15
decision influencers, 93-4
decision making, 48
Decision Making Unit, 189
decision-tree, 198
    size of sales force, *199*
declining phase, 113
deferred discount, 267
deliveries, rush, 211
Delphi Method, 156
demand variables, 39
derived demand, 173
desk research, 156
despatch department, 208
development phase, 157